Anonymous

Industrial Advantages of Houston, Texas and Environs

Also Series of Comprehensive Sketches of the City's Representative

Business Enterprises

Anonymous

Industrial Advantages of Houston, Texas and Environs
Also Series of Comprehensive Sketches of the City's Representative Business Enterprises

ISBN/EAN: 9783337191238

Printed in Europe, USA, Canada, Australia, Japan

Cover: Foto ©Suzi / pixelio.de

More available books at **www.hansebooks.com**

THE

INDUSTRIAL ADVANTAGES

OF

HOUSTON, TEXAS,

AND

ENVIRONS,

ALSO

A Series of Comprehensive Sketches of the City's
Representative Business Enterprises.

HOUSTON, TEXAS.
The Akehurst Publishing Co.,
1894.

THE CITY OF HOUSTON.

HIS continent has been productive of startling developments. States, territories and provinces have been carved from an expanse of wilderness and cities have grown up like an exhalation. Presage and opinion have been at fault, convenience and facility have been potential, and what in the old world would be considered but a short lapse of period has sufficed here to create a city with swarming thousands, replete with the products of the soil, resonant with the hum of manufacture and abounding with the treasures of art and comfort. Today a great and growing city with a population of from 60,000 to 65,000 souls stands in the midst of a rich and fertile country. Ascend to the roof of any of the blocks in the central part of the city and look at mid-day on the scenes beneath and stretching far around you; lofty buildings, beautiful churches, and a teeming myriad of population meet the sight. Boat after boat is passing along the bayou leading to the sea, from the depots freight and passenger trains come and go at brief intervals. Industry, competence and enjoyment are evinced in every quarter. There seems no merchandise but what has its mart, no interest without its representative, all facilities for travel abound, the electric car upon the paved street or the miles of walk for the passing throng. The melody of bells proclaims the fleeting hours and heralds the cessation or renewal of a multiform of industry.

While it is not our mission to enter into minute details concerning the early settlement and history of Houston, it is still proper for us to embody in a work of this character a brief sketch of the more notable facts in the development of this populous locality, from the trackless waste which it once was.

The chronicles of Houston are brief and uneventful. Its experience of the Civil War and of the period of reconstruction just subsequent, excepted, it has pursued the even tenor of its way, little delayed, if not altogether unaffected by stirring events. It came into being too late to participate in the events of the Texan revolution, and the only reminder it has of that romantic time is the name it bears. The field of San Jacinto where the patriotic Texans were freed from the domination of Mexican rule is, however, but few hours distant from the city by water. The site of the city of Houston was chosen by John K. Allen in 1836, a short time after the battle of San Jacinto had established the independence of Texas, and its name was bestowed upon it in honor of Sam Houston, the victor in that memorable encounter. The town site chosen by Allen was laid out in streets and lots and they were offered for sale in August of the above mentioned year. The advantages of the site even at that time were apparent. The city was at the head of navigation on Buffalo Bayou and was an excellent point from which to ship the products of the central part of the state. Allen

Harris County
Texas

foresaw that at this point the future railroad system of the state would center here, and his prediction has been verified in a manner far beyond his, or anyone else's, conception at that period.

In May, 1837, the Congress of the Republic of Texas met at Houston. Its sessions were held at a Capitol which had been erected by the city for this purpose, at a cost of $36,000. The Capitol Hotel now occupies the site of this structure. Later however, Austin was made the capital of the Republic and this naturally militated somewhat against Houston, for the time being. However, upon the annexation of Texas to the United States, Houston forged ahead once more, capital was attracted here and immigrants settled in the country in considerable numbers. About 1850 the

HARRIS COUNTY JAIL.

design of a railroad from Harrisburg, a settlement near by, to Austin, was conceived and its projector, Gen. Sidney Sherman, took active measures to make the project a success. Eastern and northern capitalists were induced to embark in the scheme, a charter was obtained from the legislature, containing a proviso empowering the city of Houston to tap the road at some convenient point, and the enterprise was carried along with energy. After this the citizens of Houston began to interest themselves in railroad construction and obtained charters for three roads to enter the city, the Galveston, Houston & Red River, now the Houston & Texas Central; the Houston Tap & Brazoria, now a branch of the International & Great

Northern, and the Texas & New Orleans, now a part of the Southern Pacific, or Sunset Route. The State Legislature made liberal grants to these lines and in 1861 there were 357 miles of railway centering at Houston. But the march of improvement in this direction was stayed by the outbreak of the Civil War, and Houston, just entering upon a period of great prosperity and rapid advancement, was suddenly checked in its forward career. Of course there was a good deal of business of a superficial character carried on during the four years of conflict, but it had no substantial basis. However, soon after the conclusion of peace, Houston began to advance steadily and never since has that advancement received a serious check. The population of the city in 1870 was 9,382 persons, in 1880 it was 16,513. The federal census of 1890 gave a total of 27,411 inhabitants to the city, but since then it has gone upward by bounds and leaps. In 1891 the population based on the number of names in the directory was estimated at 48,972, in 1893 58,513, and today the population of Houston and suburbs is probably between 60,000 and 65,900 people and its trade is equal to that of any city in the state. We have said enough here of the past; our business is now with the present, with living men and their daily occupations, enterprises and successes, what they are doing for themselves in manufactures, commerce and finance, and in contributing to and in advancing the general prosperity of the community.

LOCATION, CLIMATIC AND SANITARY.

Houston is located in Harris County and is about fifty miles distant from the Gulf of Mexico. It borders on the Buffalo river or bayou, which is a navigable stream for vessels whose draught does not exceed nine or ten feet. The city occupies almost a central position in the eighteen hundred miles of territory known as the Coast Country of Texas which fronts Galveston Bay and the Mexican Gulf. This area is well drained by creeks and bayous, along the banks of which are thick woods where grow large quantities of valuable timber of different varieties. The eastern limits of the city are not far distant from the great pine country of East Texas, and close at hand are immense forests of oak, sycamore, hickory, ash, cypress, magnolia, etc. While Houston can hardly claim to be a Philadelphia in the arrangement of her streets, yet is the city well laid out and most of her thoroughfares are generally wide and straight. The leading streets are paved with vitrified brick, bois d'arc, stone blocks and solid gravel. Thirty-five miles of streets have been paved within the past three or four years with the above materials and the results have been most satisfactory. The sewerage system is of the best and is based upon the most improved method and principles. The plan adopted is known as the separate system by which both surface drainage and sewerage are conducted through vitrified pipe and brick sewers to Buffalo bayou. Over fifty miles of pipe have been laid down. The city is perfectly drained, and stagnant water is never seen in the gutters, which are regularly flushed from the waterworks. No consideration is more essential to the continued prosperity and happiness of a community than health. Houston is one of the healthiest cities of the United States. Despite the fact that a large proportion of the population are negroes—a class among which sickness is more prevalent than with white people, because of crowded homes and lack of knowledge and opportunity to consider the laws of health—despite this drawback, Houston has the lowest death rate but one of all the cities of the country. In fact, it is safe to say that the prevailing sickness here is teething and old age. Much of this gratifying condition of affairs is due to wise sanitary precaution and the use of artesian water, supplied by the city water works company. A strong point in Houston's favor over many other cities is the purity and quantity of her water supply. Artesian water, when properly obtained, is well known for its purity, and chemical analysis vouches for this fact. The water is not only pure, but the supply is abundant. There are twenty four artesian wells sunk by the company, which have a capacity of from four to five million gallons per day. There are fifty-five miles of mains and thirty-five hydrants in the city service. The supply of water is not only ample for domestic use, but the company is competent to furnish all that may be needed for manufacturing purposes for many years to come. As occasion arises the capacity is increased. The pumping capacity at the present time is 16,000,000 gallons daily. The pressure used for ordinary purposes is from forty to fifty pounds to the square inch, which can be

THE KIAM BUILDING.

increased to from 100 to 120 pounds to the square inch in case of fire. This pressure is sufficient to throw a stream of water over all but one or two of the very highest buildings in the city. The company have a stand-pipe of thirty feet diameter, which is of the height of 150 feet. This is probably the largest stand-pipe in the country. They have another, twenty feet in diameter, and eighty-five feet high. Compared with other cities of the South, the quantity of water per capita and its quality far exceed the average.

Houston is in latitude 29 degrees 47 minutes north, or about a plane with Spain and Italy. The average elevation above the sea level is forty feet and the air line from the Mexican Gulf is forty miles, so that the heat of summer is cooled and the winter blasts from the North are tempered by the sea breezes of the ocean. The usual range of temperature is from thirty to ninety degrees, sometimes reaching ninety-five to one hundred degrees in summer at mid-day. Seldom it is colder than freezing point more than a day or two in succession. The average winter temperature is 60 degrees. The rainfall is about the same as the rest of the Texas Coast country, averaging about fifty inches a year. The summer weather, though warm, is very wholesome, and the winters are too mild to develop pulmonary diseases. Contagious fevers, the direst enemies of large cities, are practically unknown here, and altogether, as a healthful place of residence, Houston is to be envied by her less favored sister cities.

A CITY OF HOMES.

This designation cannot be improved upon, for after admiring the handsome residences of the wealthy, and the comfortable homes of the well-to-do, the eye of the visitor may rest with pleasure upon the homes of the mechanic, the clerk and the young business man, miles of the streets in the city and suburbs being lined with neat, but inexpensive houses, often surrounded by a plot of ground, and in many cases owned by the occupant. Land has never been held here at fancy prices, and the result has been as

RESIDENCE OF MR. WM. D. CLEVELAND.

stated. Much of this gratifying state of affairs is due to the efforts of the improvement organizations and the enterprise of the building and loan associations. The reasonable prices at which all classes have been able to obtain the great boon of owning their own domiciles has materially enhanced the welfare of the city, and apart from stimulating habits of thrift, has created a class of citizens bound up with the interests of the locality and who are content to live and labor here for the general good. A man who desires a home is not required to store his money in the cupboard or bureau, or invest it in a savings bank, where it will pay him but a low rate of interest, until he accumulates, slowly, sufficient to buy him a home, nor is he compelled to borrow, if he can, the necessary sum of his employer, or some wealthy friend, as a favor, and take his chance of being able to pay it back when due. He can place his surplus earnings in one of the associations above spoken of, where it accumulates rapidly until he has a small proportion of the necessary amount. He can then borrow the remainder of the association, buy himself a lot of any responsible real estate agent at cash prices, build a house upon it and repay the whole sum in small monthly installments—not much exceeding the rent he formerly paid.   Numerous organizations, capitalists and real estate dealers stand ready to sell really advantageous lots and build houses thereon upon the above terms, and hundreds of homes have been acquired in this way within the past few years, and the suburbs of Houston are rapidly filling up with neat and tasteful homes for the masses.

INDUCEMENTS TO MANUFACTURERS.

The right place to manufacture successfully is evidently at a point where the raw materials accumulate naturally, or can be procured advantageously, and where at the same time there are advanced and ample facilities for sending the product to market.   Situated at a focal point of many competing lines of railroad and with water communication to the sea-board added, connecting the city with the North, South, East and West and also with foreign countries, and furthermore, being a great mart for agricultural

GRAND CENTRAL RAILWAY STATION.

products, and most notably cotton, material can with facility accumulate here under the most favorable conditions.   Opportunities can here be obtained by the manufacturer superior to those of larger cities, for the reason that while equally favorable conditions in some respects may perhaps be on hand, the cost of living, and therefore of production, is lower, and that today in Houston, central and most advantageous sites for factories and shops are available at a very low cost.   This city and its inhabitants are prepared to welcome any who may purpose to make this location the seat of their operations, and to afford them every assistance which is in their power.   The manufacturer who comes here will find everything at hand for the successful furtherance of his enterprise, and as before said, a friendly and a helping hand will be extended him by every citizen of the community.   No place in the South is prepared to offer more inducements to the large and small manufacturer than does Houston at the present time, and while a center of refinement, culture and convenience, every advantage of the highest order is open to him who seeks. There is no reason why Houston should not become one of the greatest industrial centers of the country. Already much has been accomplished and her products are widely known throughout a large circuit of territory. The stranger to the city in traversing the streets and the suburbs may see establishments which would be a credit to any place; but we want more of them and there is

CONGRESS STREET.

ample room. The question might be asked, what can be manufactured to advantage here in Houston? The simplest answer, and practically a true one, is, *everything*. A thrifty population in the surrounding localities would furnish opportunities for such industries as do not require strictly skilled labor, and the large cities in direct communication with us would supply more experienced artizans than at the outset would be required, and there would be no dearth of suitable help should the demand arise. No

better field could be found anywhere to successfully operate cotton cloth
and yarn mills, cotton, sugar and rice mills, undearwear factories, woolen
mills, boot and shoe factories, hub and spoke works, a trunk factory, tan-
neries, carriage factories, barrel works, crate factories for fruits and produce,
canning factories, woodenware factory, a furniture factory, agricultural
implement works, basket works, flour mills and, indeed, almost any
description of large or small industry.   Some of the general advantages of
this city are :

FIRST.   *It is located in one of the most fertile and productive regions of*
the country and one of the most thriving and prosperous sections in the
South.

SECOND.   *It possesses admirable railroad facilities, connecting it with*
the entire country and opening up all parts for its products and shipments.

THIRD.   *It has water connections with the sea-board, bringing the city*
in direct contact with Galveston, and thus exercising an important influence
in keeping down railroad freight rates, through affording a means of
competition.

RESIDENCE OF MR. C. LOMBARDI.

FOURTH.   *It has a complete and well equipped water supply second to*
none other in a place of similar size, and far in excess of all present needs.
The city is well lighted by electricity, is efficiently policed and guarded
against fire.

FIFTH.   *A complete system of electric street cars is in operation, placing*
all parts of the city in direct and speedy connection.

SIXTH.   *The local government is based upon strict ideas of economy*
consistent with safe and secure progress, and the spirit of the people is
decidedly in favor of every measure to make the rate of taxation low,
while at the same time all public improvements are of the best character
and are well supported.

SEVENTH.   *The public school system is conducted upon a satisfactory*
basis and affords excellent advantages and facilities.   The social advantages are numerous, the tone of society healthy, and the morals of the
community generally are of the best.

EIGHTH. *The cost of living here is much lower than in most places in* the South.

NINTH. *The surroundings are delightful; the climate cannot be excelled,* there are no epidemics, the locality is generally free from prevailing sickness and the sanitary precautions are enlightened and vigilant.

TENTH. *Available sites for manufacturing are in plenty and are low* in price, and residential property is obtainable upon equally advantageous terms.

The manufacturing enterprises now located here are prosecuted with vigor, and are intelligently and successfully directed and admirably equipped. The shops and factories in the city give employment to a large number of skilled artizans and laborers receiving good wages, and it may

GIBBS' BUILDING.

be said that in Houston are employed as many as 12000 men who work in the railroad shops, compresses, oil mills, factories, etc., and in building and other public works.

The people settled in this locality are, as a rule, of the better classes found in the South, being made up of industrious and thrifty work people, while the business men and capitalists are large spirited and enterprising in contributing to the already pronounced growth and prosperity of the city. As already pointed out, the facilities afforded by the shipping conveniences, favorable location and other natural and acquired resources, assure the future prominence of Houston as a trading and manufacturing center. They have afforded and do afford the agriculturalists of this section a desirable market for their produce, and have added thousands of dollars to the value of every part of the wide expanse of rich, fertile

agricultural land by which Houston is surrounded.   This city is the natural
trading center for a locality which is noted for production of vast quantities of cotton, sugar, fruits, vegetables and other produce brought to the
city for transportation to all parts of the world.   But there is great room
for expansion, and Houston's capital though large, has its limit, and some
of the older capitalists have been trained to certain pursuits and may not
be quite fitted for a change, hence the opportunities must be filled principally by incoming capitalists and manufacturers who will, however, find
the local business men and capitalists willing to join hands with skillful
and enterprising managers.   The introduction of new manufacturing
interests will increase the opportunities of the retail merchants, and this the

PRINCE BUILDING.

latter appreciate, and they are ready to co-operate in all measures that will
bring new industries to the city.   The healthy conservatism that characterizes her leading spirits, and the persistent but not over-ambitious vigor,
which animates the younger element, are placing Houston in an enviable
position among the most flourishing cities of the South.   Rich in natural
resources, strong in credit and unhampered by burdensome taxation,
Houston offers inducements which should attract the eager attention of
capitalists seeking sound investments and manufacturers looking for a
place to locate themselves where there is an active and growing market.

What has already been accomplished in the way of manufacturing, may be learned from the following partial list of what is now made here; awning, flags and tents, bread and crackers, barrels, tanks, cisterns, lager beer, artesian ice, blank books, blueing, boilers, engines and general machinery, soda water, ginger ale, etc., brass and iron castings, architectural iron and galvanized iron products, brooms, candy and confectionery, carriages and wagons, car wheels, general railroad work, cigars and cigarettes, clothing, cornices, beds, mattresses and bedding, mosquito bars

MAIN STREET.

and fixtures, pharmaceutical preparations, electric supplies, fire brick and clay, office and bank fixtures, flowers, shrubs, trees, seeds, etc., frames and mouldings, furniture, shirts, overalls, underclothing, etc., harnesses and saddles, moss collars, bagging and cordage, steam laundry work, lumber, sash, doors, blinds and mill work generally, bricks, macaroni, sausages, monuments, tombstones, cotton seed oil, cotton seed meal and cotton seed products, paints, boots, shoes, coffee, spices, tin and sheet iron work, trunks, baking powder, pickles, creosoting work, soap, etc. Houston

is one of the largest cotton seed oil manufacturing points in America.   It is
the second largest cotton seed market in the country.   At Houston Heights,
a suburb of the city, considerable manufacturing development and growth
has been exhibited.   Here are located the Consumers Cotton Seed Oil
Mill, pressed brick and tile works, General Electric Manufacturing Co.'s
plant, spring bed and mattress factory, planing mill, hub, spoke and veneer
factory, art glass factory, furniture factory, machine shop, stove factory and
others.   Some of the above are already in operation and others are rapidly
approaching completion.   The largest iron mills at Houston are those of
the railroad companies.   The three shops of the Southern Pacific, Houston
& Texas Central and Houston East & West Texas employ about 1500
hands, and probably about 3000 men all together employed by the transportation companies.

THE WHOLESALE TRADE.

The wholesale trade of Houston has every facility for doing business,
having direct rail connection with all sections, giving the city every
advantage of competition in freights.   There is also the Buffalo Bayou with

RESIDENCE OF MR. FELIX HALFF.

good boat service and other independent vessels plying between here and
Galveston.   It is not so very long ago since all this territory was controlled
by jobbers from Galveston, New Orleans, St. Louis and other large cities,
and Houston's wholesale houses, which then operated in but a small way,
were compelled to obtain much of their supplies from these dealers.   The
result was that successful competition was out of the question.   Now a
very different condition of affairs prevails and has prevailed for some time.
Today our wholesale merchants have facilities equal to any in the country.
They buy their goods in every case direct from the manufacturers and
importers, or themselves import direct, and not only do they compete successfully with other cities, but they have almost driven their competitors
out of this market.   In a general way, it can be said of the wholesale trade
of Houston that it now occupies all the territory to which it is rightfully
entitled and in addition it is largely encroaching on the territory formerly
almost exclusively controlled by other centers.   The trade is now in a most
satisfactory condition.   Many of the houses are reaching out for new trade

as fast as they can and they have every reason to be pleased with the out-look. The merchandise brokers, who represent a number of leading mills and manufacturers, are also doing good business. It should be here noted that Houston may be regarded as the center of the sugar and molasses market of Texas. In the vicinity of the city are raised several million pounds of sugar, which is sold through Houston merchants.

THE RETAIL TRADE.

The surrounding country for a radius of from fifty to a hundred miles and including a number of towns and villages of more or less note, is almost exclusively tributary to this city in most of the lines of retail business. Besides this, Houston as the principal city in an important region of agricultural country, is the natural market for the principal part of the products of this region; thus a large amount of custom is drawn here to swell the general aggregate of its annual retail business. The trade, as a rule, is conducted by individuals and firms composed of men of enterprise, experience and integrity. The stocks handled by Houston's merchants embrace full supplies in all lines and they spare no pains to maintain their stocks as complete and varied as could be desired. Houston has no cause to apologize for either the character or goods of her retail establishments, which will compare favorably with those of any city of similar population anywhere. The stores are all well arranged, lighted generally by electricity, and many of them have handsome plate glass fronts and all modern facilities and conveniences. The above is the rule, to which there are but few exceptions.

THE FINANCIAL INSTITUTIONS.

Houston's banking business is a strong support of the manufacturing, commercial and mercantile interests of the city, and working in alliance with these interests in all their legitimate phases each appreciably influences and partakes of the tone and methods of the others. Hence the banks of the city, like her business enterprises, are noted for their sound, energetic, yet conservative management, command the entire confidence of business men and capitalists, and hold the highest rank among the financial institutions of the South. Houston's banks are the First National Bank, capital, $100,000, surplus, $350,000 ; Commercial National Bank, capital, $200,000, surplus, $31,000 ; Houston National Bank, capital, $100,000, surplus, $11,000 ; South Texas National Bank, capital $500,000, surplus, $50,000; Planters' and Mechanics' National Bank, capital, $250,000, surplus, $17,500, and T. W. House's private banking house, which transacts a large business. There is also here the Houston Loan and Trust Company, operating under a State charter. In addition to the capital and surplus the banks have substantial additional funds in undivided profits. The above financial institutions, excepting the Trust and Loan Company, comprise the membership of the Houston Clearing House. The clearings of these six banks in 1893 were $269,549,060, an advance of $43,906,763 over 1892, when they were $225,644,297. This increase amounts to a gain of 20 per cent, the largest increase in the same time of any city of the United States, and this, too, in a year which has been phenominal for mistrust and disaster. Houston's banking transaction exceed in volume those of Denver, Louisville, Kansas City, St. Paul, Minneapolis and many other places of far larger population |than this city. This fact serves to illustrate in a forcible manner the real, solid, substantial prosperity of the city—actual business transactions and not inflated wind, being the basis upon which is claimed the great advancement and progres.

of the locality. Too much stress cannot be laid on the importance of these indisputable figures, and their significance should not be lost sight of by those seeking out a place for profitable investment, and for the establishment of any description of productive industry.

COTTON.

The following matter relating to Houston's cotton facilities has been furnished us by Captain G. W. Kidd, the popular secretary of the Houston Cotton Exchange:

Houston as a Cotton Market.

First we must speak of the Houston Cotton Exchange and Board of Trade that laid the foundation for her large cotton transactions, and by the energy and business sagacity of its members, its factors and buyers, caused Houston to be recognized as one of the leading markets of the

COTTON EXCHANGE.

United States. The report of the receipts and shipments from this center are watched daily with eager eyes by the operators in all the cotton centers as they are flashed to them by wire at an early hour. And earlier in the season both the New Orleans and New York markets were controlled by her reports. Upon the floor of the Exchange may be found dealers of many nationalities, English, French, German, Greek and Americans meet there in generous rivalry, buying for New England, Liverpool, Havre,

Bremen and ports in Italy and Northern Europe.   One great attraction is the superior staple of the cotton brought here from the river bottoms; besides our soil and climate is so congenial to the growth of this king of plants. We may add, many of the uplands produce fibre that is scarcely equalled, and Harris county, within two miles of Houston, has yielded one bale to the acre that compares favorably with the highest grades.   The unequalled facilities for receiving and handling the staple are important factors. Thirteen railways ramifying the State concentrate here, and deliver the bales to five compresses, unsurpassed anywhere, that have side tracks for receiving and shipping by rail, and also for loading directly upon barges that deliver their cargoes at the Gulf.   The volume of Houston's business, in the space at our command, can be best illustrated by comparison.

RESIDENCE OF MR. R. B. MORRIS.

Since September 1, 1893, to date, taking the New York Financial Chronicle, the highest recognized authority, we find that

New Orleans received		1,581,535	bales cotton
Houston	"	953,233	" "
Galveston	"	924,510	" "
Savannah	"	847,141	" "
St. Louis	"	469,108	" "
Memphis	"	428,605	" "
Norfolk	"	410,021	" "

The above named cotton centers are enough for our purposes.   Houston is enabled to ship via New Orleans, Galveston and Velasco, and expects to have another competitive port at no distant day at Sabine Pass.

Buffalo Bayou—her tidal waterway—compels cheap competitive freights by the Houston Direct Navigation Company's barges that deliver cotton at the ship's sides in the Gulf.   The first ship that sailed for Manchester to pass through her ship canal was loaded in the Gulf Stream entirely by Messrs. Inman & Co., of Houston, and the second ship, that the fortune of the seas permitted first to enter Manchester, was also partly loaded by this great firm.

We will say just here that the Houston Direct Navigation Company's barges carried to the Gulf since September 1, 1892, 261,495 bales and it is regretted we have not the data at hand giving the cotton seed meal, oil, etc., also carried.   It is not out of place to say that Messrs. W. D.

SHEARN M. E. CHURCH.

Cleveland & Co., T. W. House, Carson, Sewall & Co., S. L. Gohlman, H. D. Taylor & Sons, Macatee & Co., Henry Henke & Co., Ziegler & McIlhenny have been established here for years as factors, with abundant means at command.   Among our buyers we have already named Inman & Co., who are constantly filling orders for home and foreign markets, their guarantee being good, not only among our home spinners, but in Liverpool, Manchester and on the continent.   Messrs. Ralli Bros., a Greek house with a world wide reputation, Messrs. C. S. Wigg & Co., C. H. Lucy & Co., Bateson, Hooper & Co., James Beckett, Alex Coghill, Jr., mostly for English account.   A. Breyer, E. S. Swift & Sons, R. T. Phillips & Co., for the continent.   Messrs. Garrow & Co. chiefly for New England spinners, but also English account.

In speaking of the Cotton Exchange and its facilities we did not say, because it could be inferred, that very full quotations are received from the home and foreign markets, and every transaction in futures in New York and New Orleans is recorded every minute they transpire, a telegraphic operator having hi; office on the floor, who also receives and transmits private dispatches.

We have appended the annual cotton receipts of Houston in bales from 1885 to 1893 :

Season ending August 31, 1885 . . . .   408,434 bales
     "   "   August 31, 1886   694,357   "
     "   "   August 31, 1897   748,036   "
     "   "   August 31, 1888   641,159   "
     "   "   August 31, 1889   675,504   "
     "   "   August 31, 1890   794,601   "
     "   "   August 31, 1891   985,084   "
     "   "   August 31, 1892 1,135,872   "
     "   "   August 31, 1893 1,119,282   "

The largest cotton receipts of Houston for a single day, and the largest of any point in Texas for one day, were 21,766 bales received at this city October 20, 1893.

Below are appended a list of the compress companies in Houston and their capacity.

Inman Compress Company, 90 inch, Morse Press, capacity 1,600 bales in twenty-four hours.

International Press Company, Taylor Hydraulic Press, pressure 2,000 tons to square inch, capacity 1,400 bales in twenty-four hours.

Bayou City Press Company, 84 inch Morse Press, capacity 1,600 bales in twenty-four hours.

New Press Company, New Taylor-Miller Hydraulic Press, power capacity 2,000 tons pressure to square inch, capacity 1,600 bales in twenty-four hours.

Cleveland Compress & Warehouse Company, Improved Taylor-Miller Hydraulic Press, power capacity 2,400 tons pressure to square inch, capacity 2,160 bales in twenty-four hours.

LUMBER.

The lumber interests of Houston are only second in importance to cotton, in the volume and value of transactions. For two hundred and twenty miles east of the city is a belt of land covered with timber, which is eighty miles wide, and extends to the Louisiana border and then beyond into that state for a further distance of fifty miles. The supply of standing timber on these lands is enormous. There are hundreds of mills in operation throughout this territory, and most of their product is shipped to this city, or is marketed through the efforts of the wholesale dealers and commission houses here. A moderate estimate of the lumber handled, sold and made up into house material by the dealers and mills of Houston would be about 100,000,000 feet. Beside this, 50,000,000 to 75,000,000 feet are shipped to Houston consumers direct from the mills. The wholesale and commision houses sell from 150,000,000 to 200,000,000 feet, though little of this comes here, but is shipped direct to its destination from the original sources of supply; the business, however, being transacted by Houston houses. In addition to lumber, mainly long leaf yellow pine and cypress, through the agency of the Houston concerns, about 150,000,000 of cypress shingles are distributed over a wide expanse of country. In speaking of the causes, which have made this the lumber center of the state, the most important is that the city alone uses more of the staple, than any other three cities of Texas combined. The admirable shipping facilities all furnish good cause for this gratifying result. We must not fail to allude here to the organization known as the Lumbermen's Association of Texas, which has been instituted to help keep the manufacturer and the dealer in touch on all matters connected with the trade, and to generally stimulate the business. Nearly all the lumber manufacturers and dealers in the state are members of the Association. Its president is Mr. R. D. Gribble of Houston, and Mr. C. F. Drake, of Austin, is secretary and treasurer. The price of lumber to consumers in Houston is about $12 per thousand feet, and shingles from $2 to $3 per thousand. We might mention here that brick and other building material are quite reasonable in price, and tend to stimulate the building trade generally. New settlers

NEW FIRST PRESBYTERIAN CHURCH.

will find every facility here, which would enable them to erect dwellings and other structures, under conditions which would compare favorably with other localities.

REAL ESTATE.

Real estate in and around Houston has assumed an active, healthy demand. With the marked increase of population, naturally there has arisen a corresponding demand for residential sites. The improvement organizations and real estate dealers have labored well, and their efforts have borne good fruit, and sales recently, in and around the city, have run into hundreds of thousands of dollars. Much in the way of improvements has been accomplished in the suburbs, and there are now many desirable sites available, which will prove of advantage as investments, as the city continues to expand and grow, or which are admirably suitable for the erection of residences, business blocks, and for manufacturing purposes. There is a pronounced and steady increase in the value of property, and there are the best reasons for the fact. There are offered today, opportunities for the investment of large sums in more commodious and extensive buildings for commercial and office purposes. Today bonuses are being paid for stores and places in which to do business. During the past year or so, some very handsome blocks have been erected here, and many more will follow this coming season. Among those recently completed are the Kiam building, the Mason building, the Shaw and Jones buildings, and the Rich building. We are reliably informed by a leading real estate agent of this city, that there will be erected in Houston, during the coming year, as follows: The new Rice office building, Hampe's new dry goods and office building, a six-story office building by the Co-operative Building Association, a new High School, new First Presbyterian church, Henry House block, two buildings erected by Frank Dunn, new building erected by Dr.

HOUSTON LIGHT GUARD ARMORY.

Logan of St. Joseph, Mo., new Troy Steam Laundry, a probability of the Houston Post putting up a fine, new structure, the property recently acquired by Judge Henry Brashear and Dow & Lucas will be improved, Dr. M. Perl contemplates erecting a handsome business structure on the old Allen homestead, Jacob Binz will erect a four or five story mercantile and office building opposite the Capitol hotel, Mrs. Selina Veith will erect a three story brick business house on San Jacinto street, C. H. Way of Brooklyn, N. Y., contemplates the erection of a business block on Commerce street, and many of our citizens are going to build new residences in various parts of the city. But we are only at the commencement, and there never was a time in the history of the city when better chances of rise and appreciation were apparent in real estate investments. There is no false boom here, nor are there inflated values, but a solid, substantial progress, which is bound to bear good fruit. Capitalists and investors, and others, who are looking for a suitable location in which to carry on their business, will do well to look in this direction towards a profitable field. With natural and acquired advantages, which are rarely equalled, Houston and vicinity are prepared to offer opportunities for the placing of capital, which must conduce to the profit of all, who are judicious in their selection of property. The field is here, and the crop will come in profusion at the appointed time.

The following is an extract from a letter written by Mr. J. H. Bright, of the firm of Bright & Co., real estate dealers. The letter was published in the Fort Worth Gazette, the Houston Post, and other journals.
*   *   *   *   *   *   *   *   *   *   *   *   *

" A number of houses, that have been erected, or are being erected, in the city of Houston for the year 1893, embraces some of the handsomest

RESIDENCE OF MR. L. M. DISNEY.

structures in the state, and in point of numbers greater than that of any two cities, being almost 1,600 separate and distinct buildings erected in the year 1893.

" There have been no bank failures, no restrictions were placed upon depositors, but at any and all times the depositors of the various banks were allowed to withdraw their balances without notification. The banks, without exception, have declared and paid their semi-annual dividends, just the same as they did in prosperous times. Instead of merchants retiring from business, new merchants have engaged in business, from other cities, to take advantage of our facilities as a distributing point, and the low rate of freight guaranteed our branches of commerce.

" A vacant business house is unknown. When one wishes to engage in business, it is necessary to have a place erected to meet his requirements. A number of large business houses are at present in the course of construction, and are all under lease for a term of years, and others are soon to follow, and applications have already been made for their occupancy.

"Houston is a city of many beautiful streets and residences. Fifty miles of streets are paved or under contract to be paved with the most durable material known.

" Houston is the second city in the United States in point of health, although it is a ' Mecca ' for the unfortunate, it being the home of several hospitals and infirmaries, and many of the deaths that occur in Houston are those of non-residents. The extreme low death rate reported by the city physician, compared with former years, is-said to be due entirely to the artesian water used by the city water works company. This magnificent plant, with a permanent capacity of over 10,000,000 gallons per day, is supplied from twenty-six artesian wells, which water is pronounced by chemists to be absolutely soft, and free from chemical or mineral properties. The stand pipe used as a reservoir is the largest in the United States.

" Houston is lit by electricity, for public uses and streets, and by gas, from works with a capacity for supplying a city of 150,000 population."

* * * * * * * * * * * *

There can be no doubt entertained by anyone, who has observed the rapid strides the city of Houston has made in the past few years, as to its continued and most successful advancement. We have epitomized at length its advantageous shipping facilities, delightful climate, admirable location, cheap sites for manufacturing and residence, good water supply, cheap living and other attractions, and need not further recapitulate. Its advance is certain, it cannot be otherwise. Evidence is not wanting of the truth of these assertions, and but a single visit to Houston by one who is not familiar with these facts is required to convince him that for the means of safe investments, for a place in whicn to carry on business successfully, for a city in which to live economically and well, Houston is unsurpassed.

THE TEXAS GULF COAST COUNTRY.

The Gulf coast country of Texas, which may be said to include the counties of Harris, Brazoria, Chambers, Orange, Galveston, Wharton, Jefferson, Fort Bend, Matagorda, Liberty and Hardin, is offering today greater inducements to the farmer, fruit grower and investor than almost any section of the United States. Here can be obtained, at a relatively very low price, lands of the greatest fertility, needing no irrigation, in the heart of a country which is progressing by leaps and bounds. In no part of the United States are thrift and industry better rewarded. Fruits can here be raised at a greater profit even than in California, as they are ready for shipment fully a month earlier than in that State, and at the same time Texas is three or four days nearer to a profitable market. Early vegetables grown here yield the best returns, and stock raising and general farming has been proved a thorough success. The locality has the best of railroad facilities and water transportation, and all parts of it are rapidly being settled with desirable and industrious people from all over the country. The general surface of the country is from fifty to sixty feet above the mean tide level, and is sufficiently rolling to afford good drainage, which is further facilitated by numerous streams of clear running water, which empty into the various bays which indent the coast of the Mexican Gulf. The soil varies somewhat in different localities, consisting mainly of red, chocolate, black sandy and dark sandy loam, all of which are very fertile and suited to the growth of any crop which it may be desirable to cultivate. The section throughout is generally sub-irrigated, which enables it to withstand drowth better than most localities. By reason of the proximity to the Gulf an ample and seasonable rainfall is assured. Good, clear water can be had at a depth of from fifteen to thirty feet in most localities. In addition unlimited supplies of the purest water is obtained from artesian

Pasture Scene, Pleasant Hill Valley, Harris County, Texas. Property of Col. Philip W. Hudson. From photograph taken Dec. 15, 1893.

wells, sunk a to depth of from 400 to 600 feet, which need no pumping. The climate of the Texas Gulf coast country is the finest in America. The trade winds coming from the Gulf temper the heat of summer and the cold of winter, rendering the temperature more equable, and free from the sudden rainstorms of the country further north. It seldom goes above ninety-five degrees in the summer and below twenty-five in winter, while the Gulf breeze makes it refreshing even in the warmest days of midsummer, and sunstrokes are practically unknown. The nights are deliciously cool, and sleep comes to invigorate the worker for his next day's toil. The country is eminently healthful, malaria being conspicuous by its absence, and pulmonary diseases gain no foothold here.

Farming, either on a large or small scale, can be prosecuted here under the most favorable conditions. Taking value and prospective advancement into consideration land may here be purchased cheaper than elsewhere in the country. The soil and climate is especially adapted to the growth of cereals, tame grasses, rice, sugar, all vegetables grown in the United States, and fruits indigenous to temperate and semi-tropical climates, also stock raising and fattening. The country is rapidly assuming the aspect of an immense garden, reigned over by the deities, Ceres, Flora and Pomona. Today South Texas is the natural home of the pear, grape, peach, fig and strawberry, and the phenominal returns realized from these crops by those who have been engaged in raising them for a

MARKET HOUSE.

number of years, together with the splendid market and shipping facilities enjoyed by this locality, will make this section, within the next five years, equal in value per acre to the lands of California. Pears do exceedingly well, those that do best being the Keifer and Le Conte varieties. They are easily propagated from cuttings. The trees will begin bearing the third or fourth year, the fifth they will yield a profit, and the sixth they will net from $400 to $600 per acre.

Strawberries have met with the greatest success, and they are the pride of the country. They are greatly in favor with new settlers, bringing a fair return the first season after planting. Strawberries grow here from February to December, although, of course, they fetch the best prices in the early spring. This fruit, when properly cultivated, yields easily from $500 to $700 per acre. Peaches will yield $800 to the acre, plums do well, also grapes, plums, raspberries and other small fruits. All kinds of vegetables can be grown on these lands with success. Two

crops of cabbages can be raised regularly, and each crop is worth $250 to
the acre.   Irish potatoes are profitable, and well looked after yield 250
bushels to the acre.   Garden peas yield about $150 to the acre, and wax
beans average $120 to the acre.   Peas and beans are early crops, and can
be followed by others on the same soil.   A good crop is sweet potatoes,
especially suitable for a new settler.   From one to two hundred bushels
can be obtained from an acre.   A well known farmer at Alvin last season
a·eraged 219 bushels of sweet potatoes to the acre.   All tame grasses do
well.   Alfalfa is raised with large success in this section, and is very

POSTOFFICE.

profitable.   That most beautiful flower, cape jessamine, has been cultivated
largely at Alvin, Brazoria county, and we almost hesitate to mention the
value of the yield, $1,000 per acre is but a moderate estimate.   Cape
jessamine buds bring 80 cents per hundred, and a three years' plant yields
from 300 to 400 buds each.   Six hundred plants can be cultivated on each
acre of land, and we leave our readers to make their own calculation.
The above figures have been supplied by one of the oldest settlers in the
country, and may be relied upon.   The yield is rather under than over
estimated in all instances.   General farming, apart from fruit and vegetable culture, is destined to be one of the leading pursuits of this section.
Stock and cattle raising and feeding for the market invites an immense

field for success, and is already being prosecuted with vigor and energy by a number of enterprising agriculturists. There is a large demand here for stock of all kinds, and the soil is eager to yield the food for their sustenance. Five months of seed time, five months of harvest and two months of rest, with often two crops per year from the same ground, are some of the advantages of this favored region. Corn, oats, cotton, sugar, rice, melons, beets and all varieties of tame grasses and cereals are never failing and prolific crops. Large and small tracts of land are offered at low prices, and on terms which render the payment easy to the settler. Now is the time to come here and partake of the opportunities and blessings with which a beneficent Providence has endowed this country, before prices rise and appreciate, as they are certain to do in the very near future. Any of the enterprising real estate agents mentioned in another portion of this volume, will be glad to correspond with all who are interested in our remarks, and they tender to settlers and investors a cordial welcome. Another thing that must be taken into consideration is that this district is no wilderness, schools for the young abound under State direction and supervision, churches are numerous, and all the refinements of civilization are at hand. Hardware and building material can be purchased here as cheap as anywhere, lumber is particularly reasonable in price, and suitable help can be obtained with facility. Special inducements are offered periodically in the way of excursions at reduced rates, and it is seldom that home seekers come here and fail to make an investment.

HOUSTON'S TRANSPORTATION FACILITIES.

Houston may be said to lead all Southern cities as a railroad center. Her position in the transportation world is most happy. A steamboat and fifteen railroad lines meet here, affording unsurpassed shipping facilities for manufacturers of any description, and for the shipment of their products, those of the soil, general merchandise, etc., to or from any part of the country, at low rates, and with facility and dispatch.

The Galveston, Harrisburg & San Antonio and the Texas & New Orleans railroads constitute the links of the celebrated "Sunset Route," of the Southern Pacific Company. These roads are of the greatest value to Houston. The Galveston, Harrisburg & San Antonio has lately amended its charter so as to make this city its terminal point instead of Harrisburg. The headquarters of these roads are at Houston, and so are their shops, where cars of all descriptions are built, as well as engines, and the various requisites incident to railroad equipment.

The Houston & Texas Central passes through twenty-seven counties of central Texas, through a highly cultivated and populous region. It has done much to advance the interests of the state generally, and it has largely stimulated its settlement. The road does a large business here ; and at Houston are its general offices and shops. A large number of hands are afforded employment in connection with its service, machine shops, car shops, round houses, creosote works, etc.

The International & Great Northern is a trunk line through Texas to Mexico. The road extends from Longview, in northeast Texas, to Laredo, on the Rio Grande, and from Palestine through Houston to Galveston. It has also several branches tapping a number of cities and small towns in the state. One of these branches, known as the Columbia branch, extends from Houston to Columbia, a distance of fifty miles. The Galveston, Houston & Henderson is a branch of the International & Great Northern and extends from Houston to Galveston, a distance of fifty miles.

Other branches of the I. & G. N. are Overton to Henderson, 16 miles; Minneola through Tyler to Troupe, 45 miles; Phelps to Huntsville 8 miles, and Round Rock to Georgetown, 10 miles.

The Houston, East & West Texas runs from Houston to Shreveport, La. This is a narrow guage road at the present time, but it is expected that a change will be made to standard guage in the near future.

The Gulf, Colorado & Santa Fe Railroad is one of the divisions of the great Santa Fe south-western system. Its terminus in Texas is Galveston, and it extends from that city to Purcell, I. T., 517 miles distant. This road, with branches, has a mileage of 1058 miles. It is connected with Houston by a branch, which opens up for the city the entire 9000 miles of the Santa Fe system, which taps the West and South-West from Chicago to San Francisco.

The Missouri, Kansas & Texas Railroad has recently been added to the transportation facilities of Houston. It has constructed here a new and handsome depot, and has adopted this city as the southern terminus of

CHRIST CHURCH.

the road. Through its means a new route has been opened to Kansas City, and to Hannibal, a connection being made at the latter place with the Burlington & Wabash lines for Chicago. The M. K. & T., or "Katy," as it is familiarly called, runs through the three states, which it has embodied in its name. It is first class in its equipment. It has 1828 miles of track, about half being in Texas. It does a large business in carrying freight, especially cotton, corn, cattle and general merchandise.

The San Antonio & Aransas Pass is sometimes styled the "Mission Route." Its eastern terminus is at Houston. It extends from this city to San Antonio, a distance of 309 miles. The road traverses a splendid farming and stock raising country, and in the vicinity of Rockport and Corpus Christi, it taps a very fine fruit growing district. The road is well equipped throughout with steel rails, iron bridges, and all modern facilities.

The Texas Western is a narrow guage road extending from Houston to Seely, a distance of fifty-one miles. It connects there with the G. C. & S. Fe.

The Houston Belt & Magnolia Park Railroad connects the city with Magnolia Park, a beautiful recreation ground of 1374 acres on the banks of Buffalo Bayou. At Harrisburg this line joins the Houston, La Porte & Northern Railroad.

The Texas Transportation Co., a local railroad convenience of large utility, connects Houston at Clinton with ocean steamers, enabling cotton, cotton seed meal and other products, to be shipped by this road to all ports of the world.

The New York, Texas & Mexican Railroad is now running trains from Beeville to Rosenberg over its own line, and from Rosenberg to Houston over the Southern Pacific system.

Besides the railroads there is a navigation company, which dispatches steamboats and barges between Houston and the Gulf at regular intervals, and when occasion demands, and there are also a number

SWEENEY & COOMBS OPERA HOUSE.

of independent vessels which ply on this stream. Much freight is shipped by this route to the sea-board, cotton especially, being sent down in barges and discharging into ocean going steamers anchored in Galveston Bay, direct, without transhipment in that city. The same applies to cotton seed oil and meal, which are dispatched to Europe by the same means. Owing to the great advantage of shipping via Buffalo Bayou, cotton is laid down in Liverpool and other European ports 48 cents a bale less than from Galveston. An advantage to Houston, of the greatest moment, connected with Buffalo Bayou is that it creates competition, keeps down rail rates, giving to this city lower rates to and from all points than is enjoyed by any other place in Texas. The principal transportation business of Buffalo Bayou has been since 1840 conducted by companies organized here. The main business is now however done by the Houston Direct Navigation Co. which has united and succeeded various transportation lines previously organized. Houston as a common point controls the freight rates of the West and the Republic of Mexico.

Some idea of the importance of Houston, as a railroad center, may be gathered from the fact that there are fifty-two regular passenger trains, and oftentimes between fifty and sixty passenger trains entering and leaving the railway depots of the city daily. From 126 to 184 freight trains are the daily average number passing through, and making Houston the terminus of their journey. Houston is the largest and most important center for railroad construction south of the Potomac river, the number of hands employed in the machine, car, creosote and repair shops here, averaging fully 5000.

EDUCATIONAL.

The public schools of Houston are fifteen in number, nine being for white scholars and seven for the colored population. The number of children enrolled are as follows : 2,900 white, 1,900 colored, total, 4,800. There is a High School for white advanced pupils, which has an attendance

HOUSTON NEW HIGH SCHOOL.

of 180 pupils, and the colored High School instructs thirty young people of African race. The graduates from the High Schools are fully competent to enter the highest class colleges or universities of the United States. The Houston public schools have for years taken the highest rank among educational establishments of the South. They have always been conducted upon non-political and non-partisan principles. The teachers are chosen because of the fitness for their positions, not because of any political influence which they may possess. Merit and good character are the only qualities taken into consideration in the selection of the instructors of the youth of this city. Besides the public schools there are a number of small parochial schools, under direction of the Catholic ecclesiastical authorities. There is also the Convent school of the Incarnate Word, where a full course of education is imparted by the sisters.

The public school structures are well built, and in them the latest and most approved methods of study are employed, and improved apparatus introduced as rapidly as possible. The Board of Education has recently spent about $100,000 in building four new brick school houses, which are perfect in model and appointments. A fine, new High School building is now being erected, and this, when completed, will fall but little, if any, short of $100,000 in cost. We should like to say here that at the expense of the board the pupils are furnished with a large amount of supplementary reading matter, judiciously selected by the teachers. In every school there is a working library, the books of which are loaned to the pupils at the discretion of their instructors. In fact, so easy and enjoyable has

HARRIS COUNTY COURT HOUSE.

schooling become here, that pupils are almost invariably found to be willing to improve their opportunities with a keen appreciation of the advantages open to them. It is generally admitted that the work done at the Houston schools will compare favorably with any city of the South.

AMUSEMENTS.

In the way of entertainments and amusements there is much to make life in the city pleasant and sociable. During the winter there are the usual church fairs and festivals. There are also social and society reunions and a number of clubs of various descriptions. There is a very fine theatre here—Sweeney & Coombs' opera house, (which we illustrate,) and the cream of the dramatic and operatic profession appears here before the Houston public. There are also a number of smaller halls in which dramatic representations, readings, *musicales*, *soirees*, etc., are given.

SOCIETIES.

The citizens of Houston are a gregarious and sociable community. They organize themselves into societies of every sort for benevolent and social purposes. Masonic, Pythian, and a variety of other worthy and useful organizations abound, and thus the people keep themselves well preserved against the rusting influence of selfishness and asceticism.

MASONIC TEMPLE.

There are here two lodges of A. F. & A. M., a Chapter of R. A. M., a Council of R. & S. M. and a Commandery of Knights Templar, a Lodge of Perfection, 14th degree A. & A. S. R. The Most Worshipful Grand Lodge A. F. & A. M. of the State of Texas also holds its annual communications in December of each year at the Masonic Temple in this city. The annual convocation of the Grand Royal Arch Chapter of the State of Texas is also held in Houston. There are very many enthusiastic members of the Masonic fraternity here, and it is a somewhat remarkable fact that the first Knight Templar dubbed and created in the State of Texas is now living, and holds an honorable position in Ruthven Commandery. The Knights of Pythias are represented by four lodges, two sections of the Endowment Rank, and one division of Uniform Rank, the Knights of Honor have four Lodges, the Chosen Friends eight councils, A. O. U. W. three lodges, B. P. O. Elks has a lodge with a large and important membership. There are also five organizations under the auspices of the

Hebrew societies, four German singing societies, seven associations in the interests of railway employees. The military organizations consist of the Houston Light Guards, with a membership of nearly one hundred, the Rutherford Rangers, a cavalry organization of about fifty mounted men. and the Houston Artillery Co., recently organized. There are also upward of fifty miscellaneous organizations, not including those connected with the churches.

MUNICIPAL.

The city's bonded debt is about $1,746,000, and the bonds command a premium in the open market, and are considered by high financial authorities to be gilt-edged securities. In 1880 when the total valuations were only $5,352,000 the tax rate was $2.70 per $100. The tax rate now on $20,000,000 valuation is only $2 per $100. The debt in 1880 was $1,501,000. or about $90.33 per capita. It is now but $1,746,000, which is less than $50 per capita. Another consideration which must be borne in mind is that the valuation is very low, less than 75 per cent of the real value, and, therefore, the ratio of taxation, $2 per $1,000, is really much less than in other cities where the assessment is fully up to the value of property. One per cent of the tax roll is devoted to the payment of the yearly interest on the city bonds, the rest to the general fund, including the school appropriation. The taxes are judiciously utilized, apart from the above, for city expenditure, salaries and public improvements. All works within the duties of the municipal authorities are thoroughly carried out, and Houston today presents the aspect of a healthy, well governed city, where law and order reigns, and where life and property are as efficiently protected as in any city of the land.

HOUSTON AND SOUTH TEXAS FAIR AND DRIVING ASSOCIATION.

Through the efforts and enterprise of Mr. Harvey T. D. Wilson, a well known financial agent, and a native Houstonian, our city can now boast of possessing one of the finest fair grounds and race tracks in the South. At this present time of writing the work of construction is well under way, and will be completed by April 8th, 1894, about the time this volume will be issued to the public. The establishment will be perfect in all its details, and will embody all improvements necessary, or which in any manner will be advantageous to an institution of this nature. The location of the grounds is all that could be desired. The distance from the center of the city is about two miles and a half, and a belt line of railway, owned by the Southern Pacific railroad, can transport any number of persons in short order, at the merely nominal expense of five cents per head. The full mile race track is located to the east of the grand stand, and within the mile course is a fine half mile track. Both are so situated that the grand stand is just half way of their straight stretches, and commands a splendid view of the finishes. The tracks are built with seventy rod stretches and ninety rod curves. The home stretch is eighty-five feet wide, curves seventy-five feet, and the back stretches sixty-five feet. The elevation of the curves is a half inch to each foot of the width of the track. The grand stand is of the dimensions of 65x150 feet, and it is provided with comfortable seats for 3500 people. The structure has five entrances, and there is a restaurant on the second floor, 30x150 feet in area. There are also, a handsome saloon on the first floor, dressing rooms for the jockeys, toilet rooms, and all modern conveniences. This stand is a distance of about sixty feet from the race track fence. The judges' and band stands, in front of the grand stand, are of ornamental design, and are admirably placed in regard to position. One hundred feet south of the grand stand, and the same distance from the track, as is that structure, is the club house.. This contains nineteen rooms, and it is provided with a second story gallery, which has a seating capacity of 250 persons. It has also handsome reception and dining rooms, and indeed everything that should make it first class and attractive in all its characteristics. Located some two hundred and fifty feet distant from the club house is a plain, substantial, but yet withal attractive building, utilized as the boarding house. It is arranged with ten bedrooms, large sitting and dining room, etc. It is utilized as the residence of the manager and for the accommodation of the patrons of the stables and the track. The stables are of the dimensions of 30x65 feet each, and they have eight feet awnings all around them. There are ten stalls in each stable, 12x12 feet in dimensions. The stables are wainscoted for a height of five feet, with two inch dressed lumber, and they are latticed over this another five feet. Above the lattice work is a shelf seven feet wide. The stables are shingle roofed, and as a protection from fire they are situated a hundred feet apart. There is here altogether, stable accomodation for fully three hundred horses, and it is safe to say that no track in the country has better accommodations for valuable horses, or conveniences where they will receive better care. These cottage stables are a noticeable feature of the establishment, worthy of the appreciation of horse owners. Special efforts will be made to establish a reputation for Houston as the choicest and most desirable of wintering places for fine horses, and such treatment will be accorded the animals as will make it the most popular spring, fall and winter quarters in the United States. The entrance to the grounds is imposing and ornamental, and there are provided the latest and most improved character of turnstiles, which are automatic and self registering. The fence which encloses the hundred and thirty-five acres of beautiful land, which constitute the extent of the grounds, is substantially built, and is close boarded for a height of eight feet. All material used in the construction has been furnished by Messrs. Lock, Moore & Co., of Westlake, La., and it comprises the best of heart Calcasieu pine, and the finest of cypress shingles. The expenses of improvements and construction up to the present time amount fully to the sum of $40,000, and at an early date convenient and elegant fair buildings will be added, at a large additional cost. Nothing in fact will be lacking to make this a model establishment of its kind, either in appointments or conveniences. The drainage has been rigidly scrutinized and supervised and it is absolutely perfect. The soil is black loam, and experts have said that this will make the track one of the fastest in the country. Altogether this enterprise is one of the greatest moment to this city and section. It will be the object of the management to attract hither the attention of the whole Gulf Coast country. Fairs of importance will be held from time to time, and a number of influential organizations have intimated their intention to make displays of a most ambitious character. The growing agricultural interests of this section needed the institution of a first class establishment of this nature, and the public are to be congratulated on the acquisition of so complete and perfect a place, where may advantageously be displayed the products of the toilers of the soil. Much credit is due to the energy and enterprise of Mr. Harvey T. D. Wilson, who is the sole owner of the property, and who has improved and built the place at his sole individual expense. The entire community is actively co-operating with him to make the racing and fair a success, and the jockey club now being organized through the efforts of Mr. Wilson, will soon announce to the world the programme of the management.

HOUSTON CITY STREET RAILWAY COMPANY.

The Houston City Street Railway Co. was incorporated October 1876, and it came into the hands of the present management in 1890, electric power being then substituted for horses and mules. Its value to the city and her material interests can hardly be overestimated. The acquisition of this improvement has been of the greatest moment to Houston, adding so much to the comfort and convenience of its residents, and largely enhancing the value of real estate in and around the city. The company are the successors to the two lines of horse railroad which preceded it, their interests being amalgamated with those of the present corporation. The railway plant and possessions are complete in all their appointments, and adequate to all demands that may be made upon them. The motive power is supplied by two large Reynolds-Corliss cross-compound engines, which have a united capacity of 700 horse power. Five dynamos are utilized to generate what electricity is required to operate the cars. The company have forty-seven cars in operation, over forty miles of track, constituting twelve separate routes. All of the cars run upon a central belt in the centre of the city, so that every car passes the office of the company, the principal hotels, the Cotton Exchange and other central points, every trip.

CITIZENS' ELECTRIC LIGHT AND POWER.

In the year 1889 began a new departure in the lighting of the city of Houston, for at that time the above mentioned company began operations, and with every facility at command has earned for the city the distinction of being one of the best lighted, and consequently among the safest for life and property in the Gulf states. The plant is located at the foot of Gabel Street, on Buffalo Bayou. The building has been fitted up by the company with one of the most complete electric light equipments obtainable. There are here three engines respectively as follows: One is of the Hamilton-Corliss pattern, and is of 500 horse power capacity; the others are a Bass engine of 75 horse power, and a Taylor engine of 100 horse power. There are ten dynamos, and the capacity of the plant is about 500 arc lights, 4000 incandescent lights, and 160 horse power for operating elevators, light machinery, etc. The company have a contract for the city for street lighting, supplying the municipalty with 150 arc lights. They also furnish light and power to hundreds of business establishments, public buildings, and private residences. There is a separate circuit used for supplying electric power for electric motors, to operate elevators and light machinery, and this is coming more and more into use, displacing to some extent steam and hydraulic power, in certain cases, being so much more economical and easy to operate. The company have altogether about fifty miles of wire in the city, and they employ about twenty men. The capital stock of the company is $200,000, and the executive officers are: Jas, A. Baker, jr., president, and A. Granger, secretary and treasurer. Mr. Baker is of the well known and leading law firm of Baker, Botts, Baker & Lovett, of this city, and Mr. Granger has been a resident here for the past fifteen years, and he devotes his personal attention to the business of the company. The service given has generally been pronounced as of the best.

HOUSTON GAS LIGHT COMPANY.

The Houston Gas Light Company enjoy every facility for supplying this city with gas of the best quality. Their plant is probably the most complete in the state. The retort house is furnished with four benches, of six retorts each, and has a capacity of 250,000 feet in the twenty-four hours. The condenser and scrubber have a capacity of 300,000 feet in the twenty-four hours. The two gasometers have a combined capacity of 250,000 feet. Besides supplying gas to Houston inhabitants, the company also deal largely in coal tar, coal, and coke, also gas stoves, heaters, and ranges of the best pattern, and most approved efficiency. Their supplies of coal both for use in making gas and for supplying the public, are obtained from Pennsylvania and Alabama. It is shipped here by sea and bayou, being unloaded from the vessels at Galveston, and re-shipped in barges direct to the doors of the company's premises. They handle a very large quantity, annually, being enabled to quote lowest rates here for the mineral. A specialty of theirs is crushed coke for family use, which is an excellent substitute for anthracite coal, being both cheaper and better. They have a new coke crusher now in operation, and they prepare coke to suit ordinary grates, heaters, ranges and stoves. The capital stock of the Houston Gas Light Company is $200,000, its executive officers being T. W. House, president; T. H. Scanlan, vice president; J. J. McKeever, secretary treasurer and general manager, and J. H. Fitzgerald, superintendent.

PROSPECTS FOR THE FUTURE.

Houston has a record of continuous growth, and it is a fair presumption that the future will present results of even accelerated expansion.

RESIDENCE OF MR. A. C. HERNDON.

Her natural advantages were at no time better supplemented by her acquired resources than now, and the opportunities to inaugurate new enterprises, and obtain homes, occupation and happiness are here open to all. This city is the home of intellectual vigor and refinement, with a past full of interest, a present full of earnestness, and a future full of brightness. Houston presents many attractions to the student, the business man and the wage earner, and greatest of all to that most practical philanthropist, the enterprising capitalist seeking safe investments in real estate, or in the establishment of productive industries. The time is not far distant when the 65,000 of Houston and environs shall be doubled and tripled, and when of the entire Gulf States it shall be what it is now to Texas, its most attractive city.

I. J. ISAACS, Editor.

The City of Houston.

Its Leading Industries and Mercantile Establishments,
with Sketches of their Foundation, History and
Progress and Notes on the Character and
Extent of their Operations.

A. C. HERNDON & SON,

General Land Agents, 1016 Congress Avenue.

In earlier pages of this volume we have discoursed at length relative to the advantages that Houston and vicinity offer at the present time for investments in real estate, whether as a means of placing money advantageously or acquiring a home on a soil, which bountifully and abundantly yields its fruit to honest toil. Among leading firms of real estate dealers and land agents here who have inducements of the highest character to offer is the firm of A. C. Herndon & Son, whose business was originally founded in 1886 by Mr. A. C. Herndon, the present style being adopted in 1890. The firm are general land agents, buying and selling city and county property. They have many tracts of great promise and value to dispose of, which have been divided up into lots and parcels to suit the convenience of purchasers. They have also valuable farm and forest lands, which are offered at prices that are bound to materially appreciate in the near future. There never was a time when Houston and Harris County property offered greater inducements. The country is rapidly being filled up, as is natural when the great value of the locality is understood. Population is increasing by leaps and bounds, factories are being established, new enterprises are almost daily being inaugurated and a solid, substantial era of progress is firmly established. There is no inflation or false boom here, the prosperity is on a sound basis, and it is probably safe to say that no city in the country has felt less the strain of hard times during the present stringency than has the city of Houston—the metropolis of the State. Every advantage is offered here to the home-seeker, a law-abiding population, solid and and substantial business houses, solvent banks, energetic enterprise, unrivaled shipping facilities, many converging lines of railroad, deep water connection with all of the ports of the world, a fruitful and prolific soil, markets for produce on the spot, the greatest cotton center in the country, pure water, well paved streets, a delightful climate, healthful location, good schools and not to continue indefinitely, we will mention, last, though not least, good sites for homes at a low price. Almost every variety of agricultural products can be grown profitably in Harris County, and the season here is much earlier than many other Southern and Pacific Slope locations. Messrs. A. C. Herndon & Co. have many desirable bargains to offer at all times in the city and neighborhood. Home-seekers and investors are invited to call on them at their office, or correspond by mail, and all enquiries will at once receive their immediate attention. The standing of the firm is such as to inspire the fullest confidence, and all transactions are based upon honor and good faith. The gentlemen comprising the firm individually, are Messrs A. C. Herndon and J. B. Herndon, father and son. They are thoroughly experienced in all matters relating to the real estate business, and sedulously devote their closest care and attention to the real interests of their clients. To the capitalist seeking a means of placing his funds where they will breed a substantial profit, to the home-seeker, either here or abroad, and to all who may be interested in real property we advise a correspondence and connection with this firm which, we are persuaded will redound to ultimate advantage and satisfaction.

WM. D. CLEVELAND & CO.,
Wholesale Grocers, Cotton Factors, Etc., and Proprietors of the Cleveland Compress Model Warehouse.

The most casual observer of Houston's commercial resources must accord to the firm of Wm. D. Cleveland & Co., the leading position. The business was originally founded by Mr. Wm. D. Cleveland in 1869, the present firm being organized in 1886. The salesrooms and offices at the present time, are located in a large concrete building of two floors and basement, 100 feet square, which is the property of the firm. Their original headquarters were destroyed by fire, April 8th, 1893. In view, however, of the great expansion of the business, the firm contemplates erecting, at an early date, a new and imposing structure which will be an architectural ornament to the city, and will combine all conveniences for carrying on their business to advantage. In reference to the stock handled by Messrs. Wm. D. Cleveland & Co., it is safe to say that for quantity and value, variety and diffuseness, quality and superiority, adaptability and selection, it cannot be excelled even at the larger establishments of the kind in metropolitan centers. Among certain of their specialties, we wish to draw atten-

THE CLEVELAND COTTON COMPRESS AND WAREHOUSE.

tion to those which bear the name "Apex" as a brand title. The geographical position of Houston is such that it forms the apex of a triangle, the base of which is the Gulf of Mexico, with the ports of Velasco and Galveston as outlets at the angles. These ports are in direct connection with Houston and serve as gateways for the dispatch of her cotton and other products to all parts of the globe. Also, as the apex of a triangle is naturally its highest point, so the goods branded by this title may be said to be of the highest standard quality. The firm put up under this distinguishing trade mark a variety of articles, such as the Apex Roasted Coffees, Apex Baking Powder, Apex Sugar Corn, Apex Condensed Milk, Apex Tomatoes, Apex Blueing, etc., and they are about to largely extend this branch of their business and to place before the trade many other goods of superior quality thus marked, which will be standard, and the quality of which they will guarantee. The firm have a special department devoted to the roasting of coffee and the manufacture of baking powder, equipped with the best appliances. They enjoy the best of facilities for procuring the finest qualities of coffee which come to this market, and they are now enabled to supply the Texas trade with fresh parched coffee of the best character, and the most delicate blends. By obtaining their goods of this firm, in lieu of purchasing from distant localities, dealers will be enabled to furnish their patrons with coffees which have not deteriorated or lost flavor in lengthened transportation. The "Apex" brand is equal to any on the market and the "Fancy Blend" will make a cup of coffee that lingers deliciously on the palate for a long time after drinking. The house carries also a very large stock of teas, which are selected especially for it by some of the most experienced tea merchants in the trade, and dealers can be assured of here obtaining the choicest goods in this line. As to the stock of domestic and imported canned goods, sauces, table delicacies, heavy groceries, etc., it is impossible for us to do more than allude to it, other than to say that the firm are strictly first-class wholesale grocers, with the most complete facilities at hand, and having at heart the best interests of the public equally with their own. Referring to the cotton departments of the house's business, we will mention that the compress and warehouse are located in the Fifth ward. It fronts on the bayou and is near the International bridge. The building is of the unusual dimensions of 600x164 feet. It is equipped with all the latest and best improved appliances for handling the staple with dispatch and economy, and the establishment is a model one in every respect. The compress is of the celebrated Taylor Hydraulic pattern, the most powerful extant, and it is very fast in its working. Its capacity is 100 bales of cotton per hour. The firm invite consignments of cotton in any quantity, and they are prepared to make advances if required, and assure quick sales and prompt returns. The firm handle about 50,000 bales of cotton annually on commission, and they also do compressing for the trade. Messrs. Wm. D. Cleveland & Co. employ about fifty salesmen, assistants and work people. They have seven commercial travelers on the road, calling on customers within the circuit of their trade. The members of the firm are Messrs. Wm. D. Cleveland and C. Lombardi, both of whom are gentlemen of thorough experience in all matters relating to the trade. To their constant efforts and close attention must be attributed the signal growth and development of the business which has drawn attention to this center as a highly favorable and advantageous market and source of supply.

HALFF & NEWBOUER BROS.,

Importers and Jobbers in Dry Goods, Notions, Boots, Shoes, Hats, Etc., corner Franklin Avenue and Fannin Streets—New York Office 22, 24 and 26 Howard Street.

A house which has done much to enhance the reputation of Houston is that now conducted under the title of Halff & Newbouer Bros., whose business originally

was established about a half century ago. The present firm assumed control in 1886. The premises occupied comprise a three-story brick building a hundred feet square. These extensive quarters are sub-divided into different departments, each containing an ample, well assorted and carefully selected stock of the various lines of goods handled by the house, which embraces a complete assortment of American and imported dry goods, notions, hosiery, gents' furnishing goods, dress goods and silks, linens, etc.; also, boots, shoes, hats, caps, etc. The house is the largest concern of the kind here and one of the largest in the State. The firm enjoy the most intimate relations with manufacturers in this country, and they are also direct in porters, with purchasing agents in prominent foreign centers of production. They ha · an office in New York at 22, 24 and 26 Howard street, in the heart of the dry goods district, and a resident partner in the metropolis is there engaged in studying the markets so that all advantageous fluctuations are availed of and the leading novelties of each season placed before patrons at the earliest date. The firm employ fifteen assistants and salesmen, several of whom are on the road calling on the trade within the States of Texas and Louisiana. The firm are also cotton factors. They invite consignments of the staple and have every facility for conserving and advancing the interests of consignors. The members of the firm are Messrs. Felix Halff, J. S. Newbouer and Ed. Newbouer. Mr. J. S. Newbouer resides in New York, attending to the interests of the house there. All of the partners may be said to be thoroughly experienced in every detail of the business. With ample capital honorably accumulated, purchasing agents in the centers of production and distribution and every facility that could be afforded by experience, credit and connections, this firm is certainly in a position to deal favorable with merchants within the circuit of its trade operations.

DICKSON CAR WHEEL CO.,
Manufacturers of "Barr Patent Contracting Chill" Car Wheels from Texas Iron, Houston.

We here draw the attention of our readers to the enterprise of the Dickson Car Wheel Co., of Houston, Texas, who are the manufacturers of an improved car wheel which has clearly demonstrated its great features of superiority and utility. The Dickson Car Wheel Co. was incorporated in 1887, with a capital stock of $75,000. Mr. J. F. Dickson, the founder, commenced business at Marshall, Texas, in 1875, and he began the manufacture of his car wheels in 1880 and removed to this city in 1886. The works at the present time cover the space of two entire city blocks, and they are very complete in character. The dimensions of the establishment are 500x250 feet; the principal building, the foundry, is 75x200 feet in area, and there is also an office building, core ovens, well equipped machine shop, fuel sheds and other minor structures. Special machinery of improved character is used and a force of about fifty skilled mechanics are given employment. The capacity of the works is 50,000 car wheels annually. The Dickson Car Wheel Co. are manufacturers of chilled car wheels made from Texas iron, both the common and "Barr" contracting chill kinds being made. About twenty years or more ago Mr. John F. Dickson, the president of the present company, was general superintendent of the Texas and Pacific Railway. At that time his attention was directed to certain properties and peculiarities of the charcoal pig iron made from Texas brown hematite ores, and it became his opinion that this iron was particularly well suited for car wheel construction. So impressed was he, that he resigned his position with the railroad and commenced the manufacture of car wheels with this iron. At the outset the tendency was to somewhat deride and ridicule him, but he had the courage of his convictions and the result proved conclusively that he was right, and now the Dickson car wheels have gained the very highest reputation for superiority in every way. It is a fact that the iron ores of Texas possess some remarkable peculiarities which make them specially suitable for this purpose. The iron used comes from Cherokee county, the "Birmingham" district of Texas. It is with economy and facility that the raw material is transported to the works, which are provided with independent side tracks and complete shipping facilities connecting the establishment with the railroad system of the city. The great feature of the Dickson wheels, made from Texas iron, is their unusual strength and great wearing properties. The company have a record of over 60,000 wheels unbroken in use and the wheels have attained the highest mileage of any in the country. In a total of two hundred and sixty wheels which for various causes were withdrawn from use by the Houston and Texas Central Railroad, the excess of mileage over guarantee was 6,009,435 miles without a broken or defective wheel among them. In fact, letters and reports from every important railroad using these wheels show a very large average of mileage over guarantee. The company's guarantee on "common" wheels is 60,000 miles, and on what are known as the "Barr" wheels 70,000 miles. We need not go into details here regarding the process by which the "Barr" wheels are made, other than to say that by means of a peculiar process in the chill they are made much stronger than the common wheel and are absolutely true in rotundity, it being impossible to make one out of round or to produce chill cracks or sweat at the throat. As mentioned above the company make their guarantee 10,000 miles higher with the "Barr" wheels than with the common wheels. There can be no question but what in all respects the Dickson car wheels, made from Texas iron, bear the palm of superiority from all others. Independent tests have demonstrated that the breaking strain of a cast bar of Texas iron is much greater than that of the best car wheel mixture of similar thickness. The Dickson wheel, either "common" or "Barr," is used on the following roads, viz: Houston and Texas Central, International and Great Northern, St. Louis, Arkansas and Texas, East Louisiana, Denver, Texas and Fort Worth, Southern Pacific System east of El Paso, Mexican International, Gulf, Colorado and Santa Fe, Houston East and West Texas and others. Inquiries directed to these corporations will substantially verify all that is claimed for these products. The reputation of the wheels has gone beyond the limits of the United States, and a demand for them is now coming from Mexico, many of the roads there having adopted them, and the company have just filled a large order for one of the leading lines in that country. The president of the Dickson Car Wheel Co., as before mentioned, is Mr. John F. Dickson, who discovered the suitability of this metal for car wheel purposes. Mr. Henry H. Dickson is vice president and secretary and Mr. Geo. M. Dickson is superintendent. These gentlemen are father and sons, and all the stock of the organization is held by its executive officers. The senior is a man of great experience in all that relates to practical railroading, and his sons have had a life-long familiarity with their present industry, with which they may be said to have grown up contemporaneously. They all give their personal supervision and oversight to the working details of the business.

THE KING BRIDGE CO., CLEVELAND, OHIO,

Houston Office, 610½ Main Street. S. A. Oliver, Contracting Agent.

The above named company has its headquarters at Cleveland, Ohio, where they have one of the largest and most important bridge and structural iron and steel plants in the United States. In this city they have a branch office, conducted under the management of Mr. S. A. Oliver, who has represented the organization here since 1874. The extent of the works is such as to afford the most ample facilities and conveniences for the construction of the largest steel and wrought iron structures in railroad and highway bridges, iron roofs, turn tables, viaducts, iron piers, trestles and girders and other description of iron and steel work, which conveniences are greatly enhanced by the utilization of the very latest and best of improved and special appliances suited for this particular class of work, the whole operations being closely supervised by men of the greatest and most practical experience in the business. The company invite references to the leading railroads and municipalities throughout the country. Among the bridges built by this company we will instance the steel cantilever bridge over the Ohio river between Cincinnati, Ohio, and Newport, Ky.; Cleveland central viaduct; draw-bridge at Oakland Harbor, Cal.; bridge across Wabash river at Logansport, Ind.; Twelfth street viaduct bridge, Chicago; Eighteenth street draw-bridge, Chicago; bridge across the Mississippi, Minneapolis; bridge over Illinois river, Peoria, Ill.; D., L. & W. R. R.'s crossing at East Buffalo, N. Y.; steel suspension bridge at Grand avenue, St. Louis; also the iron and steel work for market house at Cleveland, Ohio; the steel work on the Mines and Mining Building at World's Columbian Exposition, Chicago, etc. The above serves to illustrate the diversity of the resources and the wide-spread nature of the company's operations. They do not, however, confine their operations to large work only, but are prepared to give equal attention and care to the smallest contract. The work executed by them possesses all the advantages known to modern engineering, and they are so pronounced in their points of excellence as to have occasioned expressions of approval from leading engineers in the country. The company have completed many contracts in this section, probably more than any other single enterprise of the kind. Mr. Oliver personally supplies estimates and superintends the construction of work done in the territory under his jurisdiction, which includes the states of Texas, Arkansas, Louisiana and the territories of New Mexico, Oklahoma and Indian Territory and Old Mexico. Mr. Oliver also handles iron fences for all purposes, and he is prepared to give estimates and take orders for the same. This gentleman, besides his connection with this enterprise, is also president of the Phœnix Lumber Co., of this city. From the office in Houston is invited correspondence, and drawings, plans and estimates will be furnished free to towns and corporations or others who may contemplate the erection of bridges or any other class of work in this line.

WM. B. KING & CO.,

Wholesale Liquors and Cigars, corner Travis Street and Franklin Avenue.

This house dates back from the year 1881, when it was established at Galveston as King & Fordtran, the present designation being adopted January, 1892. From its inception but one method of business policy has been adopted, that of supplying the most reliable quality of goods at lowest prices. The premises occupied comprise a building of two floors at the above address, which are 50x100 feet in dimensions. Here is to be found a full and complete stock of the favorite brands of rye, bourbon and wheat whiskeys, gins, rums and wines of Californian and other American vineyards, and foreign goods, some of which are of their own importation, including champagnes, clarets, sherries, ports, sweet and dry wines of France, Germany and Spain, together with the finest of French brandies, English and Holland gins, Jamaica and St. Croix rums, Irish and Scotch whiskeys, Bass' ales, Guinness' stout and bottled goods of all descriptions. In American whiskeys specialties are made of "King's Gold Dust" and "King's Brookfield" whiskeys, which are the private brands of the house and which are manufactured especially for its trade. These goods are warranted pure and choice, of fine flavor, smooth and delicious to the taste. No better goods can be obtained in this market. Messrs. Wm. B. King & Co. also deal heavily in cigars, handling a full line of the choicest domestic and imported goods. The firm employ about fifteen assistants and salesmen, and their trade extends throughout Texas generally. The sole proprietor is Mr. Wm. B. King, a gentleman who is so well known as to require no personal commendation from us. The reputation enjoyed by the house for the expeditious and discerning manner in which all orders are filled merits the appreciation and approbation of those with whom it may come in contact,

BRINGHURST BROS.,
Real Estate, 313 Main Street.

The most essential qualifications for the successful prosecution of the real estate business, in addition to a thorough knowledge of values, is a strict regard for truth and honor in all transactions. A successful business record of a dozen years is sufficient guarantee that the house now under comment possesses in every respect the qualifications enumerated. The enterprise was founded in 1883 by Mr. John H. Bringhurst, and in 1889 the present firm was constituted, by this gentleman forming a partnership with his brothers, Messrs. Tom and Geo. R. Bringhurst. The senior member died in 1890, Mr. Geo. R. retired in February, 1893, and Mr. T. Bringhurst has since continued the business under the original designation of Bringhurst Bros. The firm devote their energies to the transaction of a regular real estate business, handling both city and suburban property. They have valuable tracts of fruit and farm lands for sale, worthy of the attention of the home-seeker and the capitalist. The range of properties handled is such that it varies from land as low as fifty cents per acre up to property worth a thousand dollars per acre. They have on their list at the present time some large tracts of land, which are suitable for being subdivided into very desirable farm lands. The firm's wide-spread connections, complete facilities and established reputation makes it advantageous for property owners to entrust their interests to their care. Messrs. Bringhurst Bros. sold the property known now as Houston Heights to its present owners. This property has been one of the most successful in and around Houston. The firm invite correspondence and inquiries, and will cheerfully respond, giving all particulars relative to South Texan properties. At no time have better opportunities presented themselves, and an outlay now is sure to result in ultimate profit and benefit. Mr. Tom Bringhurst is a native of Texas, born and raised in this city, which he has seen grow and expand. His father came here in 1836 and he was a participant in the Texan war, and was at one time a prisoner to the Mexicans. He was well known and highly respected, and for many years was an officer of the Grand Lodge of Texas, A. F. & A. M. Mr. Tom Bringhurst takes to-day the keenest interest in all that pertains to the welfare and advancement of the locality. He is thoroughly posted in real estate values and his advice is always at the disposal of his clients for their good and advantage. His reputation for fair dealing and reliable representations is beyond cavil, and the business he conducts is altogether entitled to prominent notice in these pages.

E. SIEWERSSEN,
Hides and Wool, Commerce Avenue and Milam Street.

Texas has for many years enjoyed celebrity as a source of supply for the rest of the country in the staples of hides and wool. This state still continues to ship these commodities in large quantities, and an enterprise in this city engaged in this department of trade is that of Mr. E. Siewerssen, who in 1888 became sole proprietor of the business formerly conducted as Hartwell & Siewerssen. This firm were the successors of Mr. T. H. Anderson, whs founded the industry in 1879. Mr. Siewerssen occupies a two-story brick building 25x100 feet in dimensions. This is used for the purpose of storage and for the curing of the hides previous to shipment. The house is prepared to buy hides and wool in any quantities, and its proprietor solicits consignments and is prepared to pay full market value for the same. Those of our readers throughout the state who may have any hides or wool for disposal will do well to consider this house before shipping elsewhere. The hides are bought green and are cured here and then packed and sent to tanners in all parts of the North and East. Mr. Siewerssen is a gentleman of much experience in the business, and he bears the reputation of being in every way a thorough, fair dealing and enterprising business man, and transactions with him will redound to the profit and satisfaction of all concerned.

MILBY & DOW,

Dealers in Coal, and Manufacturers of Hammered, Fire and Building Brick.
Office, Cotton Exchange; Yards, corner Sixth and Girard Streets; Mines, South McAlester, I. T.; Brick Works, Harrisburg.

The origin of this undertaking goes back to the year 1877, when the firm founded the first coal yard opened in the city of Houston. They added the manufacture of brick to their coal business in the year 1882. The plants and possessions of the firm at the present time are ample and important, and in the various departments a force of about one hundred men are given employment. Their coal yards are situated at the corner of Sixth and Girard streets and they cover the full space of a city block. For shipping and receiving conveniences the establishment is directly connected with the tracks of the Houston and Texas Central Railway. The firm handle all kinds of coal, generally carrying in store from three hundred to six hundred tons, according to the season. The firm are the exclusive sales agents in Texas and Mexico for the celebrated "Kali-Inla" coal, mined by the Choctaw Coal and Railway Company at McAlester, I. T. They are enabled to promptly supply this high grade of coal in carload lots direct from the mines to destination without breaking bulk. The plant for the production of brick is located at Harrisburg. Here they manufacture hammered, front, fire and building brick of the best quality. The hammered is made by a special process and by special patented machinery. It is decidedly superior to ordinary brick, will wear longer and is more sightly and impervious to water and weather. The capacity of the works permits of the production of about 100,000 brick daily. The firm also control the product of Coghlan Bros., brick works, which turn out about 20,000 bricks daily. Their hammered brick was used in the construction of the American Brewing Association's brewery, that of the Houston Ice and Brewing Company and the Milby & Dow building. The firm are in a position to promptly fill all orders to complete satisfaction, not only here in the city, but anywhere in contiguous territory. The individual members of the firm are Messrs. C. H. Milby and Andrew Dow, both well known residents of this city, who take the keenest interest in its advancement and progress, to which their enterprise has largely contributed.

HOUSTON AND TEXAS LAND OFFICE,

Trust Company Building, Main Street, corner Franklin Avenue.

The Houston and Texas Land Office was established nearly a quarter of a century ago, in the year 1872, and it has since earned a reputation of the highest character for utility, reliability and correctness. Its proprietor, Mr. P. Whitty, is a land surveyor of great experience and he devotes faithful attention and care to all matters pertaining to his profession. Everything in the way of land surveying is executed; also, the laying out of town sites, farm lands, etc. Mr. Whitty also devotes particuler energies to the making of maps of lands, towns and cities. which are carefully compiled and promptly supplied. He carries in stock maps of Houston and also of all counties in the State, and maps of the various additions and new settlements in this locality. He made the map of Raywood for the Empire Trust Company; also, laid out the lots for the Brunner Addition, the Magnolia Addition, Riverside Park, etc. A speciality of the business of this office is reports on values, and the long experience and practical knowledge of Mr. Whitty makes him eminently qualified for this work. He also devotes attention to the paying of taxes on property and to all business connected with land and real estate matters. The interests of his clients are his first care and business entrusted to him is thoroughly carried out to the full satisfaction of all who may employ his services. Mr. Whitty was City Engineer of Houston for nine years, and he has had also thirteen years' experience in railroad construction, which facts tend to assure confidence and that everything pertaining to the work he undertakes will be carried out thoroughly to completion. The standing of the house is too well known and understood for us to attempt to add to it. However as an illustration of one of the city's acquisitions and conveniences we accord to the Houston and Texas Land Office the courtesy of prominent recognition in these pages.

DUMBLE, ARMISTEAD & CRONAN,
Hardware Dealers, 217 Main Street.

This substantial house is **a** pioneer in the hardware business here and one of the oldest established enterprises of Houston. It was founded in 1871 by George Dumble, the present firm being organized in 1893. To-day it is one of the largest houses of the kind in this locality. The premises occupied comprise a three-story brick building 30x 100 feet in area, also two large warehouses, each forty by one hundred feet on Jackson St. The whole of this is utilized and the arrangements of the establishment are perfect, every article being so classified that the selection of goods becomes an easy matter and all of the wares are displayed to advantage. The comprehensive stock carried by the house embraces all the various goods in the lines indicated, and it is all procured direct from first hands. Besides every variety of articles included in the general headings of shelf and builders' hardware, the firm deal in iron and galvanized pipe, steam fittings, stoves, tinware, house furnishing goods, steel cut and wire nails, belting, packing, manufacturers' supplies, etc. They are the exclusive agents here for Giant stitched rubber belting, Munson's celebrated Eagle and Dynamo leather belting, Fairbanks' standard scales, Knowles' steam pumps, Excelsior steam injectors and other specialties of acknowledged celebrity and merit. Messrs. Dumble, Armistead & Cronan execute everything connected with tin, sheet iron and cornice work, and they have a shop especially devoted to this department. The house employs about a dozen assistants, and its trade extends throughout this city and neighborhood. The members of the firm individually are E. H. Dumble, M. H. Armistead and T. W. Cronan, all of whom are active in the management of the business, of which they have a thorough and complete experience. Mr. Cronan is an active member in the Masonic order and he has held many positions of honor and influence in the fraternity. All members of the firm are leading residents, identified with the city's advancement and progress.

M. DeLEON, C. E.,
Contracting Civil Engineer and Agent for Hinderer's Iron Fence Works and the Stewart Iron Works, 815 and 817 Commerce Street.

The important character which the facilities of Houston are assuming is exemplified, in a manner, in the establishment here of such an enterprise as that conducted by Mr. M. DeLeon, contracting civil engineer, who commenced operations at Houston in 1892. He is prepared with all facilities to furnish and submit plans and accept contracts for bridges, buildings, roofs, turn-tables and in fact everything relating to civil engineering. Mr. DeLeon is in every way experienced and competent to undertake everything connected with his profession. He is a graduate civil engineer of the Polytechnic Institute of Troy, N. Y., one of the best institutions of the kind in the country. He has made the plans for several bridges in this section which have given entire satisfaction. Mr. DeLeon is agent for Hinderer's Iron Fence Works, of New Orleans, and for the Stewart Iron Works, of Wichita, Kansas. He has at the disposal of his customers over four hundred designs of fences from which suitable selections can be made with facility, and he sells no fencing that he cannot guarantee. He will be found to be a young, energetic and practical man, conserving the best interests of all having dealings with him. Individuals, corporations and others who should require the services of a gentleman of the above profession can with safety entrust their business to his care.

SMITH, PEDEN & CO.,
Wholesale Dealers in Iron, Fifth Ward, near I. & G. N. Bridge.

Iron is the most important metal at the command of man, and the use of it in all industries is becoming greater. In fact, it would be impossible merely to mention its many uses, and we will here content ourselves with speaking of it in the forms as handled by the house of Messrs. Smith, Peden & Co., of this city. This firm was established in 1890. The premises they occupy comprise a large three-story iron-clad building, which is 120x110 feet in dimensions. The building being iron-clad, and crowned with an asbestos roof, is practically fire-proof, and as an additional protection watchmen patrol the establishment day and night. These precautions are ren-

dered the more necessary inasmuch as the firm have the property of others to guard as well as their own, the lower and third floors being at the disposal of the public as storage warehouses. Further improvements are about to be added, which will increase the conveniences of the establishment. Messrs. Smith, Peden & Co. deal heavily at wholesale in iron and steel roofing, siding, galvanized and black sheet iron, corrugated iron, nails, tin-plate, zinc, solder, iron fencing, asbestos and felt roofing; indeed, everything required in the way of sheet iron and steel for building and other purposes. Iron to-day is to a large extent superseding wood and brick in the construction of buildings, affording as it does a greater protection against the ravages of fire and also being ultimately cheaper. The firm carry an immense stock, which they obtain under the most favorable conditions from the mills and *bona fide* manufacturers, and they are enabled to offer the goods to the trade at lowest prices. The side-tracks of the I. & G. N. R. R. run to the doors of the warehouse and the tracks of other railroads will soon be added, placing the establishment in the closest connection with the railroad system of the city. The firm employ eleven assistants and salesmen, three of whom are commercial travelers on the road transacting the business of the house within the States of Texas, Western Louisiana and Western Arkansas. They have also a warehouse at Fort Worth, Texas, where they have a representative for the sale of their goods. The members of the firm, individually, are R. P. Smith, E. A. Peden and D. D. Peden, all of whom are practical in their knowledge of the business to which they give their closest personal attention. The firm have recently added to the business the handling of high grade fertilizers. These goods are particularly well suited to the growth of cotton, corn, sugar, flowers, fruits, vines, etc., and are especially adapted to Texas soils.

LEVY BROS.,
Dealers in Dry Goods and Millinery, 215 Main Street.

The inception of this business took place in the year 1888, when it was instituted by the present proprietors. At the start the enterprise was inaugurated upon but a modest scale, but intelligence, enterprise and correct business methods had their inevitable results, and to-day the establishment is one of the leading houses in its line of trade in the city. The headquarters of the firm comprise a brick building of three floors 25x90 feet in dimensions, the whole of which is utilized. On the ground floor are the dry goods, notions and fancy goods departments; on the second floor is contained the stock of millinery and millinery goods, and the third floor is utilized in the dress-making operations. At this establishment may advantageously be obtained everything included under the general headings of dry goods, notions and millinery, comprising the richest and most expensive silk and velvet fabrics down to the cheapest prints; also, furnishing goods, hosiery, linens, woolens and cottons, fancy goods, trimmings, cloaks, suits, etc. A particular specialty is the millinery department. The firm are among the first to obtain the latest novelties of the season, both imported and domestic, and hats and bonnets are made to order which are the peers, both as regards style and material, of any that may grace the windows of the leading houses either in London, Paris or New York. Another specialty is the dress-making department, which is also conducted upon the same principles, and costumes emanate from here which are perfect in taste, conception and execution. The prices throughout will be found eminently fair and moderate, tending to the satisfaction of patrons. The firm employ about twenty sales-people and assistants, who are skilled in their various departments. The entire management is sedulously overlooked by Messrs. A. M. Levy, Haskell Levy and Hyman Levy, who constitute the firm. These gentlemen are careful and experienced buyers, keenly cognizant of the requirements of their customers. They are intimately connected with the advancement and welfare of the city and are interested in a number of Houston's banking and corporate organizations. Concluding we may add that this firm enjoy the fullest consideration of the ladies of Houston and the public generally, induced by the enterprise displayed in the conduct of the business as well as because of the honorable principles of trading evinced from the start of the house and continued down to the present time.

T. H. THOMPSON & CO.,
Wholesale Dealers in Fruits and Produce, and Commission Merchants, Washington Street, near Grand Central Station.

Prominent among the business houses of Houston is that of Messrs. T. H. Thompson & Co., founded in 1887. This firm are in the enjoyment of facilities of the most complete character, which have recently been largely increased and expanded. They have just entered into possession of their own newly erected building, which has been specially arranged for the uses to which it is applied. It is three stories high and 50x125 feet in dimensions. The lower floor is fitted up with a complete cold storage plant of the latest and most improved construction and which has been put in at an expense of $8,000. There are here a number of rooms which can be regulated to temperatures best suited to the preservation of the various products handled by the house. This gives the firm large advantages and enables them to carry the largest stocks and to keep them in fresh condition at all times. Messrs. T. H. Thompson & Co. are large wholesale dealers in green and dried fruits, butter, cheese and western produce, but in addition to these lines, which they have always carried, the firm upon entering into their new building have added to their business a full line of packing house products. They are the South Texas representatives of three of the largest packers in the West, and in view of these connections are enabled to quote to the trade packing house prices on bacon, lard and hams in carloads and less than carloads. Their building is situated on the tracks of the Houston and Texas Central and Southern Pacific Railroads, which enables them to handle these goods at a very small expense. An experienced representative of Messrs. Armour & Co. is in charge of this branch of their business, and buyers of hog products will save money by getting their prices. Special attention is also given to the receiving of Texas produce. The country within the triangle formed by Houston, Galveston and Velasco is filled with fertile fruit and truck farms which yield a product the quality of which is not surpassed by any other section in the United States. Strawberries, plums, peaches, sweet potatoes, Irish potatoes, English peas, snap beans, radishes and all kinds of vegetables, and above all the finest of pears are produced here in profusion. Consignors will find the above firm is enabled to assure prompt sales and quick returns in view of the extensive character of their trade and the large influence of their wide connections. This house is one of the most important concerns in the State and have advantages to offer which are not surpassed anywhere. The individual members of the firm are Messrs. T. H. Thompson and W. H. Kirkland, both of whom have every experience of the business. Mr. Thompson has been ten years in the fruit and produce trade, and Mr. Kirkland about the same time in the wholesale grocery business. As to the standing of the firm we shall not allude to it, other than to say that they offer the First National Bank of this city as their reference. The various departments entail the services of twenty assistants and salesmen, eight of these being commercial travelers.

WASHBURN & MOEN MANUFACTURING COMPANY.
Works at Worcester, Mass., Waukegan, Ill.—Houston Branch, Geo. A. Cragin, Agent.

The reputation of the above named company is national, and their products are known from the frozen ocean to Cape Horn, and from the Atlantic to the Pacific. Yet our mission to make this a comprehensive reflex of Houston's trade conveniences leads us to devote some measure of our space to their establishment in this city. The office is located in the Gibbs' building on Franklin avenue, and the warehouse adjoins the track of the Southern Pacific railway near the Texas Transportation Co.'s depot. Here they have facilities for the carrying an enormous stock, consisting of from fifty

WAREHOUSE OF WASHBURN & MOEN MANUFACTURING COMPANY.

to one hundred carloads of their products, the quantity varying with the season of the year. They supply from this point the entire State of Texas and the Republic of Mexico. The company manufacture iron, steel and copper wire of every description and for all purposes, and they make specialties of what are known as Glidden and Waukegan barbed wire, cross head and single eye bale ties, wire rope and cable, insulated copper and iron wire, telegraph and telephone wire. They have in stock at all times, at the warehouse at Houston, plain and barbed wire, staples, hay bale ties, wire rope, clothes line, insulated wire, copper wire, wire nails, coppered steel spring wire, tinned broom and mattress wire, wire bed springs, galvanized barbless fencing, galvanized pump rod and chain, etc. Orders can be filled at immediate notice and in any quantity. The company employ about eighteen warehousemen and assistants at the Houston branch, and the almost stupenduous number of 4000 men in their factories at Worcester and Waukegan. No concern of the kind in the world approaches them in extent and volume of operations, whether in this country or in Europe. Their products are in general use not only with agriculturalists, but in many trades and industries, and the extent of their sphere of usefulness hardly has any limit. Mr. Geo. A. Cragin, the gentleman in charge of the business here, has been with the company for the past thirteen years, and he is thoroughly conversant with the demands of this section. To his efforts may be traced the success of the enterprise at this point, his constant and unremitting care being devoted to its details. Mr. E. J. Pietzcker is assistant to the manager. This gentleman has been with the company over a year and may also be considered as entirely familiar with the business. The City of Houston is certainly to be congratulated for being selected as the Southern headquarters of this enterprise, and the fact serves to illustrate what we claim generally in this volume, that Houston is today the most favorable center of distribution in Texas, and that perhaps it is destined to become the leading city of the Gulf States.

A. D. WHEELER,
General Agent New York Life Insurance Co., 405 Kiam Building.

The above named gentleman is one of the general agents for the State of Texas representing the above named company and is in full charge of the agency in this city, which has been established for some time. This office has jurisdiction over a wide range of territory, having authority to appoint sub-agents and attend to the general business of the company, and it is here to stay and share in the general prosperity which is now characteristic of this section. In reference to the New York Life Insurance Co. generally we may repeat here what is well known everywhere, and that is, that all the elements of safety, liberality and responsibility in life insurance are happily combined in it. As to its responsibility it offers the best proof afforded by a record of nearly half a century of honorable dealing, during which it has paid its policy holders hundreds of millions of dollars and has held the confidence of the public by the irreproachable equity of its business course. The wisdom and sound judgment of its management is evinced in its wonderful prosperity. On January 1st, 1894, it had cash assets amounting to the sum of $148,700,781, and its surplus by the New York standard of four per cent. was $17,025,636, among the largest of any company in the world. It had outstanding insurance of $779,156,678, and its new business for the year 1893 was $223,800,000. Each year shows an increase of business, an increase of policy holders, and what is of far more importance, an increase of surplus in ratio to liabilities. This is a significant indication of its popularity and financial strength. Its policies are most liberal in terms and with all the guarantees and privileges that experience has shown to be safe. They are absolutely free from all restrictions whatever, the only condition being the payment of the premium. The policy is incontestable from any cause after one year, allows a month's grace in payment of premiums, a re-instatement within six months if the insured is in good health, and its non-forfeiture provisions are self-acting in case of neglect on the part of the insured; after the policy has been in force five years the company will make loans thereon at the rate of five per cent per annum interest. The company is undoubtedly one of the most liberal and reliable in the world, indeed if it be not entitled to a place at the head of all similar organizations, and the advantages it offers are impossible to be excelled by any really safe and sound methods. Mr. Wheeler, the manager, will be pleased to impart all information relative to the business, and correspondence will receive prompt attention. This gentleman was formerly manager of the northeastern office at Paris, Texas, and he has been with the company four years and is in every way experienced. The New York Life Insurance Co. have already insurance in force to the amount of over fifteen million dollars in this State, and its mission of usefulness will soon be greatly extended and expanded.

S. O. COTTON & BRO.,
General Fire Insurance Agents, 119 Main Street.

No lesson has been more impressed upon the minds of property owners in important centers by the great fires that still occur than the wisdom of dividing risks through the agency of experienced and responsible underwriters, who are not tied down to any particular company and who can be depended upon to act honorably and intelligently for all concerned. Such an agency in this city is that of Messrs. S. O. Cotton & Bro., who have a wide experience of many years' standing and who have always enjoyed the confidence of business men and property owners in an eminent degree. The firm are the authorized agents in this city for the following strong list of reliable and well known insurance companies, viz: The Lancashire, of Manchester; Royal, of Liverpool; Queen, of America; New York; Phœnix Assurance, of London; Southern, of New Orleans; St. Paul Fire and Marine, of St. Paul; Macon Fire, of Macon, Ga.; Merchants, of Newark, N. J.; Fire Association, of Philadelphia; Traders' Insurance, of Chicago, and Atlanta Home, of Atlanta, Ga. This is a list of undoubted excellence, guaranteeing certain indemnity in case of loss, with assets of many millions of dollars, and Messrs. S. O. Cotton & Bro. effect insurance in each and every one of them at lowest rates. All just claims are settled by them without undue delay or annoyance to patrons. The business of the firm was originally instituted as Schmidt & Loeffler, the present designation being adopted in 1876. Mr. S. O. Cotton, the senior member of the original firm of S. O. Cotton & Bro., died about five years ago, the present co-partners being Messrs. J. M. Cotton, Rufus Cage and Stonewall Bond, all of whom are thoroughly experienced underwriters and men of well known business reputation. The operations of the firm are not entirely restricted to this city, a considerable *clientele* being also drawn from surrounding localities. We offer no apology for placing before our readers the above few details with regard to the well known and reliable insurance agency of Messrs. S. O. Cotton & Bro., of this city.

WAGLEY & CHERRY.
Real Estate, 400 Kiam Building.

Although the above named firm of real estate dealers have but recently established their present business, they are in the enjoyment of the very best of facilities, and the gentlemen comprising the co-partnership are men of the most practiced experience. They are today prepared to offer to the investing public great inducements and advantages in attractive and valuable property, which is certain to rise in value within a very brief period of time, and which is being rapidly filled up with a desirable class of settlers. Messrs. Wagley & Cherry transact a regular real estate business, such as the purchase and sale of real property of all descriptions, the collection of rents, the handling and care of estates for non-residents, the obtaining of loans on real estate, and other high class collateral security. The firm are at the present time introducing on the market what is known as Fairview Addition. This is a tract of land adjoining the fair grounds, sub-divided into 120 lots, which are offered for residential purposes. The location is delightful and healthful, and it is just at the edge of the limits of the city of Houston, with which it is connected by the electric street car system, which enables it to partake of the benefits of all the city improvements and conveniences. The firm also handle the town of Brookshire, along the line of the M. K. & T. R. R. This comprises several thousand acres, which are platted into building lots and fruit farms. It is within easy distance of the city, and although but six months old, it is already well settled and built up. The land on this property is particularly fertile, and well suited for raising strawberries, pears, peaches, small fruit generally, vegetables, garden truck, etc. The prices are low, and the terms are arranged to suit the convenience of purchasers. Enough has been said elsewhere in this volume as to the great desirability of South Texas lands, and it only remains for us to say here that Messrs. Wagley & Cherry have the very best of inducements to offer the homeseeker and the investor. The members of the firm individually are W. C. Wagley and D. B. Cherry, both experienced real estate men. Mr. Wagley is a Houston man, who has seen the advancement and growth of his native city, to which he has materially contributed. He has been identified with real estate matters here for over a quarter of a century, and may be said to be a pioneer in the profession, and probably the longest in the business of any now operating at the present time. Mr. Cherry comes from Nebraska, where he has also had a large experience. The firm invite correspondence, and in reply will clearly demonstrate the advantages they have to bestow. The house is deserving of every confidence, and may justly be considered as identified with the best interests of Houston.

PENN BRIDGE COMPANY.
Beaver Falls, Pa. E. P. Alsbury & Son, South-Western Agents, 911½ Preston Avenue.

An exemplification of the growing importance of this city is furnished in the recent inauguration here of a branch office of the Penn Bridge Co. of Beaver Falls, Pa. This company is among the most important and extensive concerns of the kind in the country, and the recent stimulation and advancement of this part of the United States makes Houston a fitting field for their labors. The company have a very complete plant at Beaver Falls employing about 800 hands, and they turn out about 20000 tons of product annually. The Penn Bridge Co. are contractors and manufacturers of bridges, structural material, and iron and steel, and they have unrivaled facilities for turning out this class of work promptly and to satisfaction. They have executed and carried out to completion some of the most notable contracts all over the country. They are now in a position to furnish plans and estimates for anything in this line, in this section, and already they have now in hand many important contracts, and are negotiating others in this territory. The jurisdiction of this office includes Texas, Arkansas, Louisiana, Mexico, New Mexico and Oklahoma, and the business here is under the efficient charge of Messrs. E. P. Alsbury & Son, who respectively are Messrs. E. P. Alsbury and A. A. Alsbury. These gentlemen are thoroughly experienced and practical engineers. They execute all the designing and estimating for the work of this office, and superintend personally all contracts. Both are natives of Texas, and well known Houston residents. The company invite correspondence from town and city authorities, railroad corporations, and others interested, and plans and estimates are promptly furnished. The company will be found to possess all required facilities, and are in a position to offer inducements of the most important character. We only touch lightly on the facilities of this organization here, our object being mainly to induce a correspondence to be opened with it, full information being cheerfully forwarded from the Houston office to all who may be interested in the subject.

THE AMERICAN BREWING ASSOCIATION,

Brewers of Lager Beer and Manufactures of Artificial Ice, between Buffalo and White Oak Bayous.

An institution of which Houston has every reason to be proud is that known as the American Brewing Association. The present organization was formed January of this current year, succeeding the Anheuser-Busch Brewing Association, who were the originators of the enterprise. The capital stock of the American Brewing Association is $350,000, the whole of which is fully paid in, and the company start clear and free from debt of any kind, there being no mortgage nor a cent of incumbrance on the property. The plant of the organization is a dual one, part being devoted to the brewing of lager beer and part to the manufacture of artificial ice. The works cover two entire blocks, occupying an area 250x500 feet in dimensions. The tracks of the

Houston and Texas Central Railway are adjacent, while the company's own side-tracks run through the plant direct to the doors of each department. The structures comprising the brewery are a brew house five stories high and 40x50 feet in area, a five-story storage house forty feet square, a four-story stock house of the dimensions of 50x80 feet, a single story racking house 50x30 feet and a keg washing house 50x75 feet in extent. The whole of these buildings are substantially built of brick and iron and are thoroughly fire-proof. The ice factory is a brick building partly one-story high and partly of two floors, which occupies an area of 250x115 feet, and it is unquestionably the largest ice plant in the South. The mechanical equipment, as regards the brewery, comprises a 150 horse power engine and several smaller engines, pumps, etc., and all of the latest improved and best modern brewing apparatus and arrangements. The capacity of the brewery is 200,000 barrels of beer annually. The storage capacity is 30,000 barrels of beer and 20,000 bushels of malt. The storage house is 140 feet high and it is the most elevated building in the city of Houston. In connection with the brewery is a bottling department, contained in a building 100 feet square, and the capacity of this department is practically unlimited. In the ice factory are utilized three 250-horse power boilers and two De La Vergne ice machines, one of the capacity of 150 tons daily and the other of 100 tons daily. The company utilize four artesian wells, sunk on the property, which together have a capacity of from 1,000,000 to 1,200,000 gallons of water daily. The quality of this water is exceptionally pure and fine. Notwithstanding this fact, however, it is all distilled before being frozen into ice, assuring beyond question an absolutely pure artificial ice, entirely free from all traces of germs or organic impurities. The fine quality of this water assists also in the manufacture of the lager beer. The cold storage buildings comprise different chambers for the storage of fish, oysters, meats, vegetables, fruits, eggs, and in fact all kinds of perishable produce. This can be so regulated that each chamber can have a temperature exactly suited to the products therein stored. This cold storage department is of great utility to the fruit, produce and provision houses of Houston, enabling them to hold their goods for a longer period to await a favorable market. The brewery is the largest in the State of Texas and the establishment is fully in advance of the times, and as an inevitable growth of scientific labor and years of patient industry the management is now manufacturing lager beer, made from pure barley malt and hops only, which is the peer of any produced in the United States. The product is shipped to all parts of Texas and neighboring States. Agencies are now being established at all leading centers, and already the reputation of the American Brewing Association is fully established. For the purpose of shipping the goods the company have fifteen refrigerator cars, built by the St. Louis Refrigerator Car Company, and these are used solely for shipping beer and ice to distant localities. The executive officers of the company are as follows: Adolphus Busch, president; I. Japhet, vice president; F. Hacker, treasurer and manager, and Louis Illmer, secretary. The directors are Henry Brashear, B. A. Riesner, E. L. Coombs, Sam Allen, Henry Fischer, A. Busch and I. Japhet. The president, Mr. A. Busch, is also the president of the world renowned Anheuser-Busch Brewing Association, of St. Louis. Mr. Japhet is a well known and prominent liquor dealer of this city. Mr. Hacker was with the Anheuser-Busch Brewing Association for five years, and he is a thoroughly practical and scientific brewer, having been identified with the industry since he was a mere lad of seventeen. He is originally from Munich, in Bavaria, where he acquired the first rudiments of his profession. He has traveled extensively in foreign countries, acquiring more or less experience in every place of his sojourn. Mr. Illmer was and still continues to be general agent for Anheuser-Busch Brewing Association, and he is well known to the trade. He was in the liquor business for about twenty years. Of the stockholders of the company about a hundred are residents of Houston, so that in every way it is a home industry, with the richest promise of rapid and extended growth in the future.

THE PHŒNIX LUMBER COMPANY,

Manufacturers and Wholesale Dealers in Lumber, Sash, Doors, Blinds, Etc., corner Liberty Avenue and Moffit Streets.

The Phœnix Lumber Company was originally founded as the M. T. Jones Lumber Company, and it was incorporated and assumed its present designation in 1889. The plant at the above address is entirely new, the former premises having been destroyed by fire May 20th, 1891. With characteristic American enterprise the proprietors, far from being discouraged, immediately rebuilt, and the establishment was again in full blast August 1st following. This was quick work, but it is quite indicative of the enterprise of the house and is singularly appropriate to the title of the Phœnix Lumber Company. The works cover at the present time an area of two blocks, upon which are erected a planing mill two and a half stories high, 150x110 feet in dimensions; lumber sheds which cover an area of 20x500 feet; a glazing room 25x40 feet; an office building 24x40; stables, etc. The mechanical equipment includes steam engines of 125 horse power, about thirty planing machines, moulding machines and a quantity of other wood-working appliances of the very best and most ingenious modern construction. From seventy-five to a hundred operatives are here given employment. The works being adjacent to the railroad, the best of shipping facilities are available. The Phœnix Lumber Company deal heavily in all kinds of lumber, carrying a large stock, and they manufacture and sell sash, doors, blinds, moulding, stair work, balusters, store fronts, turned columns, brackets, church pews, etc.; indeed, they make here from a rough sill to the finest show case. Their range of production is not excelled by any similar establishment in the South. They have achieved the highest reputation for the superior character of the work turned out, while at the same time their prices will be found altogether reasonable and just. The company utilize annually about eight million feet of lumber in addition to large quantities of shingles. They are prepared at all times to submit estimates for any description of work in their line. They always carry an extensive stock of sash, doors, blinds, mouldings, etc., to fill current orders. The president of the company is Mr. S. A. Oliver and Mr. James Bute is secretary and treasurer. These are both well known business men of this city. The manager is Mr. W. D. Mihills, and he is a thoroughly practical man, who has been in the lumber trade all his life. This gentleman gives his closest personal attention and supervision to the general details of the business. The stockholders in the company are all Houston residents, so that in every respect it is a home industry. It is also a leading exponent of the growing and important interests of the city.

BRIGHT & COMPANY.

Real Estate and Money Brokers, 317½ Main Street.

The business of Messrs. Bright & Company was established in 1890 as Thomas, Bright & Company, the present firm succeeding in 1893. The firm transact a regular real estate business, and they handle all descriptions of farm and city property. Fruit lands, timber lands and ranch lands are a specialty, and recently the firm disposed of a ranch amounting to the large sum of $100,000. Messrs. Bright & Company also negotiate loans on real estate, and they take entire charge of rentals, both of business and residence properties. They represent the interests of non-residents and they are agents here for a number of northern corporations who remit funds to this locality, where a larger percentage of interest is obtainable. The firm also have connections with European investors. Business of this character may, with complete confidence, be confided to their care. Messrs. Bright & Company are the authorized agents for the well known Dickinson Land Company, who are the owners of a valuable property in Galveston county, Texas. It is located about mid-way between Galveston, the port of Texas, and Houston, its great railroad center. The district may be considered as

MR. J. H. BRIGHT.   MR. M. M. BRIGHT.

one of the most fertile in South Texas, and as a place of residence it is eminently healthful, being entirely free from malaria. Being located on a ridge its natural drainage is unsurpassed. Within a few miles by rail and road there are over a hundred thousand inhabitants, affording a market where all farm products are largely absorbed, and in many instances are largely shipped north, this section being in some products several weeks earlier than California. For fruit growers, market gardeners and dairymen the location is unsurpassed. Homes are already being built at Dickinson (town) and a thriving village will soon be in full swing. There is abundance of pure water available, obtained from springs and wells, and an artesian well of pure and clear water is now spouting 100 gallons a minute. The soil is of the richest character, and is the finest—suitable to the growth of small fruits, vegetables, etc.— also for raising cattle, horses, etc. Flowers may be said to be indigenous, and the climate is so equable that the farmer can follow his vocation all the year round. Sea breezes from the Gulf temper the summer heat, invigorating the worker and giving him fresh life to begin the daily toil. Nor is the dweller in this region denied the luxuries of oysters and fish for generous old Father Neptune supplies them in profusion and they are easily obtained daily by rail from the seaboard which is near by. It is safe to say that purchases made at this time will appreciate greatly in value in the very near future, as the country is rapidly filling up and every week the property increases in value, Eight passenger trains pass directly through the property, connecting the cities of Houston and Galveston, and a ride of an hour or so is all that is required to reach either of these places, so that home and back in the same day is an easy task. The property borders upon Dickinson bayou on the south, Clear Creek on the north and the Gulf, Colorado & Santa Fe railway on the west, and it, for the most part consists of level and rolling prairie; upon the borders of which is the only forest growth in the county, affording plenty of cheap fuel. Messrs. Bright & Company, will be glad to furnish full information, printed matter and all particulars relative to this property. Write to them, it will be to your advantage. Leave the frozen north where the unwilling soil only yields its fruits after the hardest toil, come down to the Sunny South, to a rich and virgin soil, a delightful climate, a law abiding and industrious population, a growing and improving country, health, content and comfort. The individual members of the firm of Bright & Company are Messrs. Jas. H. Bright and M. M. Bright, both of whom may be designated as energetic and pushing business men. To the efforts of this house must be largely ascribed the making known to outside investors the real attractions and value of property in this section. The firm will be glad to accord the benefit of their advice and experience to intending investors and all who may be interested, and they earnestly invite enquiries and correspondence, to which they will give immediate attention.

NEW ORLEANS BREWING ASSOCIATION.
Houston Branch, corner Wood and Willow Streets. A. S. Ujffy, Manager.

The above well known and influential brewing association have the very highest reputation throughout the South for the superior character of their product and for the enterprise of their management. They have branches at many trade centers and the volume of their transactions is very large. Here they have an office and cold storage facilities, the latter a frame building of 50x100 feet, which has a capacity for three carloads. The association is made up of six combined breweries, which together manufacture about a million barrels of beer annually. The immensity of their operations offers the best guarantee of the quality of the product, which is largely in demand wherever introduced. In this city and vicinity an extensive business is transacted, which is steadily growing. Mr. Ujffy, the manager, was formerly a traveling salesman for a Galveston house, and he is a gentleman well known and popular in this locality. The company aim to attract and hold their patronage by supplying a first-class and uniform product and by liberal methods of doing business. Dealers will find it advantageous to enter into business connections with the organization, which has inducements to offer difficult to duplicate elsewhere. As an adjunct to the growing trade of this city the Houston branch of the New Orleans Brewing Association is entitled to its proper place in this volume illustrative of the resources of Houston.

EUGENE T. HEINER,
Architect, 610½ Main Street.

The enhanced aspect of the city of Houston from an architectural point of view owes much to the skill and taste of our architects, and among such a leading place must be accorded to Mr. Eugene T. Heiner. This gentleman has, perhaps, accomplished as much in this direction, throughout the city and State, than has any of his compeers, he being the oldest established in his profession in this locality. He began operations in this city in 1876, coming here from Terre Haute, Indiana. He has had altogether thirty years' active practical experience, and therefore it is safe to say is a proficient in all relating to his profession. He has made the plans and superintended the erection of some of the most notable structures in this city and State. Of such we will instance the Milby & Dow building, Shaw and Jones buildings, T. W. House's bank, T. H. Scanlan's residence, Charles House's residence, Harris county jail, Cotton Exchange, new Houston High School—the three latter being illustrated in this volume—and many others in this city, as well as court houses, jails and other structures throughout the State. Mr. Heiner is prepared at any time to submit plans for any description of building and to superintend the erection of the same if required. His well known reputation and thorough experience is such that it would be superfluous for us to do more than touch on the subject, but as in this work it is our mission to fully display the facilities and conveniences of the city and locality, it is incumbent upon us to make mention of this gentleman, whose professional services have done so much to beautify the city and advance its claims to be designated the metropolis of the Lone Star State.

BORCHARD, BRASHER & CO.,

Wholesale Grocers and Confectioners, 907 and 909 Commerce Avenue.

Among leading enterprises in this city a prominent place must be accorded to that now conducted under the title of Borchard, Brasher & Co. This house was originally founded in 1885 as Brasher, Reichardt & Co., the present designation being adopted January 2nd of this current year. Their store comprises a commodious three story brick building 50x200 feet in dimension, which is provided with all trade conveniences, including an elevator, and every facility is here available to advance order and dispatch in the conduct of the business. The house handles at wholesale everything usually included under the general heading of groceries, and it manufactures all descriptions of confectionery. The stock is ample, full, complete and of the best quality being invariably obtained from original sources of supply enabling the lowest prices to be quoted to the trade. While a full and complete stock is carried in all departments, the firm have obtained a wide repute in certain specialties. They handle largely foreign and domestic cigars, and they are state agents for the celebrated brands of *Duke of York*, made at Key West and for the goods of the Grand Republic factory of New York City. Special brands of domestic cigars are manufactured expressly for the house and are guaranteed by it for quality and uniformity. Other specialties in groceries have this firm's brands, and are identified with it. In all respects the facilities here available are of the best, enabling it to compete favorably with contemporaries from rival localities. The individual members of the firm are Messrs. Dan Borchard, S. C. Brasher, F. A. Reichardt and R. C. Chatham, gentlemen of thorough experience in the business. Mr. Borchard devotes his particular attention to the grocery department. He is recently from Galveston, where he was a member of the firm of Borchard, Ehrlich & Co. of that city. Of the three other members who were all of the firm of Brasher, Reichardt & Co., Mr. Brasher travels on the road, Mr. Reichardt is in charge of the cigar and candy department, and Mr. Chatham also travels for the house. All are well known in this city and locality. Mr. Reichardt is prominent in military and society circles. He is Exalted Ruler B. P. O. Elks, President State Sangerfest and Captain of the Houston Light Guards. He was largely instrumental in erecting the Armory building, a structure which adds no little to the architectural attractions of Houston. The firm employ fifteen assistants, including six commercial travelers, and the scope of their trade may be said to include the state of Texas generally. The standing and reputation of the house are such as to warrant the entire confidence of those with whom it has established business relations.

WALL & STABE.

Undertakers, Embalmers, Etc., Corner San Jacinto Street and Prairie Ave.

The sad duties of the funeral director are now performed in such a manner as practically to elevate the business from the mere name of a trade to the dignity of a profession. In Houston this branch of endeavor is represented by the firm of Messrs. Wall & Stabe, who are the successors to a business which is the oldest established of its kind in this section. The enterprise was originally founded by R. E. Pannell, some time in the "forties," when Houston was but a village. His two sons succeeded him in the proprietorship, and in 1885 the firm of Wall & Noland was instituted. In 1889 the present firm became the possessors of the business. At the above address Messrs. Wall & Stabe occupy a large two story iron covered building, which is a hundred feet square. Everything is here accomplished to relieve the family of the departed from all trouble, and from attention to petty details, so much magnified at these periods of grief. The firm are the owners of six handsome hearses, ten carriages, and thirty horses. They carry a large stock of caskets and funeral accessories, and generally may be inpected here from 700 to 800 funeral cases and caskets at all times, from the cheapest to the most expensive and artistic. They are also manufacturers of several grades of caskets for their own business. The enterprise is the largest and most important of its kind south of New Orleans. Particular attention is given to embalming, which is performed in the most scientific manner. The firm employ about fifteen assistants, which number is sometimes increased as occasion demands. The firm have carriages on hire, which they furnish promptly for weddings, funerals, calling, and other purposes. The co-partners individually are Messrs. W. S. Wall and Henry Stabe. Mr. Wall is an undertaker of many years experience, and Mr. Stabe is a practical embalmer of skill, and an expert in the business. That this firm, during its long and honorable career, has done much to raise the tone of the profession, is a fact beyond question, and in according to it the courtesy of prominent mention we confer upon it only that distinction and consideration which is justly its due.

SI PACKARD'S Troy Steam Laundry

TELEPHONE 332

912 PRAIRIE AVENUE, HOUSTON, TEXAS

The Troy Steam Laundry, owned and conducted by Mr. Si Packard, forms the chief enterprise of its kind in the State of Texas. The business was originally founded as Hamilton Bros. & Packard, in the year 1890. On April 1, 1891, Mr. Si Packard became its sole proprietor. The plant may be said to be one of the most complete and well appointed laundry establishments to be found anywhere. It is contained in a two-story brick building, 25x125 feet in dimensions, the whole of which is utilized in the business. The equipment embraces all that has been found useful in modern laundry machinery, which is operated by a 25 horse power engine and a 60 horse power boiler. The establishment is well lighted and all conveniences are available. Among the appliances are a "King" No. 5 collar and cuff ironer, the only one in the State. This machine cost $1600 and it has a capacity for ironing 100,000 pieces weekly. All washers are brass machines—the only ones of the kind in Texas, and the wringers are operated by independent engines. From the inception of the business, the aim of the management has been to do thoroughly first-class work only, and every detail of the business is carefully supervised by the proprietor in person. Every care is also taken that not only shall the work be properly performed, but that no injury shall be done to the delicate fabric and no deleterious chemicals shall be used. Agencies have been established by Mr. Packard in fifty-three towns, and business is obtained altogether from a hundred and seven different localities. The number of these agencies is being regularly increased. The laundry gives employment to forty-one persons, besides a number of teams for delivery. The present capacity of the laundry is 1,000 shirts daily, which number can be increased if required. Upwards of *five million* pieces are handled annually, and the volume of the transactions is steadily increasing. The sole proprietor, Mr. Si Packard, is a young and enterprising business man, who believes that what is worth doing at all, is worth doing well. He is a well-known and popular resident, and is a member of the Cotton Exchange, the B. P. O. Elks, Houston Light Guard, Turn Verein, R. A. R., Knights of Phytias, Post C, T. P. A. and other societies. Si Packard's Troy Steam Laundry is a very valuable part of the general conveniences of Houston, and contributes no little to its comforts and advantages.

MAHONEY & POWELL,

Contractors, 500 Kiam Building.

The great advancement of this locality has stimulated the building industry to a large extent, and availing themselves of the opportunities thus offered is the firm of Mahoney & Powell, who, January 2d, 1894, succeeded to the business originally founded as Rempe & Mahoney in 1893. The firm at the present time are in possession of the very best of facilities. Although not long in operation here this house has erected some of the most notable buildings in the city, such as the Kiam office building and Mason building, both on Main street and two of the architectural ornaments of Houston; also the Sweeney & Jamison building, adjoining the Kiam building, on Main street, and many others here and in the vicinity. The firm are prepared to submit estimates and their terms will be found as low as any, compatible with thoroughly good work. The members of the firm individually are Messrs. D. Mahoney and W. L. Powell, both of whom are thoroughly experienced in all relating to the trade. Mr. Mahoney has had twenty years' practical experience as a contractor, sixteen of which apply to Texas. He is himself a practical builder and bricklayer, and his technical knowledge is of great value in the supervision of the work. Mr. Powell has been sixteen years connected with the business, and he is no less practically conversant with all its details. The firm employ a force of men varying with the exigencies of their operations, sometimes as many as one hundred and fifty being required. The house is one of the most important of its kind in the State of Texas, having the largest contracts on their hands. The energy and enterprise which have always characterized the management is a theme of the most favorable comment, while the facilities possessed by the firm are advantages made available for the benefit of all who are so fortunate as to form business relations with the house.

CONKLIN, GEORGE & GAINES.
Wholesale Druggists, 313 Main Street.

In speaking of a house so widely and favorably known for years as that of Messrs. Conklin, George & Gaines, we cannot expect to add anything to its standing and reputation. We desire, however, to say a few words concerning the history and present position of this old established, popular and reliable firm. The business was originally established as long ago as the year 1860. The founder was Mr. R. F. George, who still continues its active manager. In 1868 the style of the house became R. Cotter & Co., in 1874 the firm of M. D. Conklin & Co., was formed. The present designation was adopted in 1884. Mr. Conklin died in 1891, and his interest has since been assumed by his widow. Mr. Gaines retired from the business about a year ago. The premises consist of a three-story brick building, of the dimensions of 30x136, the whole of which is utilized. Messrs. Conklin, George & Gaines are wholesale druggists, in the general acceptation of the term, handling full lines, but their particular energies are devoted to the manufacture and sale of a number of reliable specialties, which are identified with their trade marks, and which have a widely extended reputation. Of these we will instance: I-X-L Chill Cure, I-X-L Horse Powders, I-X-L Liver Pills, I-X-L Sarsaparilla with Iodide of Potash. They also manufacture a full line of flavoring extracts, which are of the best quality, being guaranteed of full strength, pure and free from any trace of deleterious adulterations. Other specialties made here are Tooth Powder, pure Extract Jamaica Ginger, pure Seidlitz Powders, Cinchona Tonic, O. K. Headache Cure and others. The above may be said to represent the very *acme* of excellence and efficiency, made from formulas which are the results of long experience and practical research. Dealers have realized this fact, and therefore, in view of giving satisfaction to their patrons, generally prefer them to others of similar character. All of them are standard on the market, and the reputation that the house has long enjoyed goes far to inspire confidence. As before mentioned, Mr. R. F. George is the active member of the firm, in which he has been a partner from its inception. He is a thoroughly practical man in all relating to the business. The trade of the house extends throughout a wide range of territory, into places where the excellencies of the products assure their sale. Thus the name and fame of Houston is spread abroad and advertised, demonstrating that the city is rapidly becoming a favorable distributing point, and leading source of supply.

JAPHET & COMPANY.
Wholesale Dealers in Liquors and Cigars, Corner Main and Commerce Streets.

The business conducted in Houston under the title of Japhet & Company was originally established in 1869 by the senior member of the firm. This reliable house occupies at the above address a three story brick building 30x90 feet in dimensions, which is well arranged and appointed, with all conveniences available, including an elevator. The stock carried includes some of the choicest Bourbon and Rye whiskies, gins, rums, brandies, American wines, foreign clarets, ports, champagnes, sherries, cordials, etc., and in fact everything pertaining to the trade, besides cigars of the best foreign and domestic manufacture. Much of the imported stock, in case and bulk, is of the firm's own importation, and domestic products are obtained direct from the manufacturers in large quantities, the house possessing all the advantages of ample capital with which to make judicious purchases. Messrs. Japhet & Co. are the agents in this locality for the celebrated and unsurpassed Schlitz Milwaukee bottled beer. Among the leading brands of whiskey sold here are *Hazel Nut, Nutwood, McBrayer, Greystone, Monarch,* and *Lynchburg Rye.* These goods are of the most desirable character, pure, smooth, and altogether superior. Full lines of other goods are handled, both domestic and imported. In cigars appreciation has been gained for *Beethoven, Moro-Bella ,Plutocrat,* and other brands, goods recommended and guaranteed by the firm. The trade of the house is steadily growing, both in this locality and elsewhere in the state. Nine assistants are employed, including three men on the road. The members of the firm individually are Messrs. Isidore Japhet and Daniel August Japhet. Both gentlemen possess a complete knowledge and experience of the business, gained through almost a life-long pursuit of its details. The senior member of the house has been twenty-eight years a resident of Houston, and twenty-five years in business here. He is a gentleman closely identified with the best interests of the city, and its advancement. He is also vice president of the American Brewing Association. Mr. Daniel A. Japhet is a son of the senior member, and entered the firm as a partner January 1st, 1893.

CASH & LUCKEL,
Real Estate, Loans and Investments; Houston, 306½ Main Street; Galveston, 421 Tremont Street.

Among prominent firms of real estate agents in Houston and Galveston who have favorable inducements to offer is the house of Messrs. Cash & Luckel, who, October, 1892, succeeded Messrs. Williams & Cash, who originally founded the business. The firm give their entire energies to the operation of a general real estate agency, including the collection of rents, the investment of funds and the negotiation of loans upon real security. Their facilities are of the very highest character and their operations are upon the largest scale; indeed, we believe that it is safe to say that this house is one of the most important of its kind in the State, having, perhaps, the largest list of lands to dispose of in this section. The specialty of the house is extensive tracts of cheap Texas lands, which are suitable to be sub-divided into lots and farms. No section in the country to-day presents better opportunities to the settler, the investor and the capitalist. South Texas lands are fertile and well watered and are particularly adapted to the growth of all kinds of saleable fruits and vegetables, not to speak of the facilities they offer for stock raising, dairying and for the growth of corn, cotton and other staples. Pears are especially cultivated with profit on these lands, yielding from $400 to $600 per acre when in bearing, which is attained in about five years and increases yearly, and in the meantime a living may with ease by earned in truck farming. Houston and Galveston afford the best of markets for these products, not to speak of the rapidly growing demand for Texas fruits which is coming from the North and West. The diversity of the crops in this section is remarkable, the climate is delightful and there is everything at hand to make the life of the farmer a happy one. Endorsements of the facts we have stated come on every hand from competent authorities, and to-day South Texas presents a field for the fruit grower and farmer unsurpassed anywhere, even "in the glorious climate of California," which. however, is no better than we have here. The list of properties offered by Messrs. Cash & Luckel merits the careful attention of investors, and especially Harris county lands, which are particularly desirable. Taking present price and prospective value into consideration, they are offered very cheap as will be realized upon investigation. Terms may be arranged to suit buyers, and the firm invite correspondence and they will cheerfully and promptly reply to all inquiries. The firm give their attention also to the perfection of titles and to the care of property for non-residents. The standing of the firm assures the fullest confidence, and they offer as references the Galveston National Bank, of Galveston, and the Planters' and Mechanics' National Bank, of Houston. The co-partners individually are Messrs. R. M. Cash and L. C. Luckel. The first named gentleman resides at Galveston and is a well known real estate man there. Mr. Luckel lives in this city, and he has had many years' experience of all that pertains to real estate matters. Concluding, we will but add that all representations made by this firm can with safety be depended upon, and all transactions are based upon honor and fair dealing.

C. W. ALSWORTH,
Dealer in Agricultural Implements. 911 Preston Avenue.

Reflecting the trade conveniences of Houston it is proper that some few details connected with the above house should be embodied in our pages. The enterprise was founded in 1885, and since then it has built up an important and growing trade. The premises occupied comprise a large three-story brick building 50x115 feet in dimensions. A large warehouse is also utilized at the corner of Baker and Pine streets, Fifth Ward. At the store is shown a large stock of the best and most carefully selected agricultural implements, farm and garden tools, shelf and builders' hardware, etc. The specialty of the house is the best quality of farm implements in large variety, offered at the lowest prices. Here may be obtained sulky plows, cultivators, disc harrows, shovels, stalk cutters, hoes, wagons, barb wire, steel blades, mowing machines, hay ties, hay rakes, and in fact everything needed by the farmer, planter or fruit grower. Among implements specialties are made of the celebrated genuine Avery plows and Rock Island implements, which are the peers of any extant and surpassed by none in the American market. Mr. Alsworth is a gentleman of great experience in this business, and he has a practical knowledge of what is best suited to the needs of this locality. He believes in supplying the very best that the money can buy, and thus not only gains patronage, but holds it. It is to the advantage of all visiting the city to give him a call and see what he has to offer. A correspondence with him will be promptly answered and information and descriptive printed matter immediately forwarded. Every inducement is offered, and for quality, extent of stock, fair dealing and low prices, no more advantageous purchasing point is to be found throughout this section of the State of Texas.

MISTROT BROS.

Wholesale Dealers in Dry Goods, Clothing, Shoes, Etc., and Proprietors of the Armory Department Store, Texas Avenue.

The success of this house is particularly noticeable from the fact it has been in existence here only since June 1893, and although in a sense a junior among its contemporaries, the volume of business it transacts is equally as large as is that of any of its more ancient competitors. The firm occupy for the wholesale business a three story brick building 50x100 feet in dimensions, and the stock carried here embraces everything in the way of dry goods, notions, clothing, hats, shoes, etc., etc. In fact the stock is one of the completest in the Gulf states, and the trade will find that here they can obtain for as low a price the same quality of goods as are procurable at New York, Chicago, St. Louis or New Orleans. Messrs. Mistrot Bros. enjoy the completest facilities, enabling them to procure their goods to advantage. Purchases are made direct from the manufacturers and original sources of supply, and they also import from European countries. The firm are always on the alert to obtain the latest novelties and the newest goods, in the interests of their patrons. Messrs. Mistrot Bros. are also the proprietors of the Armory Department Store located in the Light Guard Armory, at the junction of Texas Avenue and Fannin Street. This establishment was opened to the public in 1892 by Messrs. Collet, Wagner & Risser, the present firm acquiring the business in 1893. The store is admirably appointed, provided with all conveniences, and is lighted by electricity. The business is divided into a number of departments, the principal of which are as follows: dress goods, silks, linens, millinery, shoes, hosiery, underwear, cloaks, clothing, toys, gents' furnishing goods, carpets, house furnishing goods, etc. Each of these departments is separate from another, each showing the results of its own sales, and supervised by an experienced and competent manager. Messrs. Mistrot Bros. are able from their stock to equip a new home complete with everything but the sole item of furniture, but they also sell under one roof every article of ladies', gentlemens' and children's wearing apparel. Every accomodation that modern business methods have rendered necessary is provided customers at this establishment, including an electric elevator. The house employs about 50 assistants in the Armory store, besides eight in the wholesale establishment. The firm in addition to the operation of their business here, have branches at Marlin, Brenham, Bryan, Navasota, Huntsville, Cuero, and Mexia. They are also connected with the houses of H. B. Mistrot & Co., Waco and Corsicana, C. L. Mistrot at Dublin, Henrietta, Comanche, Belcherville and Hico, and E. W. Mistrot, at Ennis. The above mentioned houses, along with the Houston enterprise, constitute what is known in the Eastern market as the Mistrot syndicate, who purchase in common, thus gaining many advantages in buying, over individual houses. The members of the firm are S. P. Mistrot,

G. A. Mistrot, F. E. Mistrot and A. J. Wagner, all of whom take an active part in the business, and all are gentlemen of long tried and thorough experience in the dry goods trade. The house is the only one here which combines important wholesale and retail operations, and its trade may be quoted as a prime factor of the advancement of this city in influence and importance.

MACATEE & CO.,
Cotton Factors and Dealers in Building Materials, Etc., Washington and Fifth Streets.

An old established house, with an interesting business history, is that of the above firm, which was originally founded in 1860 as Macatee, Stafford & Co. In 1865 the title was changed to Macatee & Whitmarsh, and in 1870 Mr. W. L. Macatee assumed the sole proprietorship. The present designation was adopted in 1887, and the gentlemen associated with Mr. Macatee retired from the business in 1890, since when he has carried on the business alone, continuing, however, the firm designation. The premises occupied comprise an office, salesrooms and warehouse contained in a two-story brick building 50x75 feet in dimensions, which is Mr. Macatee's property, as well as is the entire block in which the building is located. Here ample conveniences are available for the storage of cotton and other goods dealt in by the house. Messrs. Macatee & Co. are cotton brokers, handling about 5,000 bales annually. The firm invite consignments of the staple from planters and others, ensuring quick sales and speedy returns, and making advances if desired. They have every facility for the transaction of business and for conserving the best interests of consignors. Another department is the handling of building materials, such as Portland and Rosendale cements, lime, hair, laths, fire brick and clay, drain pipe, etc. These goods are obtained direct from the manufacturers in carload lots, and are offered to the trade of the best quality and at lowest prices. Large stocks are always kept on hand and all orders are promptly filled. Mr. Macatee is a gentleman of complete and lengthened experience in all relating to the business he conducts. He came to this city in 1855 and became a clerk with Mr. T. W. Whitmarsh, who was burned out in 1860. Then Mr. Macatee, in conjunction with Mr. Stafford and E. B. H. Schneider, both clerks in the house, purchased the business which he since continuously conducted for over a third of a century. Now, this gentleman is the oldest cotton factor in Houston, and he has had the gratification of seeing the expansion and advancement of the city until to-day it is entitled to be ranked as the real metropolis of Texas.

GEORGE W. REYNOLDS & CO.,
Real Estate, 416½ Main Street.

Transacting in a quiet and unostentatious way large operations in real estate is the firm of George W. Reynolds & Co., who established their business here about three years ago. This house is in the enjoyment of the best facilities for placing large blocks of real estate on the market, and they have inducements of the highest character to offer to the investing public. The firm are general real estate agents, taking charge of estates for non-residents, collecting rents, etc. They are the owners and handlers of some large tracts of land in South Texas, which they have sub-divided indiciously, and which they offer for sale in quarter sections. These tracts are particularly well adapted to farm and fruit lands, being well located, fertile, well watered and contiguous to a favorable market. The prices at which they are offered will be found to be low considering the value, and they are sold on terms to suit. Having alluded elsewhere to the attractions of this part of Texas, we need not recapitulate, but will only say that Messrs. George W. Reynolds & Co., have at the disposal of the home seeker and investor, some of the best of these lands that are to be obtained in the State. The firm also buy, sell and exchange city property, lots, business property, etc., and they also deal in Kansas, California, Minnesota, Dakota and Iowa lands, having a very full and comprehensive list. The standing of the firm invites every confidence, and strangers are offered as reference the banking house of T. W. House, of this city. The members of the firm individually are George W. Reynolds and S. S. Reynolds, gentlemen thoroughly understanding every detail of the business. The senior partner has had fully ten years active experience of real estate matters, and S. S. Reynolds has been identified with them for nearly as long a time. The firm will be glad to hear from out of town parties who wish to investigate the opportunities now offered, and they will promptly reply to all inquiries. Concluding, let us add that the firm have every experience, ample capital and all facilities at their command to advance the interests of their clients.

CAPITOL HOTEL,

Geo. McGinly, Proprietor, Corner Main Street and Texas Avenue.

We are a nation of travelers and locomotion is distinctly an American characteristic. Out in the world, jostled among strangers, anxious and busy with business complications, the traveling man soon learns to appreciate the careful attention and hospitality which marks a really first-class hotel—which sheds contentment upon the tired soul, and which brings him comfort and repose, though he be a stranger in a strange land. The tide of travelers who are attracted to Houston will find no better

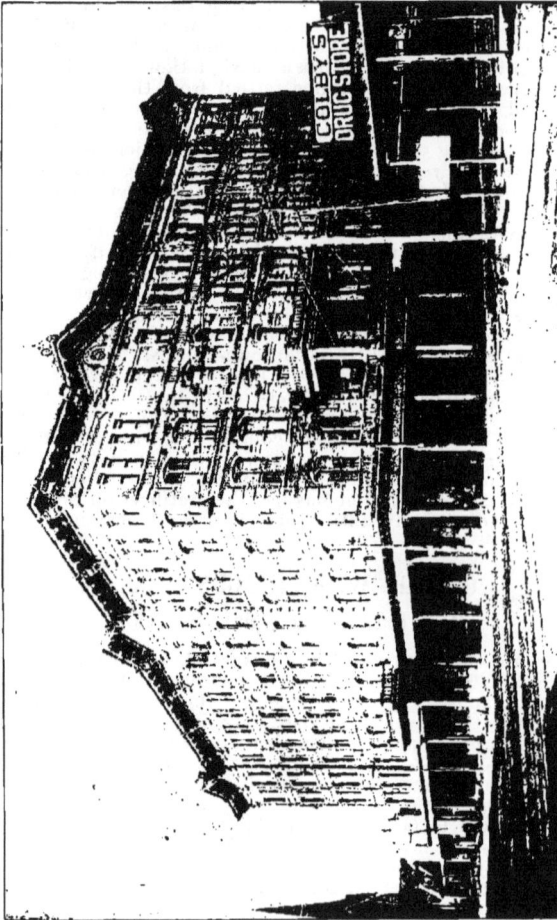

CAPITOL HOTEL.

place at which to drop anchor than at the Capitol. This house is a handsome five-story brick building, 150x179 feet in dimensions. It is centrally located, thoroughly equipped and furnished in first-class style, supplied with all modern conveniences, electric lights, electric bells, large sample rooms, bar room, billiard room, handsome parlors, and everything required to conduce to the comfort of guests. The house has a large number of sleeping rooms, handsomely decorated, and furnished well and completely. The tables are bountifully spread and the most exacting can find an ample supply of both substantials and luxuries wherewith to satisfy the inner man. The regular rates are from $2.50 to $3.00 per day with special rates to commercial travelers. The Capitol hotel was built in 1882 by M. A. Grosbeck. Mr. Geo. McGinly has been the proprietor since 1884. This gentleman has been in the hotel business for nearly a half a century and nothing connected with hotel matters are unfamiliar to him. He was proprietor of the Tremont House, at Galveston, for six years, also of the Beach Hotel in that city, the Grand National Hotel, now the Everett, at Jacksonville, Florida, the Kimball House at Atlanta, Ga., the Stockton at Cape May, and several others. He was but a lad when he started in hotel life, but he commenced in a good school—at the far famed Astor House of New York City. The house's hospitality is a theme of favorable comment with the knights of the grip and other occasional visitors to the city. Therefore, on landing at Houston take the bus which meets all trains and descend at the Capitol and see for yourselves how well mine host McGinly knows "how to keep a hotel."

HOUSTON ICE AND BREWING COMPANY.
Office and Brewery Corner Washington and Fourth Streets.

The Houston Ice & Brewing Co. was incorporated in 1887, with a capital stock of $250,000 fully paid up. The plant is of a very complete and extensive character. It is located on both sides of Washington and Fourth streets, and on one side covers an area of 200x150 feet, and on the other is of the dimensions of 150x150 feet. The principal buildings on the property are the brewery proper and ice plant, five stories high and 100 feet square in extent, a two story boiler and engine house, 50x100 feet, a single story wash house, 60x100 feet, the bottling department, 60x70 feet, a stable, 50x70 feet, and an office building, 50x60. All of the above are built of brick, except the office. The power for working the plant is obtained from a fifty horse power engine, and there are two improved ice machines, respectively of 120 tons and 60 tons capacity. All of the machinery and appliances are of the newest and best that can be obtained, conducing greatly to the high quality of the product, and to the low expense of operating. The capacity of the ice plant is 100 tons daily, of the

brewery 60,000 barrels annually, and of the bottling works forty barrels daily. The water, both for the manufacture of ice and lager beer, is obtained from three artesian wells, one of which is 800 feet deep, the others being respectively 300 feet and 150 feet in depth. The total capacity of the three is 300,000 gallons daily. The water thus obtained is of the utmost purity, yet nevertheless, it is all distilled before being used in the making of the ice, thus insuring absolute purity. This water is particularly well suited to the manufacture of lager beer, and no doubt contributes to its high quality. The company take pride in the fact that they are enabled to supply the home market with a home made product; at the same time, that owing to its excellence, it is largely in demand in localities distant from the city. Only the best quality of hops, the finest malt and the purest water constitute the ingredients, and it is manufactured according to the most approved scientific methods under the supervision of a past master in the art of brewing. The company's beer is known by the general brand name of "Magnolia." The bottled goods brands are "Extra Pale," "Southern Select," and "Standard." The beer is shipped to all parts of the state, and the brewery being located on the line of the Houston & Texas Central Railroad, with its own side tracks direct into the works, the best of shipping facilities are available. At the present time the Houston Ice & Brewing Co. have agencies and distributing points at Galveston, Velasco. Willis, Richmond, Navasota, Warden, Hempstead, and other places. These branches are about to be added to in various localities. The executive officers of the company are H. Hamilton, president, B. Adoue, vice president, and H. Prince, secretary and treasurer. The above are all well known residents of this city. The stockholders are all Houston people, and the enterprise is essentially a Houston industry. Mr. Fritz Kolb, the brew-master, is a thoroughly scientific and skilled brewer. He is originally from Germany. where he acquired his present knowledge of his profession. The establishment employs in the various departments about eighty workmen, the amount of wages thus annually distributed being of large benefit to the locality. Supplying the people of Texas with a pure, delicious and sparkling beverage, which really has no superior, and which therefore commends itself to the trade. it advertises abroad the name and fame of the city, drawing attention to it as the real metropolis of Texas, and the distributing point of the state.

HOUSTON BARREL AND CISTERN FACTORY.
Corner Dowling Street and McKinney Avenue.

Among the most important manufacturing enterprises of this city must be classed that of the above mentioned company. The business is also one of the oldest established here, having been originally founded as a private enterprise in 1872. The incorporation of the present company transpired in 1889, the capital stock being $25.000. The plant covers a half block ; the factory being an iron-clad building of 75x250 feet. The machinery and appliances are of the best and latest improved character, power being furnished by a thirty horse power engine and boiler. From fifty to seventy-five skilled mechanics and others are employed at the works. The Houston Barrel and Cistern Factory manufactures everything in the way of tanks, barrels, cisterns, including oil and molasses barrels, beer kegs, etc. The entire work in all its details is executed on the premises. The staves and headings are cut by special machinery designed for the purpose, the remainder of the work being done by hand labor, the result being first-class products in every respect. The material used is oak and cypress which come from the forests of Louisiana and Arkansas, within a convenient shipping radius. The company's business is not confined to this city, large quantities of the goods being dispatched to various parts of the state and beyond. The company make and sell from 20,000 to 30,000 barrels annually, over 1000 cisterns, and a large number of beer kegs. They supply all the breweries in Houston. The establishment is the only steam factory of the kind here and its facilities are complete, enabling them to quote the lowest prices. The executive officers are P. R. Carson, President ; A. F. Meyer, Vice-President ; T. W. House, Treasurer ; E. Blaffer, Secretary, and C. H. Hoencke, Superintendent. The management of the business is in the hands of gentlemen of the highest standing in the community, and it is conducted with a spirit of enterprise and energy which has been a prime factor of its success.

S. E. McASHAN,
Cotton and Wholesale Grain, 107 Main Street.

The staple agricultural products of this section of the country find a favorable outlet and market through the enterprise of the above mentioned house, which was established by its present proprietor in the year 1889. Mr. S. E. McAshan is in the enjoyment of the best facilities to advance the interests both of the producer and buyer. He invites consignments of cotton in any quantities and will purchase the same outright for cash, giving the highest current prices, or he will handle the staple on commission, selling it in transit or storing it at warehouse, as the occasion should arise to insure the most favorable market rates. Consignors will find their best interests well served in dealings with this house. The interests of his patrons are in every way rigidly conserved and nothing is left undone to obtain for them every advantage that legitimate methods could procure. Mr. McAshan also deals heavily in grain, which is obtained direct from original sources. Only sales at wholesale are made, and that too in carload lots, which are shipped direct to the purchaser without breaking bulk. Mr. McAshan is a gentleman thoroughly qualified by experience for the conduct of a business of this character. His standing in commercial circles is of the highest. In conclusion, we may be permitted to remark that the business is conducted upon a policy of fairness and liberality, and those interested will find that relations once entered into with the house will conduce to advantages difficult to procure elsewhere.

F. W. HEITMANN & CO.

Wholesale and Retail Heavy Hardware, Tinners', Blacksmiths', Machinists', and Railroad Supplies, Etc. 113 Main Street, and 114 and 116 Fannin Street.

This business was originally founded in 1865 by Mr. F. W. Heitmann. Mr. F. A. Heitmann, his son, became a partner January, 1889 and that year, on the third day of October, the senior member of the firm died. The business, however, has since been continued by the son, under the original designation of F. W. Heitmann & Co. From quite small proportions it has advanced to its present important character. The premises occupied consist of a three story brick building running through the entire block and having frontage on the two thoroughfares mentioned in the heading. It is of the dimension of 25x150 feet on the one side and 50x100 on the other. The comprehensive stock handled includes heavy hardware, tinners,' blacksmiths,' machinists,' railway and mill supplies, bar iron, sheet iron, iron pipe and fittings, belting, hose, wood split pulleys, saw mill supplies, etc. The entire establishment is filled from ground floor to roof with goods, the premises comprising over 20,000 square feet of floorage area. The facilities of the house include obtaining all goods direct from manufacturers and first hands in all instances, and specially advantageous arrangements are enjoyed with manufacturers of certain specialties. The firm are state agents for the following well known houses: E. C. Atkins & Co., Saw Manufacturers, Indianapolis; Bannantine Galvanized Iron Company, St. Louis; Gardner Governor Co., Quincy, Ill.; Metropolitan Injectors, New York; H. R. Worthington, Steam Pumps, New York; Cleveland Rubber Works, Cleveland, Ohio; Reeves Wood Split Pulley Company, Columbus, Indiana; Bradford Leather Belting Company, Cincinnati, Ohio; Niagara Stamping and Tool Company, Buffalo, N. Y.; Michigan Lubricator Company, Detroit, Michigan; Magnolia Anti-Friction Metal Company, New York; N. & G. Taylor Co.'s Old Style Roofing Tin, Philadelphia, Pa. The firm make a specialty of the equipment of saw mills which they are well prepared to furnish throughout with all machinery and appliances, upon a reasonable scale of charges. Mr. F. A. Heitmann has been brought up to the business and thoroughly understands every detail connected with it, and what today constitutes the trade demands. He may be quoted as one of our most enterprising business men. He is a director of of the South Texas National Bank and is interested in other banks here. He is also a member of the B. P. O. Elks and the Turn Verein. With a reputation extending over a period of nearly thirty years, this house occupies a position in mercantile circles to which we can add little, and which entitles it to be ranked as an exponent of Houston's most progressive establishments.

CHAS. P. SHEARN.

Dealer in Corn, Hay, Grain, Etc., 618 and 620 Travis Street.

The trade in grain, hay, corn, etc., may rightfully be regarded as one of the most important branches of industry that occupies the attention of our people. A well known and reliable house, devoted to the wholesale and retail branches of this trade is that of Mr. Chas. P. Shearn, which was founded in 1887 as Barrell & Shearn, the present proprietor assuming sole control in 1890. The premises occupied for the business comprise a brick building 45x118 feet in dimensions, which affords ample accomodation for the storage of a large stocks of products, and excellent facilities for the prompt filling of orders. Nine employees and six teams are required for the conduct of the business, and the trade transacted is very extensive throughout this city and vicinity. The house deals in corn, oats, bran, hay, grain, feed stuffs, etc., and a large stock is always to be found on hand, often as much as from 4000 to 5000 bales of hay, and particularly heavy stock of feed and grain. The connections of the house with producers and shippers are such, that the most advantageous inducements are offered to the trade and customers, and the reputation of the house for sedulously caring for the best interests of patrons is well understood and appreciated. Mr. Chas. P. Shearn, the proprietor, is a well known resident of this city. He represents the Third Ward in Houston's city council, and is also interested in other business enterprises here. He is possessed of a thorough knowledge of the business to which he devotes his active supervision and attention.

J. O. DAVIS.

Civil Engineer, 310½ Main Street.

In all growing and improving localities the services of the skilled civil engineer are essential, to plat and lay out the ground for new settlements before placing them on the market and before the public. In this city this profession is represented by Mr. J. O. Davis, who has had an experienced and practical familiarity with its details and duties for a period extending over eight years. He is originally from Denver, and he is a graduate of the University of Illinois, at Champagne. Mr. Davis' services have been availed of in this locality in the laying out of part of the improvement known as Houston Heights, all of the Denver addition, the town of Webster, the town of Genoa, the town of Almeda and others. Thus it will be seen that he has taken no small part in the improvement of this section. He is prepared at all times to give his services to anything pertaining to civil engineering, the platting of sub-divisions or town sites, also making maps and surveys, etc. Property owners and corporations can entrust their interests to the care of this gentleman with the full assurance that they will be well conserved and fostered. He bears the reputation of being prompt, reliable and altogether trustworthy, and we commend him to all who may require performed anything of this character, assured that it will be carried out to entire satisfaction.

J. N. QUINN,

General Manager Texas Branch Anchor Oil Works of New York, Office, 906 Franklin Avenue.

The Anchor Oil Works of New York rank, in the character and quality of their lubricating oils and lubricators, second to none other in the country. Their business in this city, and headquarters for the State, is under the efficient charge of Mr. J. N. Quinn, who is a gentleman of long and practised experience, of all details relating to the trade. The premises utilized comprise an office at the above address, and a warehouse adjacent to the Santa Fe Railroad, affording excellent shipping and receiving facilities. The products of the company embrace a variety of high grade lubricating oils and greases, which are commended by consumers for superior quality and economy in use. They are in active demand and favor wherever placed on the market. Lubricating oils and lubricators for every mechanical purpose, cylinder and machinery oils, are all produced by the company. A large stock always on hand ensures the prompt filling of orders and the satisfaction of patrons. The house also deals in packing, hose, belting, mill supplies, etc., of approved quality, obtained direct from original sources. The president of the company is Mr. C. E. Steck, of New York, and Mr. F. G. Steck, also of that city, is secretary and treasurer. Mr. J. N. Quinn, the manager here, was for sixteen years manager of the Southern branch of the National Oil Works and Mill Supply Company, of New York. Of this period he was located eight years at New Orleans, and eight years in this city. He has been about a year in his present position. Mr. Quinn is a member of the Masonic Fraternity, also of the Knights of Pythias, Knights of Honor and other societies. He is also a member of the National Society Marine Engineers and National Society Stationery Engineers. He was formerly in the United States Navy and is a G. A. R. man.

ALEXANDER, DARLING & CO.,
Real Estate, 502 and 503 Kiam Building.

There are but few cities in the country which give more promise of permanent progress and solid prosperity than does the city of Houston. On every hand are signs and indications of an expansion which is both healthy and permanent. The population of the city and district necessarily advances to keep pace with the growing prosperity, and desirable property in the heart of the city daily becomes more scarce and difficult to obtain. There is no trace of false boom or fevered inflation here, and judicious investments in real estate do not mean simply an unfathomable hole in which to drop money; on the contrary real estate in and around Houston has an actual and tangible value, which experiences an actual and growing increase year by year. Prominently engaged in placing before the public opportunities for acquiring real estate upon a highly favorable basis, is the firm of Messrs. Alexander, Darling & Co., founded in 1892. These gentlemen are the owners and handlers of a tract of improved property known as Brunners addition, which is situated on Washington Street, in the northwestern part of the city. It comprises two hundred acres of ground, which is laid out into lots and blocks for residences. These lots are sold at a reasonable price, either for cash or on the popular installment plan, so as to allow worthy persons of moderate means an opportunity to obtain a home, and the terms are arranged to suit the convenience of purchasers. The lots are sold under proper restrictions, which will insure the quiet and comfort of residents, and no nuisances or undesirable neighbors of any kind, will be allowed a foothold on the property. Brunners addition is connected with the center of the city by an efficient electric car system, a good school is within a few minutes walk, there is an ample supply of pure water, and the drainage is excellent, being equal to the best in the city. Building on the property has gained considerable headway; already has been erected about fifty handsome modern residences, and about a hundred more are arranged for and will soon be built. Special inducements are offered to those who will build at once, liberal assistance being tendered. Taking present value and prospective advancement into consideration, the property is offered on very low terms. Messrs. Alexander, Darling & Co. also control a large tract of the finest farm and fruit lands in Southeast Texas, and are headquarters on colonization. Special railroad rates are furnished at all times to parties in the North wishing to move to this section, or wishing to make a visit to investigate its resources, climate and other attractions.

C. GRUNEWALD,
Dealer in Pianos, Organs, Etc., 310 Main Street.

The above emporium of music is one of the leading ones of the State and contains a stock of goods worthy the attention of the most fastidious. The business is one of the oldest established in Houston. It dates back to the year 1872, when it was founded by Mr. Renzo Grunewald. In 1879 the proprietorship became vested in the hands of Mr. Louis Grunewald, of New Orleans. In 1880 Mr. Cliff Grunewald became the manager of the business in this city, and in 1882 he became its proprietor. Two years later, at New Orleans, was formed the L. Grunewald Co., Limited, and this organization took stock in the enterprise here, and Mr. Cliff Grunewald was also interested in the general business of the company. Later he bought out their interest in the Houston establishment and has since conducted it entirely on his own account. The house carries a large stock of pianos and organs, the product of some of the leading manufacturers of the country. They are the sole agents here for the Knabe, Fischer and Mehlin pianos and the Mason & Hamlin, Storey & Clark and Dyer & Hughes organs. The above may be said to be renowned for their splendid tone and power, good workmanship and general excellence. The house also carries a complete assortment of classical and popular sheet and book music and musical publications of American, English, French, German and Italian origin, and the facilities of the house are such that the most favorable terms are obtained here. Pianos and organs are sold on the installment plan when required and easy payments give every facility to people of moderate means to obtain these now almost indispensable articles of household comfort and enjoyment. Mr. Cliff Grunewald, the proprietor, enjoys an experience of the business extending over nearly his whole life, both in this country and in Europe. He thoroughly understands the public demands and is altogether able to satisfy every legitimate requirement. He is an accomplished pianist and vocalist and a composer of dance music of considerable merit. He is very popular in social and society circles and is a member of the B. P. O. Elks, Knights of Pythias, Turn Verein, German-American Society, Grunewald Quartette, Houston Light Gnards, Catholic Knights of America, and is of the choir of the Church of the Annunciation.

BRAZORIA LAND & CATTLE COMPANY.

Home Office St. Louis, Mo.   Houston Office Kiam Building.   Office also at Alvin, Texas.

Thn Brazoria Land & Cattle Co. was incorporated in 1885, with a capital stock of $260,000. The office at Alvin was opened in 1887, and that at Houston was instituted in the year 1892. The president of the company is Mr. Wm. McMillan, of St. Louis. Mr. H. A. Lloyd, secretary and general claim agent of the Wabash Railroad, is also secretary of this organization. Mr. L. M. Disney, the general manager here, divides his time between the offices in this city, and his duties on the property of the company. Among the names of the executive officers and directors of this corporation will be found those of some of the best known and most prominent in the country. Mr. C. H. Hayes, general manager of the Wabash Railroad, was for many years secretary of the company, and he is still one of the directors, as is also Ex-Governor Francis of Missouri. The management is in the hands of gentlemen of unquestioned sagacity and probity, and their connection with the undertaking assures every confidence. The Brazoria Land & Cattle Co. some years ago purchased what was known as the Talmage lands, which were originally the property of the late Mr. A. A. Talmage of the Wabash Railroad. This gentleman's widow is now one of the principal stockholders in the organization. When the company acquired the property it comprised 183,000 acres of land, but they have since sold much of it to other companies and corporations. The property is

MR. L. M. DISNEY.

situated between Alvin and Houston and Velasco, covering nearly all the territory contiguous to the Santa Fe Railroad between Clear Creek and Alvin, and between Alvin and Arcola. On these lands are now located the thriving towns of Alvin, Manville, Pearland, Superior, La Conte and Malvern. The unsold portion of the property is in no way inferior to that already disposed of. This has now been laid out into fruit and farm tracts of from five acres and upwards, thus affording opportunities for persons of the most modest means to make a home and a living on the land. The company offer special inducements of value to *actual settlers*, who are willing to live and labor on the soil. To such, highly advantageous terms will be offered, in the way of low prices, with long time accorded to complete payments. The location of the property is admirable. There is at hand the best of railroad facilities, opening up the entire country as a market. The fruit lands of South Texas are now rivaling those of Southern California, and the finest pears this country produces are now raised in this section. Strawberries are shipped by the hundreds of car loads to the North and East, and one consideration should not be lost sight of, and that is, that the season is early than in almost any other part of the United States. The cities of Houston and Galveston, near by, furnish splendid local markets for all sorts of truck, small fruits and vegetables, nor is the country less adapted for stock and cattle raising, grass lands, corn and cereal cultivation, dairying, cotton culture, and in fact almost every description of agricultural pursuit. The company have devoted large sums to the improvement of the property, and these improvements are continually going on ; over thirty miles of road have been graded, up to the present time, with deep ditches on each side, and three grading machines are still kept steadily at work. Water of

the purest quality is everywhere attainable for domestic and agricultural purposes, and indeed there is nothing wanting that should retard the success of settlers. Mr. L. M. Disney, the manager, has laid out on the property two experimental farms of over a thousand acres, for the special purpose of illustrating the possibilities of the land. Thus intending settlers can observe for themselves what may be accomplished, and they need accept only the evidence of their own eyes, as to what can be obtained from the soil. On these experimental farms may be seen growing many varieties of crops, and particularly has success been pronounced in grains and tame grasses. The company invite inquiries and investigations from all over the country, and they will be glad to enter into communication with all interested, and demonstrate to them the value of the inducements and advantages offered. The manager, Mr. L. M. Disney, has a wide experience in the handling of real estate of this character. He is a man of push and energy, and is never satisfied with small results. We believe, at the present time, that he is the right man in the right place ; thoroughly proficient and capable to advance and foster those interests entrusted to his care. We have been accorded the privilege of an interview with this gentleman, and we were convinced by the logic of facts, that all that is claimed for this property will fall nothing short of actual realization. Mr. Disney will be pleased to give his time and attention to visitors to Houston, who may wish to give the matter investigation, and we are assured that a half hour spent with him will result in profit and advantage.

PLANTERS AND MECHANICS NATIONAL BANK.

The Planters and Mechanics National Bank was organized November, 1890, and although of but comparatively recent establishment it is not by any means the least important. It has a capital stock of $250,000 with a surplus of $17,500 in addition to other funds of undivided profits. The transactions of the bank include the regular routine of all banks chartered under the National Banking Act, such as loans and discounts, receiving deposits and making prompt collections at all points in this country and Europe. The bank has reliable correspondents in all leading centers of the United States, the most prominent of which are Hanover National Bank, New York ; Continental National Bank, St. Louis ; Hibernia National Bank, New Orleans ; and First National Bank, Kansas City. The report of the Planters' and Mechanics' National Bank, dated February, 28th, 1894, develops the business of the bank as follows ; Loans and discounts $395,715 ; deposits, over $340,000, and circulation $45,000. The bank has also a savings department, receiving deposits of small sums of money and paying interest on the same. The present officers of this prosperous institution are President, T. J. Boyles ; First Vice-President, R. B. Morris ; Second Vice-President, H. Prince, and O. C. Drew, Cashier. The Board of Directors includes the following : T. J. Boyles, R. B. Morris, George A. Race, Louis Tuffly, F. Halff, E. L. Coombs, H. Prince, John H. Kirby, O. C. Drew, C. H. Milby and J. M. Cotton, all gentlemen whose prominence and success in their various vocations are the best possible guarantee of the stability and soundness of the Planters and Mechanics National Bank, and gives assurance that it will continue to be, as it hitherto has been, one of the most flourishing banking institutions of the state.

DAN CROWLEY.
Importer and Dealer in Builders' Materials, 814 Commerce Street.

Among industries closely allied to the building trade, worthy of special recognition, is that conducted by Mr. Dan Crowley, who commenced operations about fourteen years ago. At the above address he occupies a two story building, covering an area of 25x100 feet, where all required conveniences are available. The house handles everything in the way of builders' materials, such as lime, plaster of paris, hair, laths, Acme, Portland, Rosendale and Louisville cements, fire brick, sewer pipe in all sizes, garden tile, land plaster, soapstone, fire clay, etc. The house enjoys the best of facilities for procuring supplies, obtaining them direct from manufacturers and importers. Mr. Crowley represents some of the most eminent houses in the country, always handling reliable goods, which he can guarantee. In all departments he is in a position to offer the best of inducements in the way of quality and price, and he transacts one of the most important enterprises of the kind in this section. Mr. Crowley is an old time resident, and a popular citizen of this community. He has been here twenty-six years, coming to Houston from Memphis, at a time when the place had but fifteen thousand inhabitants. He was formerly a contractor, and today is a practical and skilled architectural modeler. Mr. Crowley is assisted in the management of the business by Mr. M. Burke, who has been with the house for about eight years, and is thoroughly experienced. This gentleman gives his full attention to the various details of the enterprise.

E. C. CRAWFORD,
Teas, Coffees and Spices, 1010, 1012 and 1014 Texas Avenue.

Probably few articles that enter into daily consumption as articles of food are so difficult to obtain of good quality and purity as are teas, coffees and spices. There are in all sections concerns whose reputation for manufacturing superior goods are well known, and there are often others who are equally notorious for opposite characteristics. Among the leading houses of the first-class no concern in the South bears a better reputation than that of Mr. E. C. Crawford, who established his business in the year 1878. Since that period the enterprise has steadily progressed in importance and influence, and to-day ranks among the first of its kind in the State. The premises occupied for the business comprise a two-story brick building 75x100 feet in dimensions. The coffee roasting and spice grinding departments are supplied with roasters and mills, all of which are of modern construction, operated by a gas engine of 10-horse power. The house is in possession of ample facilities for producing goods of the highest quality at the lowest prices, and being content with a reasonable profit, its customers may depend that they can here obtain first-class goods of the highest value at low figures as anywhere. Mr. Crawford manufactures and deals both at wholesale and retail in teas, coffees, spices, etc., baking powder and blueing. His goods are warranted pure and unadulterated, and are sold all through South Texas. The "Crawford" and "Fairy" brands of baking powder, like the other products, are in large favor with dealers and the public. He roasts coffees for the trade and grinds spices, putting up the goods under the name of the "Texas Coffee, Tea and Spice Company," which is a synonym of excellence. The capacity of the establishment permits of about one and a half tons of coffee and other products being daily turned out. This house was the first in this State to roast coffee and grind spices for the trade, and as such must be regarded as the pioneer of an important line of business in Texas. He also was the first direct importer of teas to Texas, and to-day this department is a very particular one, insuring here the best varieties of the leaf "which cheers but does not inebriate" that comes to this market. Mr. Crawford is also the proprietor of "The Wonder Store," corner Main street and Texas avenue, where is sold to the trade and public "everything for everybody" at wonderfully low prices. Mr. Crawford is from Fayetteville, Arkansas, and has been a resident of this State since he was eighteen. He is one of the best known and most popular of our citizens. He is Worshipful Master of Holland Lodge, A. F. & A. M.; Worthy Patron of Ransford Chapter, Order of Eastern Star, and he was the originator of the Chapter of Eastern Star in this city. He is also Treasurer of Protection Council, No. 17, Order of Chosen Friends; Treasurer of Inter-State Building and Loan Association, and is a member of nearly all the Masonic bodies and many other societies. Mr. Crawford was one of the men who saw the coming prosperity of Houston and prophesied it being what it has since become, the "Hub" of Texas and the Southwest. In his business he has always been and continues to be solicitous to maintain the well established reputation of the house, and by integrity and live methods to still further augment its scope of usefulness.

HENKE'S ARTESIAN ICE & REFRIGERATOR COMPANY.
Third and Railroad Streets.

This enterprise was established about ten years ago, when it was instituted by Mr. H. Henke, as a refrigerating plant. The building utilized is 150x100 feet in dimensions, and it is completely equipped with the best of appliances, including three refrigerating machines, respectively of eighty tons, eight tons and three tons daily capacity. The company manufacture the purest ice, made from filtered artesian water, which they dispose of in the city, and ship abroad to other localities. The establishment is also fitted up as a cold storage warehouse, with rooms of various temperatures to accomodate all kinds of perishable products. The executive officers of the company are H. Henke, president, Wm. J. Lemp, vice president, and C. G. Pillot, secretary and treasurer. The first and last named of these gentleman are of the firm of H. Henke & Co., of this city, and Mr. Lemp is the celebrated St. Louis brewer.

COLEMAN & SCHULTE,

Jobbers of Packing House Products, on Railroad Street between First and Second Streets.

Based upon the supply of the necessaries of life the extension and increase of the above branch of trade bears a direct relation to the general prosperity resulting in improved facilities for the supply of the demand thus created. An enterprise recently established at Houston, bearing out the above facts, is that of Messrs. Coleman & Schulte, founded September 1st, 1893. It starts on its career with every facility at hand, and it is doubtless destined to figure prominently among the leading wholesale houses of this city. The premises occupied are located in Allen's warehouse, an area of 50x100 feet being utilized. The firm are jobbers in packing house products generally; also flour, meal, mill feed, produce, etc. They enjoy the most intimate and advantageous relations with leading manufacturers in various sections of the country, enabling them to offer the choicest goods to the trade at the very lowest current prices. Messrs. Coleman & Schulte are the sole agents for the "Royal Owl," "Diamond Dust," "King Cotton," "Ocean Wave" and "Sea Gull" brands of flour, which may be regarded as standard goods, equal to any, of the same grade, made anywhere. They are also Texas agents for the Anglo-American Provision Company of Chicago, Ill., the Sioux City Packing Company of Sioux City, Iowa, T. M. Sinclair & Co., Cedar Rapids, Iowa, and the St. Josephs Oat Meal Mills of St. Joseph, Mo. These houses have a national reputation for the products which have long been in established demand on the market. The specialty of the house is the sale of goods in car load lots which are shipped from the mills direct to the purchaser. Smaller quantities are promptly despatched from the warehouse in this city where large stocks are always carried to fill immediate orders. The warehouse being adjacent to the railroad there is no delay, and but the minimum cost of handling. The members of the firm, individually, are Robert Coleman, Sr., Robert Coleman, Jr. and R. A. Schulte, gentlemen thoroughly understanding the business in every detail. Dealers and jobbers will do well to investigate the facilities and inducements which this firm have to offer at their disposal.

ELECTRO-GALVANIC SANITARIUM,

Kiam Building Annex.

The value of electricity as a curative agent for many of the ills which human flesh is heir to, is generally understood and conceded by all who have any pretensions to latter day science. But we are of the opinion that to avail ourselves of the benefits that this wonderful fluid offers to mankind, it must be administered intelligently under the auspices and direction of those who make a specialty of this particular line of treatment. In this city at the present time Drs. Mrs. Balfour and C. H. Warner, afford to the public the greatest facilities in this direction. Their Electro-Galvanic Sanitarium in the Kiam building annex is provided with all conveniences and facilities, which enable them to give to patients a full and proper course of treatment, under the most favorable conditions. Our purpose here is simply confined to pointing out to our readers the fact that such an establishment exists here in the city, and to advise them at the same time to make such inquiries and investigations as will be sure to establish the verity of all that is claimed for and by the institution. The electro-galvanic treatment, when judiciously administered, often succeeds after medicine and all other means have failed, and combined with massage, vapor and medicated baths, its results are often simply marvellous. Surgical operations performed, assisted by the influence of electricity, are far more efficacious in certain cases than otherwise, the pain also being considerably lessened. As regards the use of baths, the value of them is even yet but imperfectly understood. The old Romans were wiser than us, and they had public baths in the most insignificant of their towns throughout their domains. Modern science has improved upon their methods, and combines with vapor baths various medicinal influences, which greatly enhance their utility. Under the care of Drs. Balfour & Warner alleviation and cure is effected of a large number of chronic and other diseases, notably throat and lung diseases, blood poisoning, nervous diseases, affections of the kidneys, female diseases, neuralgia, gout, rheumatism, etc. In obesity the best of results are obtained, the patient losing flesh without the slightest injury to health. Special treatment for all skin and blood diseases is also given. Balfour's Complexion Bleach has had a great success, and insures a brilliant complexion without injury to the skin. We have not the space to devote further to the subject, but as before said, refer all interested direct to headquarters, where they will meet with all attention and courtesy. The Electro-Galvanic Sanitarium was established in this city January 1, 1894. It occupies nearly an entire floor of the Kiam building annex. The proprietors are Dr. Mrs. Balfour and Dr. C. H. Warner. Dr. Balfour has received her education at some of the finest massage institutions in the country, and she is eminently qualified for her work. Dr. Warner is a graduate of a high class medical college at Gottingen, Germany, taking his degree there in 1858. He has made a life long study of his special vocation, and among other places he has practised at Hot Springs, Ark., and for some years had an establishment at Galveston, where they are endorsed by and refer to the leading professional and business residents of that city.

R. D. GRIBBLE & CO.,

Planing Mill and Dealers in Lumber. Office and Factory, Fifth Ward. Office also in Cotton Exchange Building.

Among houses which are prominent in the lumber trade of this state is that of R. D. Gribble & Co., whose business was originally founded about seven years ago as Temby, Lyons & Gribble, the present designation being adopted about four years ago. The plant occupies two city blocks covering an area of 200x 600 feet. The buildings erected on this property are a planing mill 200x150 feet, two lumber sheds, one 30x175, and one 30x200 feet, a handsome office building, forty feet square, and a sash and door warehouse 30x80 feet. The machinery and appliances here in use are of the best and most complete character, there being over forty ingenious and modern labor saving woodworking devices all of which are of the latest improved character. The firm manufacture and sell lumber of

MESSRS. R. D. GRIBBLE & CO.'S OFFICE AT THE FACTORY.

of all descriptions, shingles, sash, doors, blinds and mouldings, also heart cypress tanks and cisterns, and they execute everything in the way of mill and turned work, bills cut to order, etc. Their facilities enable them to turn out the very best of work promptly, at the lowest prices. The factory is adjacent to the railroad, enabling them to receive raw material and ship their goods with facility and economy. One of their specialties is the construction of heart cypress tanks and cisterns, and in this department they have a special reputation and the best facilities. The firm employ a force of from twenty-five to sixty-five workmen, the number varying with the season of the year, and handle about two thousand carloads of lumber annually. The members of the firm are Messrs. R. D. Gribble of Houston, and O. T. Lyons of Sherman, Texas. These gentlemen are also of the well known firm of Lyon & Gribble, one of the largest lumber houses in the state. Their principal office is in this city and they have offices and yards at Alvarado, Anna, Bellevue, Bowie, Belcher, Commerce, Denison, Dallas, Gainesville, Hillsboro, Howe, Henrietta, Honey Grove, Ladonia, Nacona, Noble, O. T., Sherman, Saint Jo, Tom Bean, Wolfe City, Whitesboro. Closing this sketch, let us add that the business is conducted upon principles of strict commercial integrity and liberality, and the products are invariably the result of the employment of first-class material and superior workmanship, executed under practical and competent supervision.

J. C. S. MORROW & CO.,
General Real Estate Agents, 512 Main Street.

Today South Texas presents a field for the settler and investor second to no other section in the country. In an earlier part of this volume we have gone into this subject fully. and we now offer some few details relative to the real estate business as conducted here by Messrs. J. C. S. Morrow & Co., who commenced operations December 1st, 1893. The firm have an office at the above address, on the street floor, under the Capitol Hotel. It is thus well located and easy of access. The energies of the house are given to the transaction of a general real estate business, the collection of rents and the taking charge of properties for non-residents and others. Messrs. J. C. S. Morrow & Co. devote particular attention to the placing on the market of city and suburban lots and plats, fruit and farm lands, suburban acreage, etc. They have the best of facilities for the disposal of the same to advantage, their connections and *clientelle* being wide-spread and extended. They have at all times on their books properties of the above character to dispose of, which are sold upon terms as may mutually be agreed upon. Property owners entrusting their interests to their care may do so with the utmost confidence in the full assurance that their true interests will be conserved in every available manner. The house invites references to the well known firm of Wm. D. Cleveland & Co., wholesale grocers and cotton factors. of this city. The members of the firm individually are Capt. J. C. S. Morrow and F. L. Blumer. Capt. Morrow was formerly of Georgetown, Texas, and for eleven years was with Messrs. Wm. D. Cleveland & Co. He served during the civil war as captain of a company which was the first that left Williamson county and earned the honorable title he now bears. He married a daughter of the late Gen. Sam Houston. Mr. Blumer is from Omaha, Nebraska, and was in the real estate business there. He has had a large experience. He was at one time a member of the Omaha city council. To investors and capitalists they have valuable advantages to offer, and they solicit a personal interview or a correspondence, the results of which no doubt will ultimately prove of benefit and profit to all concerned. Both gentlemen are thoroughly qualified for their present undertaking, and they may be said to be energetic and reliable business men, meriting every confidence bestowed upon them.

HERBERT E. FULLER,
Real Estate, 400 Kiam Building.

To the efforts of the real estate men of this city, much credit is due for demonstrating the advantages available in this section, and we now accord a few lines to the business presided over by Mr. Herbert E. Fuller, whose office is located at 401 Kiam building. This gentleman is the agent and manager of what is known as Oak Lawn, a tract of land located on the Harrisburg road just outside of the city limits. This property comprises about a hundred acres which has been platted into building lots, and which are offered to the public at prices from $250 and upwards per lot. Oak Lawn is one of the most desirable of all Houston's additions. It is delightfully situated on high ground and is surrounded by shade trees. It is on the south side of the bayou away from all odors to contaminate the atmosphere, and while close to the center of business it is free from noise, dust and smoke of railroads and factories. The electric street railroad runs within a very short distance, and in a very short time the property will be directly connected with the city by an extension of the line. Improvements have been introduced on the property at a considerable cost, and the tract is provided with culverts, graded streets, and other conveniences. The owners of the property have now $20,000 on hand, waiting to be used in the erection of houses, which will be built to suit purchasers, payment being accepted in installments, upon terms to suit. Oak Lawn forms, as it were, the watershed between two systems of drainage, and therefore is eminently healthful and free from malarial odors or contamination. The prices asked for the lots are very low, taking into consideration the admirable location, the improvements introduced, and the fact that the value is certain to appreciate within a short time. More than $10,000 worth of lots have already been disposed of to Houston residents and the addition is rapidly being sold to the most desirable class of citizens. Here, therefore, is the best opportunity presented for obtaining a site for a home at a low price, and in a charming neighborhood, healthful and convenient, easy of access and in every way desirable. Mr. Fuller has also for sale good and cheap farm and fruit lands in various parts of the Gulf Coast district of Texas, the California of 'the South. He will be glad to correspond with intending home-seekers and investors, and will demonstrate to them the great value of the inducements offered by the locality, which are surely founded upon a solid basis and justified by, solid facts which cannot be questioned. Mr. Fuller is a gentleman of modern business ideas and unimpeachable character and those who may enter into business relations with him will find all transactions based upon fair dealing.

REPSDORPH BROTHERS.

Manufacturers of Awnings, Tents, Etc., 706 and 708 Main Street.

In our compilation of this work on the resources and business interests of Houston, we have been forcibly impressed by the diversity of their character; and some without making ostentious display are conducting enterprises of marked utility, obviating all necessity for Houston's people to go outside for supplies in the various lines. Among such is the business of Messrs. Repsdorph Bros., which was originally instituted in 1878, by Mr. John H. Repsdorph, the father of the present proprietors, who succeeding him in 1892, adopted then the present firm designation. They occupy a two story building at the above address, which is 42x100 feet. Here they have all conveniences, employment being given to ten or more assistants. The firm are manufacturers of tents, tarpaulins, awnings, flags, horse, dray and wagon covers, etc. In the way of tents and awnings, a large variety of styles are made, as required, and all the products may, if desired, be made mildew proof, by a special process, only used by the firm, and which is certain and infallible in its application. The firm devote particular attention to work executed to order, either in duck or in canvas, and all favors received are promptly fulfilled, and to the entire satisfaction of patrons. An interesting fact worthy of mention, with regard to this firm, is that they are authorized by the weather bureau at Washington to report the weather signals in this city, and each day they display the signal flags, according to telegraphic instructions received from the capital. The individual members of the firm are B. Repsdorph and E. Repsdorph, the latter of whom may be said to have had a life long experience of the business. They thoroughly recognize the fact that in this class of work none but the very best of materials, and the most careful workmanship would withstand the strain of wind and weather, and they aim to entirely merit full appreciation and confidence. The prices will be found to be based upon a moderate scale, leading to a continuance of a trade connection once established.

THE LATE MR. JOHN H. REPSDORPH.

J. R. MORRIS' SONS,

Wholesale and Retail Hardware, Agricultural Implements, Mill Supplies. Stoves, Tinware, Etc.—Offices and Salesrooms, Main Street.

This house was originally founded by J. R. Morris in 1847, and in 1886 the firm of R. B. & B. P. Morris was formed. Mr. B. P. Morris retired February, 1893, and the present designation was adopted the same year, Mr. R. B. Morris, however, being sole proprietor. Mr. J. R. Morris, with whom the present and last past generations of business men were most intimate, was the continuous owner of the enterprise for the forty years preceding his demise. The premises occupied for the business consist of an extensive three-story building on Main street, which is of the dimensions of 67x135 feet. The firm also utilize a large warehouse in the Fifth Ward, which is two stories high and 75x125 feet in dimension. The stock includes heavy and general hardware in all its branches, machinists', mill, factory and mechanics' supplies, agricultural implements and tools of the best character and quality, iron and steel, stoves and ranges in large variety, tinners' stock, tools and supplies, belting, packing, powder, arms, ammunition, plumbers' supplies, cornice work, etc. An immense stock and complete variety in all lines are carried, specialties being made of mill, fretory and manufacturers' supplies, sanitary plumbing and engineering, etc. The firm em ploy forty-two clerks, salesmen and assistants. The proprietor of the enterprise, Mr. R. B. Morris, devotes his close personal attention to the supervision of the business, of which he possesses a life-long experience. He is also Vice President of the Planters and Mechanics National Bank of this city. Concluding, we will but say that for so long a period a prominent factor of Houston's industrial development, this old time and honored enterprise has contributed certainly as much as any other to the material prosperity and development of the community.

JOHN FINNIGAN & CO.,
Hides, Wool, Etc., Houston, Texas and New York City. Houston Office, 601 Washington Street. New York Office, 90 Gold Street.

One of the most useful vocations of the day is that of the large dealer in hides, wool, etc., for it is by means of his efforts that the producer finds a ready market for his product, and the manufacturer obtains the raw material from which he fashions the finished goods, which ultimately are made up into materials which serve to clothe all classes of the community; engaged largely in this department of business here is the firm of Messrs. John Finnigan & Co., whose enterprise was established about twenty years ago. From the start the industry has continued to expand and develop until today it may be ranked among the more important houses of the kind in the state. The premises occupied for the business in this city comprise an office at the above address with large warehouse facilities on the railroad tracks, in the Fifth ward, the buildings and yards here located covering an area of about two acres. This affords the best of conveniences for carrying large stocks which are collected from all parts and are held here awaiting shipment. The firm deal extensively in hides, skins, wool, etc., and the highest market prices are paid for these staple articles of commerce. The goods are bought outright, or may be consigned to the house, and to all who have products of this nature to dispose of, it offers superior advantages, enabling them to have quick returns, the connections of the firm being such that a ready market is assured. The firm has branch establishments at many points in Texas, enabling producers to find a market near by without having to go to the expense of shipping to a distant market. The principal branches of the firm are at San Antonio, Galveston, Dallas, Waco, El Paso, Eagle Pass and Laredo. These feeders enable them to obtain large quantities of hides and wool annually. They have an office in New York City, at 90 Gold street. Messrs. John Finnigan & Co., invite correspondence, to which they will promptly reply, showing therein the manifest advantages of dealing with them. The members of the firm, individually, are John Finnigan and R. E. Paine, both of whom possess a complete knowledge of the trade, acquired through active experience. Any extended personal comment of them would be superflous; but of the house we say that it has always been conducted upon a policy of fairness and liberality, tending largely to the profit, advantage and satisfaction of all who may form business relations with it.

S. T. SWINFORD,
Lumber Commission, 914 Franklin Avenue.

The importance of Houston's lumber trade demands special reognition at our hands, aside from that of a general character, which will be found in an earlier portion of this volume. In this connection we are led here to allude to the business carried on by Mr. S. T. Swinford, as a lumber commission dealer, and who, although established as recently as July, 1891, has built up an important and growing trade throughout the State. Mr. Swinford confines his business strictly to wholesale transactions with dealers only. He represents some of the best known mills in the South, such as M. T. Jones & Co., of Lake Charles, La.; Bradley-Ramsey Lumber Co., of Lake Charles, La., and other important lumber and shingle mills in leading lumber sections. The product is furnished to the trade in car-load lots in dimensions and lengths to suit, direct from the mills to destination. He supplies both rough and dressed lumber—all Southern pine—and shingles. He invites correspondence from lumber mills and he is in the enjoyment of the best of facilities for placing their product on the market to advantage. To dealers he has also valuable inducements to offer, especially in the way of high quality product, reasonable price and the promptness with which all orders are filled. He caters especially to the trade of Texas, and it certainly will be to the advantage of all interested to enter into correspondence with him. Mr. Swinford has long been familiar with the lumber business, and he has been connected with a large number of the principal mills in this section. He was formerly with the house of D. R. Wingate, of Orange, Texas, and he has had business affiljations with as many as fifteen mills in this State. Socially he is well known here, and is a member of the Knights of Pythias and other secret organizations. In his business policy he may be said to be liberal, prompt and in every way reliable.

74 THE CITY OF HOUSTON.

G. W. BALDWIN,
Wholesale and Retail Bookseller, Stationer. Etc., 409 Main Street.

The above enterprise was founded in 1870 and it is entitled to the distinction of being the oldest established house of its kind in the city, and also in importance and reputation it stands second to none here. A three-story brick building is utilized for the business, and here is contained a large and full stock of standard books, school books, books of poetry, travel, biography, etc., as well as a very complete line of novels, periodicals, etc. The house also deals in everything in the way of commercial and society stationery, office supplies, etc. A large stock is carried of holiday gifts in the season, also wedding and birthday gifts, cards, etc. A particular feature of this business is the circulating library of many thousand volumes, comprising the standard works of popular authors and all the latest fiction of the day. Base ball supplies and sporting goods comprise another department and all requirements in these lines can be filled here with facility. Mr. Baldwin also makes a specialty of the following: Barnes' ink and mucilage, Houston society note paper and envelopes, Baldwin's lead pencils, Humboldt Library of Science, Automatic Roll Paper Cutter, Russell-Morgan's playing cards, rubber stamps, etc. The facilities of the house in every department are complete, the goods are well selected and are of the best and the prices are as low as the lowest in the city. The proprietor entirely understands every detail of the business. He is a well known resident of the city, interested in its welfare and advancement and identified with some of its prominent institutions and organizations.

WM. BUCK & CO.,
Wholesale Produce Commission, 208 Milam Street, Houston, and 24th Street and Strand, Galveston.

The above enterprise was established first at Galveston during the summer of the past year and the branch in this city opened its doors for business January 2d, 1894. The house enters upon its career with all facilities available, and already it has clearly demonstrated its ability to attract and hold an important trade. Messrs. Wm. Buck & Co. are wholesale commission merchants generally, and they make specialties of fancy produce, butter, eggs, poultry, etc. They are now in a position to invite consignments of produce in the largest quantities, assuring to farmers, producers and others quick sales, the highest market prices, prompt returns and fair business treatment. If required, liberal advances will be made by the house. Messrs. Wm. Buck & Co. are about to open branches at New Orleans and other places, so that the outlet for goods will be greatly extended. Any description of Texas produce will thus through this house find a ready market, and the unexcelled fruits of this locality will become better known to consumers throughout the country. Mr. Wm. Buck, the head of the concern, is a gentleman of energy and push, and he has the utmost confidence that our products can hold their own against all competition. Dealers will find at all times at his establishments the choicest produce in their season. Speaking in this volume of the most enterprising houses in each branch of commerce, we may say that in produce commission trade certainly a leading position is due to that conducted under the title of Wm. Buck & Co.

J. B. BEATTY.
Lumber Commission, Cotton Exchange.

An important acquisition to the lumber trade of Houston must be chronicled in the enterprise of Mr. J. B. Beatty, who commenced operations January 2, 1894. The house handles what is known as Calcasieu Long Leaf Yellow Pine, and he represents the products of Perkins & Miller Lumber Company, West Lake, La.; Lock, Moore & Co., West Lake, La.; Norris' Mills, West Lake, La., etc. All of these are producers of a high grade of long leaf yellow pine lumber, the total products of the establishments agregating 75,000,000 feet annually. The business has been established at this point solely to introduce this lumber to the manufacturers and dealers of Texas. Mr. Beatty's facilities are more than ordinarily favorable, as dealings with him are practically the same as dealing with the producers. The prices quoted are the lowest, and shipments are made in carload lots direct from the mills to destination. Mr. Beatty is enabled to assure the prompt filling of orders however large, there being practically no limit of his capabilities to carry out the largest contracts. Mr. Beatty comes here from West Lake, La., the fountain head of these products, and in that place he has been engaged in the lumber trade for the past ten years. He has every experience, no detail of the business being unfamiliar to him. As to his standing, we shall not refer to it. other than to say that the utmost confidence may be reposed in all representations made. The location in Houston of this new enterprise, advances the legitimate aspirations of the city to be designated the real metropolis of Texas.

THE KEELEY INSTITUTE.
Corner Preston Avenue and Fannin Street.

It would be practically impossible, with the limited space at our disposal, for us to accord anything like real justice to the wonderful results of the treatment for inebriety, identified with the name of Dr. Leslie E. Keeley, of Dwight, Ill. The fame of this system is now spread over every part of the North American continent, and has penetrated into Europe and other divisions of the old world. Our object however in alluding to the subject in this volume is simply to inform our readers that a branch institute exists in this city, and has its doors wide open to all who desire to become free from the chains and shackles of intemperance. Until comparatively recent years it has been the custom to regard undue indulgence in liquors and other stimulants and

narcotics, almost as a crime. This course is a great mistake. The craving for stimulants is less a crime than a disease, and like most diseases not organic, can be cured under proper treatment. The system and remedies in vogue at the Keeley institutes have now so successfully and emphatically demonstrated their wonderful efficacy that only sceptics and interested persons deny their great mission of usefulness, after having investigated. The evidence of thousands who today walk the land free men through their aid is evidence that is unmistakeable, and this evidence is on hand in every part of the country. The Keeley Institute in this city is established here to cure persons having the drink, opium, morphine, chloral, cocaine and tobacco habits. The system adopted is the best that could be devised. It includes the taking of the celebrated remedies, joined to a judicious voluntary sequestration, under practiced and competent care and observation. An experienced specialist is in charge, who has received his training direct from the parent Keeley Institute at Dwight, Ill. This is Dr. A. P. Stewart, Jr., who is still a member of Dr. Keeley's personal staff. This gentleman gives to each individual case a watchful and close personal care, the result being no failures, except through the disinclination of the patient to faithfully follow the given directions and instructions. The treatment is mild and harmless and leaves no injurious effects such as loss of appetite, prostration, loss of sleep or symptoms of dementia. Mr. S. E. Arnold is the manager of the Institute, and he co-operates with Dr. Stewart to do all to make the inmates comfortable and contented, and to sooth the nerves of patients disorganized by excesses, and persuade them to persevere along the golden path which leads to a renewed and re-invigorated rejuvinescence. The cure is easy and absolutely safe under all circumstances. At the Institute there are accomodations for fourteen resident patients, and many more can receive treatment here and reside in boarding houses in the neighborhood. Often the Institute has the care of forty patients at the same time. This is the only Keeley Institute in Texas, and the only place in the state where the Keeley remedies are administered, and persons come here from all over the state. The building is admirably located in the heart of the city, and is a two story building of 100x150 feet in dimensions. Over the doors may been seen displayed the following inspiring legends: "Drunkenness is a disease that can be cured; the drunkard is a sick man and not a criminal," and "Medical, not penal treatment, cures the drunkard." Correspondence is invited from all over the state, and all enquiries will be promptly met and particulars immediately forwarded. We do not doubt that a retirement of a few weeks under the care and influence of this veritable health resort will free those enthralled from their bonds, give them new life, and make their surroundings once more rosy hued and happy.

CHAS. E. SEMPLE & CO.
Real Estate and Investments. 914 Franklin Avenue.

The city of Houston, and the country all around and about it, present opportunities at the present time, either for investments or occupation, second to no other section in the United States. Among real estate firms who are engaged in demonstrating the above advantages to the public of the United States generally, is that of Messrs. Chas. E. Semple & Co., who are the successors to the firm of Sherwood & Semple, established during the past year. The house transacts a regular real estate business, handling city, county and farm property generally. The firm have a long and complete list of these properties for sale, which are offered at lowest prices, and upon terms to suit the purchasers. They have good agricultural and fruit lands to offer, well located, from four to ten dollars per acre; and other lands from two dollars upwards. At the present time they desire special attention to the Phillips addition north-east from the city, and at the north of the bayou. This is platted into building lots, and is sold on terms to suit, at low prices. They have also desirable fruit lands in Galveston, Harris and Liberty counties, which they offer in lots of from ten to two thousand acres. These lands are particularly well suited to the growth of fruits and vegetables, and especially for the cultivation of strawberries, pears, truck, etc. The climate is healthful and most delightful, the cities of Houston and Galveston near by, afford the best of markets, the soil is fertile, farming can be carried on all the year round, there are but very rarely any frosts, the heat of summer is tempered by the sea breeze from the Gulf, the society is good, there is plenty of pure water to be obtained, and last, though not least, the price of the land is comparatively low, and quite sure to advance in value within a short time. Texas fruits are in the market several weeks before those of California, and the distance to the North is less from here than from there. Messrs. Chas. E. Semple & Co. invite correspondence, and will promptly furnish all information, printed matter, etc. It is now just the time to invest, even if occupation be somewhat deferred, as prices are sure to advance during the coming year. Mr. Chas. E. Semple is the sole member of the above firm. He is originally from Pennsylvania, and he has had a number of years experience of the real estate business. He is eminently a reliable business man in whose representations every confidence may be reposed.

PALACE MEAT MARKET.
H. Edwards, Proprietor. 214 Travis Street.

The trade in meats, fish, poultry, etc., is more than ordinarily well represented in Houston by the Palace Meat Market, conducted under the proprietorship of Mr. H. Edwards, who started his enterprise in 1893, and which has already gained a high place in the estimation of the discriminating public. The premises comprise a three story brick building, 30x100 feet, which is really handsomely appointed and arranged, with every regard to heathfulness and cleanliness. All conveniences are at hand, including improved refrigerators, so that patrons can be expeditiously supplied at the shortest notice, and at all seasons of the year, with the finest quality of beef, pork, mutton, lamb, veal, poultry, game, sweetbreads, fish, oysters, etc. The latter are supplied both in bulk and in shell, the varieties handled being the celebrated Berwick and Corpus Christi oysters. Mr. Edwards caters to the finest trade in the city, and the establishment has already become headquarters for choice supplies in this line, at the same time that the prices will be found altogether fair and reasonable. The proprietor is a gentleman thoroughly understanding the business and all its details. He is originally from Corpus Christi, and has established his enterprise here with the conviction that a really superior market, keeping only the best quality of products, was a necessity to the convenience and comfort of our permanent residents. The success he has deservedly met with has verified the truth of his ideas, and the house is one which is well worthy of patronage and appreciation. Fair and honorable methods of trading are here the invariable rule, coupled to courteous treatment and prompt attention to business.

W. L. WETENKAMP,
Real Estate, 310½ Main Street.

The importance of real estate interests in a rapidly growing community such as Houston and vicinity present at this time, can scarcely be over estimated. It is therefore incumbent that the business shall be represented by a class of houses as have every experience, and assure every confidence. Of such our attention is now directed to the enterprise of Mr. W. L. Wetenkamp, who commenced operations September, 1893. This gentleman devotes his energies to a general real estate business, making a specialty of city property and rentals. He has on his list a number of desirable properties at the disposal of the public, and he is prepared to take the entire charge of real estate of any kind for non-residents, paying the taxes, collecting the revenues and remitting the proceeds. He also negotiates loans on real estate security, finds lucrative and safe investments for capitalists, and acts faithfully and intelligently in the best interests of his clients. The public may with confidence entrust their business to his care, assured that all representations made, will be honestly and faithfully discharged. Mr. Wetenkamp comes to this city from Denver, and he thoroughly understands the real estate business, with which he has been identified for the past ten years. As an exponent of the growing importance of this locality, an enterprise of the above nature is entitled to due recognition in this volume illustrative of the resources of Houston and environs.

THE ACME LUMBER AND MANUFACTURING COMPANY.
Dealers in and Manufacturers of Lumber, Sash, Doors, Blinds, Etc., 2206 to 2218 Nance Street.

The Acme Lumber Company was organized and incorporated March, 1893. The company are the possessors of a plant which may be said to be of a most complete and improved character. The works cover an area of about three acres, upon which

are erected the following: A planing mill of three floors and basement, which is 72x126 feet in dimensions, with boiler and engine house attached, 26x44 feet. A two-story structure 50x60 feet is used for storing lumber, and there is an office building 20x36 feet. Besides the above there is a hardware store and sash and door building of the dimensions of 20x50 feet and other minor conveniences. The power for operating the factory is obtained from a 100 horse power engine, and a boiler of the same capacity. The equipment of the mill embodies machinery and appliances of the latest improved and best construction, enabling the very best description of products to be made, and sold at lowest prices. The Acme Lumber and Manufacturing Company deal in all kinds of lumber, carrying large stocks of the same. They also make and sell sash, doors, blinds, mouldings, frames, turned and scroll work, and all kinds of special work to order, as may be desired. Nothing is left undone at this establishment to advance perfection, economy and dispatch in the production of the specialties. From forty-five to fifty skilled workmen and laborers are employed in the several departments, which are under the practical and experienced supervision of competent superintendents and foremen. The best of shipping facilities are available, the plant being adjacent to the railroad. The company utilizes annually about eleven million feet of lumber, and a trade is transacted throughout this and neighboring sections. The president of the company is Mr. Sam Allen, and Dr. T. J. Boyles is vice-president. Mr. V. E. Appleby is general manager, and Mr. H. F. McGregor is treasurer. These gentlemen are well-known and influential residents of this city. Mr. Appleby, the manager, is essentially a practical man, with fifteen years active experience in this branch of the business. Concluding this sketch, we will add that in every way the enterprise is conducted in such a manner as to attract and hold a large and increasing permanent patronage.

J. W. HASKINS & CO.,
Wholesale and Retail Grocers and Importers of Wines, Liquors, Etc., 909 and 911 Prairie Avenue.

This is an old established and reliable exponent of the business interests of this city. The origin of the enterprise goes back to the year 1873, when it was founded as Mellinger Bros. The present firm was instituted in 1888. The premises occupied for the business comprise a two-story brick building 90x100 feet in dimensions. The firm are wholesale and retail grocers in the widest acceptation of the terms, carrying full stocks in all lines, including staple and fancy groceries, provisions, etc. Their facilities are of the very best, enabling them to quote the lowest prices to the trade and public. All goods are of selected quality, and among their specialties is Chase & Sanborn's coffee, the agency at Houston for this celebrated product being in their hands. The firm transact an important railroad business, supplying railroad and other contractors with all requisites for feeding their workmen. Messrs. John W. Haskins & Co. make a special department of handling wines, liquors, ales, porters, etc. These goods they obtain straight from the manufacturers in this country or import direct from Europe. They handle very choice lines of these goods and carry full supplies both in bulk and in case. Dealers and consumers can depend upon obtaining from this house pure and unadulterated wines and liquors at prices that will compare favorably with those of any house in this section. The firm employ ten salesmen and assistants and four teams for deliveries. The individual members of the firm are Messrs. John W. Haskins and Edward Browne, well known residents of this city. The enterprise they conduct stands high in business circles here, equally as regards its facilities, standing and commercial reputation.

L. BRYAN & CO.
Real Estate.   402 and 403 Kiam Building.

The business of this house was founded in 1892, and it now enjoys the full confidence of property owners, investors and settlers. The firm are the sole agents of what is known as the Fair Ground addition, which consists of about 100 acres of land platted and laid out into building lots. The great advantage of this property is that it is within the city limits, and enjoys all the conveniences therein derived, such as city water, electric light, gas, etc. It is connected with all parts of Houston by the electric street railroad. The addition is well graded, and all improvements placed on the property. The lots are sold at a low price, on terms and time to suit customers. Houses are put up for lot owners if desired, and convenient time accorded for repayment. There never was a time when an investment of this kind promised better, and never were better and more favorable inducements offered to people of moderate means, to relieve them from paying rent, and enable them to become the owners of their own domiciles. Messrs. L. Bryan & Co. also handle the property known as the Empire addition, which is about a quarter of a mile outside of the city. This is a tract of 40 acres, platted into building lots, with improvements now being introduced. The street car line is adjacent, and either for investment or occupation, this property will be found highly desirable. The value is certain to appreciate within a short lapse of time, and at the price at which the lots are offered, a certain profit is sure to accrue. Houston today is the most progressive city of the United States. It is the greatest railroad center of the South, with a dozen competing lines entering the city. Manufacturing establishments are being inaugurated every month, it is the center of one of the richest fruit and agricultural regions in the country, population is growing, and withal there is no boom, but a steady and healthful expansion, which is permanent and consolidated. Messrs. L. Bryan & Co. have also on their list, fruit and farm lands in the rich Gulf coast country, which are sold on terms to suit. They also have other desirable city and suburban property, and real estate of all kinds. They devote special attention to the collection of rents, and the care of property for non-residents, giving to the interests of their clients their full and close attention. All representations are based on honor, and fair dealing is the rule from which there is no deviation. The firm invite the attention of land owners and capitalists to the fact that they have all facilities for placing on the market desirable tracts of land, whether for individuals or corporations, and to plat and lay out the same advantageously, and generally to attend to all details connected with the care and sale of such properties. The members of the firm individually are Louis Bryan and Mrs. Bettie Bryan, who thoroughly understand the business in all its details.

POLEMANAKOS BROS.,
General Confectioners and Dealers in Fruit, Cakes, Cigars, Etc., and Manufacturers of Pure Ice Cream, corner Main Street and Prairie Ave.

The firm of Polemanakos Bros. commenced business recently with all facilities at hand and with the determination to handle only such a class of goods as shall rank superior in all respects. The store is a handsome one, well located and convenient, and it contains a full and particularly fine stock of confectionery and candies, American and foreign fruits, cigars of choice brands, all the popular brands of smoking and chewing tobacco, peanuts, etc. Particular attention is due to the exceptionally fine line of imported confectionery and candied fruits, which are not equaled in the city. These are obtained direct from foreign countries especially for this house, which has already made a reputation for these products. Another special department is the manufacture of pure ice cream and candies. These goods are delicious in flavor, entirely free from adulteration and deservedly popular. Messrs. Polemanakos Bros. make the above fresh every day, so that the public may always obtain here ice cream and candy equal to the best in the city. The firm are the wholesale agents in this city for the celebrated A. No. 1 brand of Virginia peanuts, which are selected for their quality. A department to which we desire to call attention is the oyster parlor in the rear of the store, where these delicious bivalves can be obtained in the finest condition. The prices in all departments will be found moderate, and the proprietors give their close attention to the business. Both a wholesale and retail trade is transacted, and it is safe to add that the establishment promises to become a permanent and valuable feature of the business interests of the city.

KING & KUHLMAN,
Commission Merchants, Proprietors Houston Corn Mills and Dealers in Grain, Hay, Etc., 107 Main Street,

A very important enterprise allied to the food and feed trades of the city, is the well-known firm of King & Kuhlman, who April 1, 1889, succeeded to the business originally founded by Mr. Robert E. C. Wilson, about ten years ago. The facilities of the house are in every way favorable and complete. The sales rooms are contained in a building 25x125 feet in dimensions, and they have also a warehouse and corn mill adjacent to the track of the I. & G. N. R. R. The mill is equipped with the best of milling appliances, and is operated by a 65 horse power engine. The capacity is about 500 sacks of meal every ten hours. They transact a regular produce commission business, handling all descriptions of farm products, and assuring quick sales and prompt returns. Specialties are made of cotton, hay, grain, seeds, mill stuffs, etc., and large stocks are at all times carried both at the store and mill. In hay and grain a stock of the value of $5,000 and upwards is often carried. To producers the firm offer every inducement and will make very liberal advances if desired; on grain they will advance nearly the full value before a sale is made. To the trade and the public they can assure the best quality of products, the lowest current rates, and the prompt filling of orders to satisfaction. The business entails the services of seven men, as well as five teams for local delivery. The members of the firm individually are Messrs. F. R. King and H. H. Kuhlman, both of whom possess a complete knowledge and experience. They have every facility at command to attract legitimate patronage, and conserve equally the interests of producer and consumer.

SAM RAPHAEL. "HAPPY SAM,"
Dealer in Cigars and Tobacco, 512 Main Street,

An exemplification of the enterprising character of Houston's business houses is typically furnished by the above mentioned establishment, which was instituted in 1880 by Mr. Mose Raphael, the present proprietor assuming control in 1889. This store has always been regarded as headquarters by all who are fastidious in their choice of cigars and tobaccos and who desire the best and and the fullest value for money. The establishment is well located on the street floor of the Capitol Hotel, convenient for residents and for visitors alike. Here will be found a full and complete stock of all the popular brands of smoking and chewing tobaccos, besides a choice selection of imported and domestic cigars of the best and medium qualities. In addition Mr. Raphael carries a fine and large stock of pipes, pouches, smokers' articles, etc., in full variety and of best quality. Only the most reliable goods are handled, no cheap trash finding a place here under any circumstances. A specialty is made of the house's own brand of "Happy Sam," one of the best five cent cigars in the market, and which has gained celebrity all through this section. These are made specially for Mr. Raphael by a responsible firm of manufacturers, and he is particularly critical in the quality of the goods to ensure the use only of the best of

selected leaf, and that the workmanship and general get up of the cigars shall leave
nothing to be desired. The proprietor, rejoicing in his cognomen of "Happy Sam,"
is well named, as he is happy in the satisfaction of his patrons, who also are happy
in being able to obtain a really fine cigar at a moderate price. The establishment
may be classed as the leading retail tobacconist of Houston.

GAUT & THOMAS,
Real Estate, Loan and Investment Agents, 310½ Main Street.

The real estate business in all important and growing centers, is rightfully regarded
as one of the prime factors of advancement, especially by property owners and those
seeking judicious investment. One of the oldest established and most reliable houses
in Houston engaged in this department of endeavor, is that now known as Gaut &
Thomas. The origin of the business goes back to a period of about thirty years ago,
when it was founded by a gentleman of the name of Foster. After his death the
enterprise was continued by his widow, Mrs. Cora Bacon Foster, the present firm
assuming control in 1893. The business of the house consists of the handling of city
lots, suburban acreage, farm and fruit lands, and the general details of a first-class
real estate agency. A specialty is made of large tracts of land, suitable to be sub-
divided into smaller properties, and the facilities of the firm in this regard are of the
best, their connections being wide and their opportunities favorable. Messrs. Gaut &
Thomas are prepared to make sales and exchanges of the largest properties, they also
negotiate loans, make investments for non-residents, collect rents, pay taxes, etc.
There never was a time in the history of Houston and contiguous territory when investments in real estate presented greater opportunities. Capitalists will find that here
opportunities are offered which cannot but result in profit, if only availed of under
the auspices and advices of those who thoroughly appreciate the situation. Messrs.
Gaut & Thomas are prepared to offer the benefits of their experience to intending
investors, and to those who have lands which they wish to advantageously place on the
market. The firm individually consists of Messrs. R. B. Gaut and A. U. Thomas, both
of whom have every experience. Mr. Gaut has for some years been indentified with
real estate interests in this section, and Mr. Thomas was formerly cashier of the State
National Bank of Vernon, Texas, and he is au fait with all pertaining to finance and
investments. The principles of business regulating the conduct of this enterprise,
are based upon mercantile honor and fair dealing in all transactions. Those forming
relations with this house may rest assured that their interests will be carefully considered and ably guarded in all transactions.

A. HAMPE,
Dealer in Dry Goods, Etc., corner Prairie Avenue and Fannin Street.

There are few dry goods establishments in the State more justly popular than
that of Mr. A. Hampe, who in 1887 became sole proprietor of the business founded as
A. Hampe & Co. in 1884. Mr. Hampe has recently entered into possession of new
quarters, which greatly add to his conveniences and facilities. These comprise a
building at the above address, which is substantially constructed of brick and is three
stories high. It is situated at the corner of Fannin street and Prairie Avenue and admirably located. It has been erected specially for Mr. Hampe, under the superin-
tendence of Architect Heiner. The structure at the present time is three floors in
height, but two more will soon be added, making one of the finest five-story buildings
in the city. The lower floors are utilized by Mr. Hampe in his business and are
50x100 feet in dimensions. In being the owner and occupier of his own premises,
the proprietor is enabled to largely diminish expenses and to quote the lowest prices
to patrons. The establishment is splendidly appointed in every way and is sub-
divided into departments as follows: Silks, dress goods, trimmings, white goods,
domestic and staple goods, linens of all kinds, corsets and ladies' underwear, hosiery,
notions fancy and staple, cloaks and ready-made goods for ladies, misses and children, and a number of minor sub-divisions. Mr. Hampe is in the enjoyment of the
best facilities to enable him to offer the finest goods which come to this market. All
goods manufactured in this country are obtained direct from the mills, and Mr.
Hampe goes to New York twice a year in search of novelties and attractive wares.
He imports direct much of his foreign stock and notably linens and hosiery. While
in all departments the choicest goods are carried, a specialty is made of laces and
embroideries, for which this house has a well established reputation. Mr. Hampe is
thoroughly experienced in all relating to the business he conducts. It has always
been his aim to offer the best of inducements to his patrons and to please them in
every available manner. Altogether it is but just to quote this house as an exponent
of the enterprise, activity and progress which characterizes the interests of Houston.

J. MANGER.
Builder. 1006½ Congress Avenue.

There is no feeling more firmly implanted in the heart of the average American citizen than his desire to become the owner of the house he lives in. To aid him to achieve this desired result is an object very worthy of commendation. Such a course is being pursued by Mr. J. Manger, who commenced his present business about a year ago, and we are glad to say has met with much success. He is formerly from Galveston, but realizing the great advancement of this locality, he decided that it offered a congenial field for his labors. Mr. Manger builds houses for anyone who is the owner of a lot in or around the city. He accepts the payment for the same in installments to suit the wishes of his patrons. By this method persons of restricted means become their own landlords, and at the end of a given period have no rent to pay whatever, even to themselves, and they become the unfettered owners and occupiers of their own domiciles. Mr. Manger will build homes from the plans of his customers or he will furnish plans, as may be desired. Already has he put up a hundred and ten houses in this way, and by the time that this work makes its bow to to the public, this number will be augmented. Mr. Manger operates entirely with his own capital, and accords to his patrons the benefits thus derived. To his efforts may be largely ascribed the expansion of the city, and its increased facilities for new comers. He invites correspondence, and will easily be able to demonstrate the desirability of his system. Why pay rent year after year, when by the disbursement of but little more money, in monthly or quarterly installments, it becomes easily possible to be the owner of your own fireside? A connection with Mr. Manger will develop this fact, and he will be found to be in every way liberal, enterprising and honorable in all transactions.

WM. A. MOORE,
Merchant Tailor, 514 Main Street.

It may not be uninteresting to masculine readers of "THE INDUSTRIAL ADVANTAGES OF HOUSTON" to receive some information pertaining to matters of attire,—"for the apparel oft' proclaims the man"—which may result in future advantage. In this connection a few lines relative to the business of Mr. Wm. A. Moore will be of interest. This gentleman established his present business in the Capitol Hotel in 1886, and the store is well appointed and arranged in every way. Here may be inspected a full and complete line of imported fabrics, including the very latest novelties of each season along with the standard lines of goods which never change. Mr. Moore imports direct his cloths and materials, obtaining them from the most celebrated mills in France and England, the well known house of Dormeuil Freres of Paris and London, supplying him with large quantities. A considerable number of employees, expert in their various departments, are employed by Mr. Moore, who supervises every detail of the business with solicitude and experience that ensure perfection, and a product so tasteful as to defy criticism. Mr. Wm. A. Moore, the proprietor, is well known to the entire community, and all who are fastidious and correct in matters of dress generally designate him as "my tailor." Those who favor the house with their orders, may depend upon obtaining in the first place, choice and tasteful fabrics, elegant styles, perfect fit and superior finish in make up and *tout ensemble*, while the prices are invariably governed by a spirit of moderation, for which the concern has gatned a thoroughly established reputation.

WILSON, PUDOR & SLOSSON.
Real Estate. 915½ Congress Avenue.

Engaged in making patent to the public the advantages and attractions of this favored locality, is the enterprising and reliable firm of Messrs. Wilson, Pudor & Slosson, who founded their business January 2, 1894. These gentlemen transact a regular real estate business, buying, selling and exchanging all kinds of city and farming property. They are the sole handlers of Magnolia Heights, a tract of land located about a mile and a half from the city limits. It is situated on the banks of the Buffalo Bayou, on which it fronts for a distance of about a mile and a quarter. It is about 1300 acres in extent, and it is opposite the beautiful Magnolia Park. It has been platted into town lots, and also into sites for manufacturing, and fruit farms of ten, twenty and thirty acres. The work recently done by the United States Government in widening the river at this point gives here a depth of twenty-five feet of water, so that large steamers can easily discharge freight at the new leeves to be constructed at Magnolia Heights. The location is admirably suited for any description of manufacturing industry, and already a furniture factory, a box factory, an agricultural implement works, and others are making arrangements to locate here. The land is well elevated, well drained, rich and fertile, and it is within a mile of the largest cotton compress in the world. It is offered to the public in fruit farms and lots, at the very lowest prices, and on easy terms, and it may be said to be one of the most advantageous sites in this locality. Messrs. Slosson & Wilson, of this firm, also control the town of Webster, located on the I. & G. N. R. R., between Houston and Galveston. The town is on Clear Creek and Clear Lake. It comprises 4300 acres of land platted into fruit and truck farms. Although the town is less than one year old, already over a hundred persons from the North have purchased fruit farms on this property, and the place has, even at this early date, a school with fifty scholars, churches, eleven miles of graded streets, the finest artesian well in Texas, with a three inch pipe flowing 150,000 gallons of pure, soft water daily. From the lake may be obtained the best of fishing, and there is plenty of game in the neighborhood. Webster is already the largest town on the I. & G. N. R. R., between Houston and Galveston, and it has a proper railroad station, post office, and telegraph offices open day and night. This section of the state is quickly being filled up with an industrious, frugal and law-abiding population. South Texas today is the magnet which attracts all who wish to better their condition, and who prefer sunny skies all the year round, to the frigid temperature and blizzards of the North. Here the waters of the Gulf temper the atmosphere, and there are no great extremes either of severe heat or severe cold. The fruit farms of South Texas pay well, yielding crops from $400 to $600 per acre in value. The town of Webster is among the best of these lands, and the prices will be found to be low, and the terms offered meet the convenience of purchasers. The members of the firm of Wilson, Pudor & Slosson individually are Messrs. Robt. E. C. Wilson, O. M. Pudor and W. B. Slosson, all of whom are gentlemen of thorough experience in all relating to real estate matters. Mr. Wilson is one of the best known of Houston's citizens, identified for many years with its advancement and progress. Mr. Pudor is from Kansas City. Mr. Slosson was the director and manager of the Texas car exhibit, which travelled over the country showing the products and resources of the great Lone Star state. The firm enjoys a reputation and a standing of the highest character, ensuring the fullestconfidence of all having dealings with them. Briefly let us add in conclusion, in a dual sense, that the field is here, the soil is rich, and it requires but resolution to pluck the golden fruit.

S. ANDERSON,
Photographer, 403½ Main Street,

Perhaps the oldest established photographer now carrying on business in the State of Texas is Mr. S. Anderson of this city, who originally commenced at Galveston as many years ago as 1851. He has had a gallery in this city for the past ten years, and today stands high in the appreciation and patronage of the public. During all these years he has not been wool gathering, but has seen the results of many innovations and changes, and has adopted all of them which he deemed were of real value to the art. At the above address he has a well located gallery, and from here he turns out everything in the way of fine photography, including childrens' pictures, outside work, views, etc. All appliances and apparatus pertaining to the profession are here in use, and the utmost care and skill are exercised to produce the finest specimens of photographic work that could be desired. Mr. Anderson's prices will be found altogether reasonable, and he is prompt and courteous in his dealings with his patrons. In illustrating the varied interests of this city it is right and proper that we should accord a due measure of our space to an enterprise which has been for so many years identified with South Texas, and as a pioneer of the art photographic in this locality, Mr. Anderson is entitled to special recognition at our pen.

L. T. NOYES,
Dealer in Safes and Builder of County and Bank Vaults, and Jails, corner Congress Avenue and San Jacinto Street.

In the departments of business as indicated by the heading, it appears to be an established fact that Mr. L. T. Noyes is supplying the southern sections of the country with safes and vaults which can defy the ingenuity of burglars and the ravages of the flames under any circumstances that are likely to arise in towns and cities. He also has achieved wide celebrity as a successful jail builder, exponents of his skill in this line being found diffused over a wide range of territory. Mr. Noyes established his business here in 1876, and occupies as offices and salesrooms a two-story building at the above address which is 100x50 feet in dimensions. He is Texas agent for the renowned Diebold Safe and Lock Company, of Canton, Ohio, who are by far the largest and most complete manufacturers of safes and vaults and steel and iron work for jails and prisons in the world. Their reputation is national and therefore requires not a word of commendation here from our pen. Suffice to say briefly that their work in every way is unsurpassed anywhere, and this fact is well understood and appreciated all over the country. We have not the space to enumerate here the large number of bank and county vaults installed by Mr. Noyes in Texas, Louisiana and other States; also, jails constructed by him throughout the country. We will mention, however, that about fifty county vaults can be seen in successful operation in Texas and Louisiana towns alone, and about a hundred fine, strong and secure jails may be inspected in this and neighboring States, which are the results of his operations. He is perpared at short notice to submit plans and specifications on all classes of fire and burglar proof vaults, safes, county and city jails, prisons, etc., and to tender for the same and carry out all contracts satisfactorily to completion. The house carries on hand a large stock of safes, doors, locks, etc., to fill immediate orders. Correspondence from banks, corporations, municipal authorities, individuals; etc., is solicited and prompt replies may be depended upon, together with printed descriptive matter and all particulars. Testimonials from the highest sources are in the possession of the house which vouch for the superior character of the work done. Mr. L. T. Noyes is a well known resident of this city, who requires but little personal comment at our hands. He is identified with Houston's interests and is also stockholder in several banks and business establishments in various parts of the State. The enterprise he conduts has done much to advertise abroad the name of the city as a prominent source of supply and headquarters of the Lone Star State.

HOUSTON GENERAL ELECTRIC COMPANY,
Houston Heights.

The above named important enterprise was founded October, 1892, and incorporated as a stock company May 5th, 1893. It is unquestionably an enterprising addition to the industrial facilities, tending to demonstrate the advantages of this locality as a producing center. The company utilize a new and complete plant erected specially for their use. This comprises a two-story brick building of 32x75 feet, located at Houston Heights, which is equipped with all required appliances and apparatus of the best character. The company are electrical engineers, contractors and manufacturers, and they have every facility for furnishing all kinds of electrical supplies, dynamos, motors, fans, lights, power and house supplies, fixtures, lamps, etc. They also undertake contracts for light, heat and power plants, electric light wiring, electrical gas lighting, burglar and fire alarms, bells, calls, annunciators, watchmen's clocks, etc. The company also do in a thorough manner all kinds of repairing, electro-plating, etc., and they devote particular attention to the re-winding of armatures, converters, etc. As an exponent of their present facilities we will mention that they installed the complete lighting plant for the Velasco Oil Company, the Empire Oil Company, of Temple, Texas, and several others equally as large. They furnished and installed all the wiring, lamps, etc., for the American Brewing Association here, re-wiring and overhauling the Merchants and Planters Oil Mill plant and dynamo. They put in the entire arc lighting plant and wiring at Houston Heights; also, at the residences and hotel there. They wired the Mason building, the residences of A. P. Root, J. S. Price, Dr. Knox, Col. J. W. Jones and many others. They have put in electric fans and executed other electrical work, including the repairing of a station apparatus and machines for electric plants throughout the State. The president of the company is Mr. S. Van Etten, and Mr. L. M. Kilburn is secretary and treasurer. Both of these gentlemen are from Omaha, where they have had an extended and practical experience of the business. The company as operated under their auspices is in a position to promptly furnish anything in their line, complete all contracts to satisfaction, and that too, upon a most reasonable scale of charges. They invite enquiries and correspondence, and will promptly and cheerfully reply.

Corporations and individuals will find their interests promoted by a connection with this concern when contemplating the installation of electrical plants and appliances of any character. After April 1st their city office and show room will be located in the Mason building on Main street, where they will be pleased to answer all enquiries relative to their work. Their factory telephone number is 570 and city office No. 400.

COLBY'S "MOSS ROSE" RESTAURANT.
408 Main Street.

Colby's Restaurant was founded in 1885, and today no place in the city is better known or better appreciated. The premises comprise a building 25x100 feet in dimen-

sions. It is fitted up with improved appliances in the way of culinary apparatus, and employment is furnished to twenty-seven waiters and assistants. Every delicacy of the season isobtainable here in the best condition, and at truly popular prices. Meals are served attwenty five cents a head and lunches from ten cents upwards, and it is really astonishing to see the quantity and quality which is set before the customer. It has been asked many a time in Houston, how is it possible for the proprietor of this establishment to serve food at the prices he does? The secret is no secret. It is simply that Mr. Colby is content with a small margin of profit, preferring large sales to large profits on a limited business. The food here is well served, well cooked and of the best quality. Mr. F. C. Colby, the proprietor, is a Houston man, and a resident of this city from his boyhood. He has been quick to anticipate the public demand,-and it is gratifying to know that his efforts have met with success. Colby's restaurant is never closed, day or night, and when in Houston, and wanting a square meal, visitors can do no better than in bestowing their patronage upon this go-ahead and enterprising establishment.

HAYES & ROBERTS.
Auction, Commission, Sale and Feed Stable. 110 Milam Street.

An enterprise recently established, and one which bids fair materially to add to the trade conveniences of the city, is that which was inaugurated January 2, 1894, by the above mentioned firm. These gentlemen commenced business under especially favorable conditions, and with the very best of facilities available. At the above address they occupy premises which comprise a new brick two story and basement stable, which covers an area of 50x100 feet, and attached to this is a commodious mule yard. The stable is constructed with special reference to the uses to which it is applied, and embodies all modern improvements and conveniences. The firm devote their attention to the sale of horses and mules on commission, and they invite consignments of these animals in any number. Houston at the present time is a very favorable market for the disposal of horses and mules. All around Houston has lately grown up a thriving agricultulal population, who come here as the natural market for all their needs. To consignors shipping horses or mules to this market, the firm offer the very best of inducements, and they will meet the stock on its arrival, and give it their personal attention. Good accommodations for the animals are available on the premises, and the firm make the best interests of their customers their first consideration. Sales are held Wednesdays and Saturdays, and they are always attended by a large number of bona fide buyers from Houston and this section of the state generally. The members of the firm individnally are Messrs. Frank Hayes and L. H. Roberts.

Both are experienced men in all relating to equine matters. Mr. Hayes is a native of Houston, and thoroughly understands the requirement of this market. Mr. Roberts is recently from Kansas, and he officiates as the auctioneer at the bi-weekly sales. With all facilities at hand, stable room for over 100 horses, large accomodations for mules, complete experience and ample capital, this house is eminently in a position to transact business favorably for patrons. Correspondence is invited, and all enquires will receive prompt attention.

GEO. W. STIEFF,
Southern Representative of the Charles M. Stieff Piano of Baltimore, Md., Houston office, 612 Main Street.

The above named enterprise was established in this city about two years ago. The headquarters of the business and the factory are located at Baltimore, Maryland. The Houston branch has been instituted for the sale and distribution of the products throughout Southern territory, and an additional branch is being established at Fort Worth. Mr. Geo. W. Stieff, in whose hands is the management of the Southern business, is a member of the firm who are manufacturing these improved and desirable musical instruments, and he is personally an expert in the business. He has adopted this city as his home in view of its mild and equable climate, at the same time that he devotes here his full time and energies to his business. The establishment where the Stieff pianos are made adopted at the outset, as a cardinal principle, that it would employ none but the best, whether of raw material or skill to mould it into a handsome and harmonious whole. At Baltimore this fact is apparent, and is evidenced in the use of the best and latest improved appliances and apparatus, together with the highest skilled labor procurable in the United States. The results are pianos which embody all perfection of tone, action, touch, construction, workmanship and excellence. All of the best and most desrable features of piano construction are noticeable in these instruments, as well as others of signal merit and utility peculiar to them alone. Testimonials have been received from all parts of the country forcibly pronouncing on the excellence of the goods. The Stieff received the highest honors at the Philadelphia Centennial Exposition, the highest honors at the Paris Exposition, and two gold medals at the World's Industrial and Cotton Centennial Exhibition at New Orleans, in 1884-5. To cap the climax at the great Columbian Exposition at Chicago, they received a Medal of Merit and Diploma of Honor, which thus for the fourth time emphasized their pronounced superiority and value. About three hundred instruments have already been sold from this office. Mr. G. W. Stieff may be accorded much credit for this gratifying success, and as before hinted, he is a proficient both in the theory and practice of piano manufacture. He is thus able to demonstrate to the public the really superior character of these instruments. The firm sell both to the trade and the public, and four commercial travellers are kept continually on the road. Mr. Geo. W. Stieff may be addressed both at the Houston and Fort Worth establishment.

GUY & COOKE,
Photographers, 501½ Main Street.

The enterprising and reliable photographic house of Messrs. Guy & Cooke furnishes evidence of the fact that it is not only the old established concerns, which alone control the bulk of patronage here. This firm established their present business July, 1891, and today it is hardly too much to say that they are leaders in all matters pertaining to photographic art in this city. At the above address they have a well appointed and thoroughly equipped gallery and studio, where are in use the latest and best methods and apparatus connected with the profession. The leading feature of this establishment is the high quality and finish of the work, which may be pronounced fully equal to the best exponents of the art displayed in the studios of the most celebrated photographers of metropolitan centers. All descriptions of photography are here performed, and the firm have obtained much success and repute in taking childrens' pictures. They have every facility for photographing outdoor views, public and private buildings, interiors, etc., and promptness is a distinguishing feature of the business. The members of the firm individually are Henry Guy and C. F. Cooke. The first named is a long time resident of this State, and Mr. Cooke is from the North. Both gentlemen are thoroughly proficient both in the theory and practice of photography, and are fully up to the times in adopting all novelties which they deem of real value. Notwithstanding the excellence of their work, the prices here will be found all that is just and reasonable. The majority of the photographs from which our engravings have been made are the work of this house, and afford an example of the versatility of their resources.

GEO. E. DICKEY,
Architect, Kiam Building.

A gratifying feature of the marked improvement in good taste which has been characteristic of the United States during the past quarter of a century is evinced in the beauty of the architecture which graces our cities and towns throughout the country. For this result we have to thank, in a great measure, the educated culture and skill of our architects, who in every way are the peers of any in European countries. In this city the profession is ably represented by Mr. Geo. E. Dickey, who commenced business here about sixteen years ago. With one exception he is the oldest established architect in the city, and the fruits of his labors are conspicuous all over Houston. This gentleman has been actually engaged in his profession for a period of twenty-eight years, and he is practically conversant with every detail connected with it. We select here a few of the more notable exponents of the work of this gentleman. He designed the plans and supervised the erection of the Capitol Hotel, Light Guard Armory, H. & T. C. Railroad station, Scanlan building, Sweeney & Coombs' building, First Presbyterian Church, the Shearn M. E. Church and other churches, and many other fine churches and public buildings elsewhere in the State. Of private residences worthy of mention built by him are those of S. K. Dick, Hon. J. C. Hutcheson, T. W. House, banker, A. P. Root, president First National Bank, etc. Mr. Dickey is prepared at prompt notice to submit plans and estimates and superintend the erection of any description of building, public or private. All favors extended him are certain to be met with an appreciative discharge of all responsibilities and obligations, and the work carried out to entire satisfaction. To him is largely due the growing metropolitan aspect of the city, and we apprehend that there will be in the future a marked expansion of his career of usefulness.

JOSEPH DAWSON,
Manufacturing Confectioner and Fancy Baker, Etc., 615 Main Street, Masonic Temple.

The above is one of the best known and most popular of the business establishments of Houston. The origin of the enterprise was in 1879. Mr. Joseph Dawson became the sole proprietor in 1881. He, however, was a member of the original firm. At the present time the business is carried on at the above address, but Mr. Dawson will occupy this spring his own new building at the corner of Capitol and Fannin streets, which has been specially constructed and arranged for the business. By means of this new departure the facilities of the house will be greatly enhanced and extended, in keeping with the requirements of a constantly expanding business. A noticeable feature of the new establishment will be a beautiful garden, enclosed under glass, with a tiled floor and handsomely decorated. This will be utilized in serving ice cream, soda water, confectionery, etc. There is no question that this will become a favorite place of resort with the residents of the city. Its institution is an act of enterprise which is sure to be appreciated as it deserves. The general business of this house consists of the manufacture of all varieties of fine confectionery, candies, fancy cakes for weddings and other festivities, soda water, etc. A specialty is made of ice cream and ices for family use. These are made of all flavors and are shaped in forms if desired. Only strictly pure ingredients are used and nowhere in Houston is to be obtained more delicious and desirable products of this character. The proprietor has been identified with this business for fifteen years, and he has every experience. His aim has always been to please his patrons by manufacturing none but the purest, finest and best, and his reputation in this regard is thoroughly well established and appreciated.

LEWIS & ROSENBERG.
Dealers in Clothing and Gents' Furnishings. 218 and 220 Main Street.

Houston is noticeable for the complete facilities of the stores along her main thoroughfares. Particularly is the clothing trade well represented, and among prominent houses in this line is that of Messrs. Lewis & Rosenberg, which was established October 1886, and which at once became a popular resort with all who desire first class clothing, equal to custom made, at reasonable prices. The business premises comprise a large two story brick building of 50x100 feet dimensions, well appointed and completely stocked with a fine and large selection of clothing, gents' furnishing goods, hats, caps, trunks, bags, etc. It has always been the distinguishing policy of this house to give the fullest value for money, and to derive its emolument rather from large sales at a small profit than from a limited business, with high prices. Thus the house enjoys a very large and growing patronage, derived from the uttermost confines of the city, and from the neighboring localities in South Texas. Messrs. Lewis & Rosenberg obtain their supplies from some of the most eminent manufacturers in the country, under specially favorable conditions, which place them on the same basis as *bona fide* makers of the goods. The firm are agents here for the well known Hammerslough Bros., clothing manufacturers of New York city, for the world renowned Youman's hats, for the Manhattan shirts, for Hamburger Bros. & Co.'s, of Baltimore, stout and lean suits, and other goods of great merit and undoubted quality. The proprietors of the business are Messrs. A. G. Lewis and I. Rosenberg, gentlemen who have for many years been connected with the clothing trade, and they thoroughly understand what are the public demands, and they are prepared with all facilities at command to fill these requirements.

NEW HUTCHINS HOUSE.
Corner Franklin Avenue and Travis Street.

The above well known hotel may be classed as a landmark of the city, having been a familiar object with residents and visitors for the past third of a century. It was originally built in 1860. It was opened as a hotel about 1866. Since that time it has been improved and remodeled, and today it ranks as one the best hotels in the South. Like good wine, the Hutchins House grows better as it grows older, and especially is this so since it has been in the hands of Messrs. Kiber & Gueringer, the present proprietors. The New Hutchins House is most conveniently located, and enjoys a very large patronage from the traveling public. The building is of brick, five stories

high, and it covers an area of 150x150 feet. Every accommodation which administers to the comfort and convenience of guests is provided, and the house is thoroughly equipped and furnished throughout in first class style. The hotel contains about a hundred and twenty rooms for guests, besides elegant parlors, reading, billiard and bar rooms, sample rooms for commercial travelers, etc. The *cuisine* of the New Hutchins House is one of the prominent features of the hotel, and is always maintained at a high standard of excellence. The rates are $2, $2.50 and $3.00 per day, according to location and magnitude of apartments. The proprietors, Messrs. Kiber & Gueringer, have been in possession since November, 1893. Mr. Kiber came here from Chicago, where he had the De Soto Hotel of that city. Mr. Gueringer has been in the hotel business all his life. His boyhood marked the commencement of his career in this walk of life. He was chief clerk at the Capitol Hotel in this city, for some time, also at the Beach Hotel and Tremont House at Galveston, and later was proprietor of the Hotel Velasco at Velasco. But few men in the hotel business are better known than the proprietors of this house, and none better deserve the good will and patronage of the traveling public. The most elegant Turkish and Russian baths in the South are in this hotel.

J. C. HOOPER & CO.,
Real Estate Agents and Managers of the Almeda Town Site and Fruit Farm Company; Office, 307½ Main Street.

The firm of Messrs. J. C. Hooper & Co., of this city, commenced operations in the handling of real estate in this section in October, 1892, and they have today at their disposal inducements of the greatest value to offer to the investor and settler. The firm are part owners and general managers of the Almeda Town Site and Fruit Farm Company, with offices in this city and at Almeda. This company consists of R. T. Hicks, cashier First National Bank, Pittsfield, Ill.; Hon. Harry Higbee, vice-president same bank, and State senator from Pittsfield, Ill.; Dr. Willis P. King, head surgeon Missouri Pacific Railway, Kansas City, and the resident managers. Almeda consists of a town site of two hundred acres, located ten miles south of Houston on the I. & G. N. Ry. It is situated on high land, is well drained and is particularly well located. In the town of Almeda has already a good hotel, postoffice, a good school and over twenty resident families, and indeed all facilities for establishing a good and comfortable home. The town is platted, and building sites are offered the public at low prices and upon terms to suit. Special inducements are offered to actual settlers. Adjoining the town of Almeda are valuable fruit lands, owned by the company. This property has been divided up into fruit farms of five acres and upwards. To those who mean business and who are willing to work faithfully, a competence is assured, even to those who purchase the smallest of these farms. Almeda has the finest location, the best soil, the most excellent natural drainage, combined with the most extensive improvements now being constructed around any fruit center in this district. The company have here a fruit farm of 640 acres, 300 of which are already in cultivation and is planted with pears, peaches, plums, apricots, grapes, etc. This farm is not only a source of profitable revenue to the company, but it also serves as an apt illustration of what can here be accomplished in the way of fruit culture. Almeda is located between the cities of Galveston and Houston, which afford splendid markets for all kinds of produce and fruits, and the time is rapidly approaching when Texas fruits, and especially pears, will be as well known in Northern markets as are to-day those of California. An advantage which these fruit lands have over those of the Pacific Slope is that the season is much earlier here, strawberries being ripe in February and pears in the latter part of June. Messrs. J. C. Hooper & Co. invite correspondence and will be pleased to reply promptly and furnish all information. The individual members of the firm are Messrs. J. C. Hooper, who resides at Houston, and J. W. Hicks, who looks after the interests of the company at Almeda. Mr. Hooper is originally from Kansas City, and he has had fifteen years' experience of real estate business. Mr. Hicks was formerly of Pittsfield, Ill. Both gentlemen devote their full time and energy to the interests of the business. The public may depend that no misrepresentations will be made by them under any circumstances. Today in South Texas are springing up all around fruitful farms, which are giving to their owners a good livelihood, and that honest independence which is the pride and boast of American citizenship.

W. A. REICHARDT.
Wholesale and Retail Grocer, 501 and 503 Travis Street, and 902, 904 and 906 Prairie Avenue.

The merchants of this city engaged in the grocery trade have every reason to be proud of the part they have taken in the development of the commerce of Houston in the past quarter of a century. The above house has fully accomplished its share, and it may be quoted as one of the oldest established in the trade. The enterprise was founded in 1870 as W. & A. Reichardt, and in 1880 the proprietorship was assumed by Wm. Reichardt. In the year 1889 Mr. W. A. Reichardt became sole proprietor. The premises occupied consist of a two story building 50x100 feet in dimensions. The stock includes a specially full and desirable line of groceries, provisions, canned goods, liquors, cigars, etc., which are offered to the trade and consumers at lowest market prices. In whiskies Mr. Reichardt has his own brands, which he can specially reccommend. These are "Montreal White Rye," "Old Racket," and others. These goods are of fine quality, and are in every way desirable. This house forms an apt illustration of the possibilities of trade in Houston, and today stands prominent as one of the most reliable here. The sole proprietor is Mr. W. A. Reichardt, who is well fitted by a long course of practical knowledge to the conduct of the business. He was one of the original members of the firm founded in 1870. He is a gentleman of sterling business qualities, quick to recognize and supply all tne wants of the trade, and he has, during his many years of residence in this city, identified himself with the best interests of the community.

A. F. LINCOLN,
Dealer in all Grades of Furniture, Etc., 701 and 703 Travis Street.

Not only the rich, but those of moderate means, make up the trade of a locality, and a concern which in its particular line is prepared to satisfy the wants of all, is a valuable contribution to the conveniences of the city. In the furniture trade this position is filled by the house of A. F. Lincoln, who, in July 1891, succeeded to the business originally founded as Gifford & Lincoln in 1883. The store at the above address is among the finest and most commodious here. It comprises a four story brick building, 50 x 100 feet in area handsomely fitted up, with all conveniences, including an elevator. The stock handled by the house includes the finest specimens of fine furniture, worthy to grace the parlors or boudoirs of the wealthiest, down to the plain, but substantial furniture, suitable to the requirements of the laborer and toiler. Besides furniture, the house also deals in house furnishing goods, lamps, framed engravings, stoves, mattresses, baby carriages, refrigerators, lace curtains, bedding, sewing machines, and in fact everything required in the household. Mr.

Lincoln will make sales either for cash or on the installment plan. In the latter case the usual mode is to pay a fifth of the value of the goods on delivery, and the remainder in five periodical installments. Mr. Lincoln obtains all his goods from first hands under specially favorable conditions, enabling him to offer the very highest value for money expended. He is prepared to submit estimates, and take contracts to furnish houses, hotels, etc., from basement to attic, and that too, upon terms of a most satisfactory character. The business transacted by the house is large and growing, and includes not only Houston, but much of the contiguous territory. The proprietor is a gentleman thoroughly understanding his business, which he has elevated to a leading place among advantageous purchasing headquarters here.

W. F. HOPKINS,
Real Estate, Preston Avenue, Opposite Court House.

In pursuance of our object to thoroughly illustrate the advantages and attractions of this city and district generally, we have denoted much space relative to the subject in an earlier part of this volume. But to enable our readers to avail themselves of the opportunities offered, we now devote a brief space to the real estate business as carried on by Mr. W. F. Hopkins, who established his enterprise in 1884. This gentleman posseses a thorough knowledge of real estate values, and all pertaining to the business generally. From this office is transacted general real estate operations, including the handling of farm and fruit lands; a specialty, however, being made of city and suburban properties. Mr. Hopkins has invariably on his list desirable real estate of this character, which is offered at low prices and upon terms to suit. Attention at this time is particularly directed to the Fairview addition, which offers inducements to home seekers and investors of a highly attractive nature. The property is west of Main street, and is situated delightfully on high ground, east of the Southern Pacific Railroad and adjoining the Fair Ground extension. The lots are well drained and require no filling up. One advantage connected with this property, is that it is closer to the business center of the city than any other first-class addition, and there being no railroad tracks to cross constitutes an additional attraction. The approach to the property is through the best part of Houston, and the section is rapidly filling up with fine residences, and it is not far distant when this will become one of the most desirable suburbs of the city. The electric street car line is about to be extended to the addition along Tuam and Fairview avenues to the Southern Pacific Railroad, giving every lot the best of facilities and placing the property within a twelve minute ride of the Court House at an expense of five cents. Improvements of importance are now approaching completion, and altogether it may be said that here is an opportunity to make an investment which is sure to realize a handsome profit in the near future, or to acquire a site for a home in the midst of delightful surroundings. The lots are sold at $300 and upwards for each, the amount to be paid for in installments and upon terms to suit. The time to buy is now when prices are low, and as the population of the city grows, which it is doing by thousands every year, it is certain that values must rise and appreciate. Mr. Hopkins is a well-known resident of this city, who is known for his integrity and fair dealing. Intending home seekers and investors can do no better than consult this house and become partakers in the great advancement and prosperity which is characteristic of Texas' most attractive business center.

THIRD WARD LUMBER COMPANY.
Corner Hutchins Street and Walker Avenue.

The resources of the city of Houston are greatly enhanced owing to the facilities afforded her citizens for obtaining at a low price all materials connected with the building trade. The lumber industry is especially well represented here, and engaged in the business we find the Third Ward Lumber Company, which instituted their business in 1892 and which was incorporated as a stock company March, 1894, with a capital stock of $20,000. The plant of the company covers about half a block. On the property are lumber sheds and planing mill and all conveniences for carrying on the business to advantage. Steam power of the capacity of fifty-horse power is employed to operate the machinery and appliances, which are of the latest and best, employment being furnished to a force of twenty operatives and five teams. The company handle all kinds of lumber and shingles, and they have every facility for supplying the trade and public with mill work of all descriptions. They are prepared to promptly fill all orders in this line, and that too at lowest prices. They carry a full stock, amounting to about $10,000 in value, so that no delay ever accrues from insufficiency of supplies. They always have on hand rough and dressed lumber, sash, doors, blinds, mouldings, etc., and a large number of feet are annually utilized in the business. Altogether the facilities of this house are of the best and the interests of their customers will not suffer at the hands of this company. Mr. Leigh Hutchins is president and treasurer of the concern and Mr. M. J. McRae is secretary. The first named gentleman is also general manager. He is thoroughly experienced in all relating to the business to which is directed his closest supervision. Altogether this house is entitled to take rank not amount the least important of the growing trade conveniences of this city, and it is worthy of the full appreciation of the trade and public.

M. V. WRIGHT,
Florist: Office, Main Street: Gardens, Washington Avenue and Glenwood.

The love of flowers is inherent in every refined intelligence, and the tendency of the times is to encourage the development of that love to its greatest possible extent. The art of the florist is one of the most beautiful ot professions, requiring exquisite taste, skill and experience, and in none are these combined to a greater extent than in Mr. M. V. Wright of this city. This gentleman established himself in business about thirteen years ago and has since met with the greatest success in the growing of beautiful and rare plants, shrubs, flowers and bulbs. His gardens, which cover over two acres, are located on Washington avenue, near Glenwood, where he has a large area under glass and many green houses, where may be found a choice collection of bedding and house plants, cut flowers and bouquets, as well as rare plants for decoration and for propagation. He also has an office and greenhouse on Main street for taking orders and for distribution. His establishment is of a most attractive character. It comprises a beautiful array of garden lands, laid out in a handsome manner. A noticeable feature is the display of aquatic plants which grace the front part of the grounds. Mr. Wright has also eighteen acres of ground under cultivation at Alvin, Texas. Eight of these are devoted to the growing of jasmins, of which he makes a particular specialty. He also grows and supplies to customers berry plants, ornamental shrubs and trees, magnolias, etc., as well as floral designs for festivals, presentations, weddings, funerals, etc. His trade is by no means confined to this locality, shipments being made to all parts of the country. During May and June he dispatches daily, quantities of jasmins to as many as seven or eight States, and he has even sent shipments of these beautiful flowers as far as Paris, France. His facilities are complete in every department, affording him every advantage. Mr. Wright is quite devoted to his art, in which he enjoys a large experience that is always employed for the benefit of his patrons, and his liberal and enterprising business policy has made his establishment a pleasant and advantageous one with which to form relations. The enterprise has grown from the smallest of beginnings to important dimensions, due to the pursuance of the above enlightened methods.

CHAS. C. RUGERS,
Importer and Dealer in Wines, Liquors and Cordials, 1105 Congress Avenue.

The fermented juice of the grape has been used and enjoyed by man since the days of Noah. The use, and not the abuse of this gift of Providence, is beneficial, but to obtain good wine in perfection and purity is the main thing, however, and in indicating an establishment where no spurious goods are allowed a place, we are conferring a real boon on our readers. We here refer to the establishment of C. C. Rugers, who June, 1893, became the sole proprietor of a business originally founded by his father, C. W. Rugers, in 1872. The store occupied is 22x70 feet in dimensions, is of two floors and contains a large stock of wines, liquors and cordials, of the very best quality and and of absolute purity. A specialty is made of California wines, a stock of all grades and various vintages being handled. Mr. Rugers purchases these wines in large quantities and lays them down to age and mature, and his father before him having always followed the same course, he has on the premises some choice matured goods, from two years old and upwards. He also handles a selected assortment of fine domestic and imported goods. The house caters to a large family trade, and to supplying wines and liquors for medicinal uses. No spurious and imitation goods are handled, only the pure juice of the grape scientifically manufactured, as regards wines, and other articles obtained direct from responsible houses. A unique feature of this establishment is a bar at the rear which is built up and decorated with sea shells and marine curiosities. The effect is particularly striking and remarkable, and visitors to the city will be well repaid by a call, at the same time they will be able to refresh the inner man with good stuff, "which cheers but need not inebriate." Briefly, in closing this notice, let us add that this establishment, in its entirety, is eminently reliable, conducted in a strictly honorable manner, and offers the public products of the very best character obtainable.

WM. HUNTER.
Real Estate.   Office Hutchins House.

The above well known and reliable real estate agency is one of the most prominent enterprises of the kind here; and its proprietor, Mr. Wm. Hunter, devotes his energies to the handling of ranches, large bodies of unimproved lands, farms, suburban and city property. He has large properties for sale in various parts of Texas, and his list includes tracts of land from those of less than twenty-five acres in area up to a 55,000 acre ranch. Most of these are first class fruit and farming lands, and are offered under conditions of more than usual attractiveness. He also handles city and suburban property, which he is enabled to offer at low rates, and upon favorable terms. Before embarking in the real estate business here, Mr. Wm. Hunter was engaged in farming operations. He is therefore doubly qualifid for his present enterprise, thoroughly understanding the real value of the properties. All statements made by Mr. Hunter may be relied upon as correct in every instance, and no misrepresentations are made under any circumstances. Mr. Hunter is a native of Texas, belonging to one of the oldest and most honorable families in the state. His father settled in 1822 on the spot where the town of La Porte now stands. During his life Mr. Hunter has seen transpire many great events connected with the history of his native state. Two of his brothers took part in the Texas War of Independence. When his father settled here there were but two or three American families in the state, and no one dreamed even that it would become the great country it has now attained. Mr. Hunter is well known as the "Old Texian." He is sixty-three years of age, and though perhaps some may consider him old in years, he certainly today is young in heart, brain and enterprise, and may be quoted as one of the livliest and most energetic real estate men we have among us. While it is not necessary to allude to the standing of this concern, it will be in order for us to mention that Mr. Hunter invites references to the Hon. Senator Richard Coke, Waco, Texas, or Washington, D. C., Hon. Senator Roger Q. Mills, Corsicana, Texas, or Washington, D. C., Hon. F. R. Lubbock, Austin, Texas, Hon. Ex-Governor John Ireland, Seguin, Texas, T. W. House, banker, Houston, Texas, and others, Mr. Hunter invites correspondence from capitalists and others, and extends a hearty welcome to strangers and investigators of the advantages of this city, and Texas generally.

OLLE J. LOREHN.
Architect.   404 Kiam Building.

The above named gentleman commenced business in this city November 1st, 1893, with every prospect of success, and with all facilities available. He is originally from St. Louis, and he is an architect of ten years practical experience, and amply qualified in every way for the successful practice of his profession. He invites the patronage of capitalists, and all who contemplate the erection of any description of public building, business establishment, private residence, etc., and he will be pleased to promptly submit plans, and generally to superintend and supervise the erection of the same. Mr. Lorehn was the supervising architect of the American Brewing Co.'s buildings—an illustration of which appears in this volume—a group of structures which invites the admiration of all visitors to the city. He has also supervised the building of a number of residences in Houston. Mr. Lorehn is also entitled to be cited as an artist in architectural matters, and he makes his own completed water color sketches, which are very effective in illustrating proposed buildings.

He made a handsome design for the new Houston High School, which although not accepted received much commendation. Mr. Lorehn is popular in the city, and he is a member of the Knights of Pythias and other societies. Let us say in conclusion, that all employing the services of this gentlemen may do so with confidence, and that pleasant and advantageous relations are certain to result from a business connection.

G. W. GAINES,
Druggist, 602 Main Street.

The pharmacy of which Mr. G. W. Gaines is the enterprising proprietor may be classed as one of those new industries which are infusing fresh blood and increased vitality into the city of Houston. It was instituted in 1893, and already has it gained a place in the favor and patronage of the public. The store comprises a three-story brick building 25x86 feet in dimensions, and the stock is large and complete, embracing a full line of drugs and medicines, which are warranted strictly pure and of the best quality, together with a complete assortment of all standard proprietary medicines, toilet articles and requisites, perfumes, fancy goods, druggists' sundries, etc., all of which are offered to the public at lowest possible prices. Special attention is paid to the accurate compounding of physicians' prescriptions, and this department is considered as a highly important feature of the business. Mr. G. W. Gaines, the proprietor, is a skillful pharmacist and practical druggist, holding a certificate from the State Board of Pharmacy. He has been closely identified with the drug business in this city for the past fourteen years, and was formerly a member of the firm of Conklin, George & Gaines, a well known wholesale drug house here. In every way, therefore, he is eminently qualified for his present vocation, and his success in it is, consequently, hardly a matter for surprise. He is courteous, patient and attentive in all transactions with patrons, and we are safe in predicting for his establishment a wide career of usefulness in the future.

DR. B. T. PERKINS, D. D. S.,
Dentist, 408 and 409 Kiam Building.

The public generally do not consider the fact that the health and soundness of the teeth often reflect the health of the body. If we do not have sound teeth we can not masticate our food properly, and insufficiently masticated food induces indigestion and dyspepsia and the hundred ills they bring in their train. The experienced and skillful dentist of to-day can arrest and repair the deficiencies of the teeth, or if too far gone can replace them with others which, although of artificial construction, will well serve their purpose. A recent acquisition to the professional gentlemen practicing dentistry here is evidenced in the business of Dr. B. T. Perkins, whose office and surgery are located in 408 and 409 Kiam building. This gentleman established himself at Houston December 1st, 1893. He devotes his energies to the regular practice of a dental surgeon and performs all descriptions of dentistry, including bridge and crown work, etc. He is possessed of every skill and experience that a thorough technical education and successful practice could impart. He is a graduate of the Indiana Dental College, of Indianapolis, and he has followed his profession successfully for a number of years at Anderson, Ind. He will be found eminently reasonable in his charges, and every case, however trivial, will receive his most careful attention. Satisfaction is guaranteed in every instance to all who may accept the tender of his services.

J. M. GEISELMAN,
Meat Market, 415 Travis Street.

One of the best known business men of our city is Mr. J. M. Geiselman, who has now been established in his present commodious and convenient premises since the past year. This is a store of 30x60 feet which is fitted up with all conveniences suitable to the business. Mr. J. M. Geiselman handles everything in the way of fine fresh meats and vegetables, including the choicest cuts of prime beef, mutton, lamb, veal and pork, poultry and game of all kinds, and vegetables in season. A specialty is made of Kansas meats which are shipped to him direct, and which are fully equal to the best which comes to Houston. In fact in all lines nothing inferior is to be found at the establishment, at the same time that the prices will be found to be as low as the lowest. The All Day Market, as this store is designated, is open all day so that housekeepers can obtain their supplies at any hour, and are not restricted to ordinary market time. Mr. Geiselman has been identified with this branch of business for fifteen years, and he is an excellent judge of what is choice in its lines. He is well known for honest methods and fair dealings, and in every way enjoys the confidence of his patrons. He is at the present time a member of the city council, and chairman of the market committee. His establishment is not by any means the least of the business conveniences of our city.

GIBBONS MANUFACTURING COMPANY.
Merchant Tailors and Manufacturers of Shirts, Underwear, Etc. 518 Main Street.

Among representatives of the best trade of the city, and one of the leading concerns here which have been foremost in promoting the standard of elegance in dress, is that of the above mentioned organization, which January 11, 1894, succeeded to the business originally founded by Mr. Geo. A. Gibbons, in 1867. This gentleman is today the active manager of the enterprise as at present constituted. The president of the company is Mr. R. B. Morris, Mr. C. J. Wright is vice president, Mr. B. R. Latham is secretarg, and Mr. J. W. Crate is assistant secretary. These gentlemen are among the most influential and best known of the residents of this city. Mr. Gibbons is both practical and proficient in every detail of the business, and he has acquired a high reputation as a master in the art of fine tailoring. He has had thirty years experience of the industry. The establishment is well known for the marked good taste displayed in the selection of the stock, which is without a supertor in the city as to quality, variety, extent and style of goods, giving patrons assortments from which to choose, not excelled even in metropolitan centers. The materials are of the house's own importation, and are made up into garments to order at prices most moderate, and in style after the latest New York and London fashion plates. Besides custom made clothing, the company also make fine dress and other shirts, underwear, etc., which fill all requirements, and attract the notice and full appreciation of the

MR. GEO. A. GIBBONS.

most fastidious. The store is centrally located, in the Capitol Hotel building, the manufacturing departments being on Texas Avenue, where a suitable number of skilled custom workers are employed. The trade of the house is not confined to this city, but extends through a wide range of territory. Correspondence is invited, and samples will be promptly sent upon application. As an interesting fact, we mention here, that Mr. Gibbons had on exhibition at the Merchant Tailors' building at the World's Fair, a very fine exhibit of gentlemen's custom made clothing, which received the highest commendation for style and workmanship. It was also shown in New York city, where it received merited praise from competent critics.

BOTTLER BROTHERS,
Dealers in Books, Periodicals, Stationery, Etc., 74 Main Street.

One of the most enterprising and progressive houses of Houston is that conducted by the firm of Bottler Brothers. This establishment was instituted here in the year 1886, and it has since attained to a leading position in the trade. The firm occupy premises at the above address, comprising a store 25x60 feet in dimensions. This, they utilize as headquarters, and they also have branch establishments in the Hutchins House, and on Preston avenue. The firm deal in a general line of books and stationery, carrying full stocks in all departments, which are selected with great care, and are offered to the public at lowest prices. They make a specialty, however, of paper covered novels, of which they carry in stock as many as 25000, a number probably not excelled in any establishment south of Chicago. Any book of this kind published anywhere in the country can be procured here as soon as issued. The firm are essentially up to date in the conduct of their affairs as will be readily seen upon investigation. Messrs. Bottler Brothers also handle all the leading periodical and daily papers of all the principal cities. The firm have the news privilege on the Houston, East &

West Texas railway, and they run agents along the entire line. The house is known by its unique trade mark of a horse shoe with the number 74 in the center, and many of their goods have this insignia stamped upon them. In every way this firm is in a position to entirely satisfy their patrons, and the eminence they enjoy is due to the constant and close attention to the details of the business displayed by the proprietors, Messrs. Will Bottler and Eugene Bottler, both of whom have had a lengthened experience of the line of trade with which they are identified.

NATIONAL OIL WORKS AND MILL SUPPLY COMPANY OF TEXAS,

Headquarters, New York City; Houston Branch, 111 Fannin Street.

What we claim for Houston is a favorable center of supply, is again emphasized in the location here of the Houston branch of the National Oil Works and Mill Supply Company, whose headquarters are located at New York City. This company has also branches at New Orleans and St. Louis. They are extensive manufacturers of lubricating oils and greases, and the works at New York are on a very large scale, the products being in demand throughout the country. The offices and warerooms here are at the above address, and comprise a two-story building 30x75 feet in dimensions. All facilities required are here available, and sales are made. from this point throughout Texas and Arkansas, three commercial representatives being kept constantly on the road. The company are manufacturers of lubricating oils and greases of the highest quality and efficiency. Among the more noticeable of the products we will mention National Ex cylinder oil, Lone Star Engine oil, Compress cylinder oil, Sublime machinery oil, Sublime engine oil, Extra dynamo oil, Zero Ammonia pump oil, etc. They also make car grease, castor oil, axle grease, and sell waste, mill supplies of all kinds. They carry at the Houston establishment full stocks at all times, and ship also in carload lots, either direct from the factory in New York or from the New Orleans or Houston depots, as may be advisable. The quality of the goods is well recognized by the trade, and all who have used them, and a sample order will conclusively demonstrate this fact. The prices will be found to be all that is reasonable for goods of the high character, such as those which are the products of this concern. In every respect the facilities are complete, and insure the prompt filling of all orders. Mr. Louis Schwartz, who is in charge of the Houston branch, has been with the company seven years, and he is thoroughly experienced and well qualified for the duties of his position. The business under his charge is of great utility to this locality, and therefore is specially entitled to mention in any work claiming to illustrate the trade conveniences of the city.

"LATHROP."

Stationer and Printer, 1109 Congress Avenue.

We now devote a brief space to the enterprise conducted under the terse title of "Lathrop's." The origin of the business dates to the year 1881, when it was instituted as the Houston Book and Stationery Company. Mr. G. T. Lathrop, the present proprietor, was at the head of the original concern, which was established as a branch of his New Orleans house, where he began in 1866. He assumed the sole control of the Houston enterprise in 1893. The premises occupied comprise a three-story brick building 25x60 feet, all of which is utilized for the stationery departments. At the rear is a printing office of 25x50 feet. The stock carried includes every thing in the way of commercial and society stationery, books, etc., including blank books, office supplies, gold pens, standard and school books, news department with all the latest periodicals, a full line of fancy goods, etc. A specialty is fine stationery for fashionable correspondence, and in this line the house has facilities fully equal to any of its contemporaries here. Another special feature of the business is the book exchange. Mr. Lathrop buys, sells and exchanges new and old books, and always has a large stock on hand at the disposal of his patrons. He also manufactures a number of specialties for school use. In the printing department he is well equipped with all appliances, and stands ready to execute anything in the way of job printing, society printing, etc., in the highest style of the typographical art. Another department of importance is in rubber stamps, which he manufactures in all varieties. Anything in this line can be obtained to perfection, and vulcanizing every day he is enabled to fill all orders promptly and to the satisfaction of the public. In all departments this house will be found fully abreast of the times, selling and manufacturing the best class of goods at really fair and reasonable prices. Mr. G. T. Lathrop, the proprietor, is a gentleman of wide experience of the business with which he has been actively identified for the past thirty years, and the enterprise he conducts is one of the most useful and progressive we have among us.

CARLTON & CO.,
Wholesale Grain and Commission Merchants, 102, 104 and 106 Travis Street.

The above named enterprise was founded November 1, 1893, with ample capital and complete experience on the part of its management. The premises occupied comprise a brick building 75 feet square, where all conveniences are available. The firm are wholesale grain and commission merchants, handling principally grain, hay, corn, oats, cotton seed meal, flour, meal, salt, etc. A specialty is made of unbroken carload lots, shipments being direct from first hands to the purchaser in some instances. The connections of the house with consignors and producers are such as to enable it to offer the greatest inducements, and the lowest current rates, a fact now understood and appreciated. A stock of all the above mentioned staples may always be found on hand to fill immediate orders, often as much as five carloads of hay being in store, and other staples in like proportions. The firm handle on commission country produce generally, and they invite consignments of the same in any quantity, and quick sales and speedy returns may generally be depended upon. Altogether the facilities of the house are such that dealers will find it highly advantageous to enter into business relations with it. The members of the firm individually are Messrs. J. E. Carlton, of Tyler, Texas.; Chas. Hawkins, of Jacksonville, Texas, and Sid Carlton, of Houston. These gentlemen are all thoroughly practical men in their experience of the business and its details. They are all well-known and popular residents of the communities in which they live. Mr. Hawkins is prominent in society organizations, being a member of the Masonic Fraternity, the Knights of Pythias, Odd Fellows, Legion of Honor, Knights of Honor, and other societies. The standing of the firm is beyond our criticism, and the utmost confidence may be reposed in them.

OCHILTREE & COOMBS,
Auctioneers, Opera House Block.

An exemplification of the enterprise of Houston's business concerns is furnished by the firm of Ochiltree & Coombs, who began operations here September 1st, 1893. The business of this house comprises that of a general auctioneer and commission agent. The firm are prepared to sell advantageously at public sale everything in the way of household furniture and effects, stocks of merchandise, etc., and they are the recognized auctioneers for the railroads and public companies centered at Houston, who have unclaimed freight, etc., to dispose of. Their sales are well attended by the general public who realize the advantages placed here at their disposal. The firm's services are not confined to this city alone, but they are in request all over the state. They may be quoted as entirely reliable and deserving of all confidence, their business policy being based upon honor and fair dealing. Major W. B. Ochiltree was raised in Houston, having come to this city when a child, in 1843. He began business as an auctioneer in 1866 a :d for twenty years was auctioneer for the well known firm of Sweeney, Coombs & Fredericks. Mr. R. L. Coombs, his partner, is a son of Mr. E. L. Coombs who is a member of that firm. Major Ochiltree is a brother of the well known Tom Ochiltree, whose sayings and doings are quoted all over the country. The father of these gentlemen was secretary of the Republic of Texas, and also its attorney-general, under Anson Jones, who was president of the Republic. Thus it will be seen that there probably is no man in Houston today who has been more prominently identified with the growth and development of this city than has the senior member of this firm. But few are better known and enjoy more the good-will of the community. Those who may have goods of any kind to dispose of can certainly do no better than place them in the hands of these gentlemen, who will do all in their power to assure prompt sale and profitable returns.

HOUSTON MARBLE WORKS, T. E. BYRNES,
Monuments, Tombs, Headstones, Etc., Corner Fannin and Franklin Streets.

The aboved named enterprise is one of the oldest established and best known in this locality, it having been founded over a third of century - in the year 1858, and it has always enjoyed the confidence and consideration of the public to an eminent degree. The plant at the above address comprises an area of 150x75 feet, and consists of office building, show rooms and sheds. The Houston Marble Works manufacture and sell marble and granite monuments, tombs, headstones and statuary, also tiles, table and counter tops, iron railings, etc. At the works all required tools and appliances are available, and a force of about a dozen workmen are given employment. Only highly skilled operatives are employed, and only such a class of work is turned out as shall meet with the full appreciation and favor of patrons. The Houston Marble Works have erected a large number of monuments, etc. in this and other localities in the State. Of such worthy of mention are monuments to the memory of B. A. Shepard, Geo. F. Baker, the firemens' monument at Glenwood, Houston; also Col.

Jones, Judge Masterson and wife's monument and many others. Mr. Byrnes imports direct the most beautiful statuary from Italy, the home of this art. He has supplied statuary distinguished for artistic conception and design and shipped it to Woodville, Texas; LaGrange, Texas; Jacksonville, Texas, and other places throughout this State and State of Louisiana. Mr. Byrnes is one of the oldest business men of this city, and has been a resident here since 1856. His facilities in all respects are of the best, and all representations made may implicitly be relied upon. Plans and estimates are cheerfully furnished, and the public can depend upon here obtaining the promptest and most courteous attention in all instances.

A. P. NIELSEN,
Pharmacist, successor to John Hagemann, 503 Main Street.

The above well known and popular drug establishment was originally founded as Heyer & Schuchard in 1885. In 1886 Mr. G. W. Heyer became the sole proprietor. In 1887 the style of the firm was Hagemann & Martin, and in 1889 Mr. John Hagemann assumed control. This continued until 1893, when Mr. A. P. Nielsen became the owner of the business. The store located at the above address is handsome and convenient and covers an area of 27x60 feet. Here at the disposal of the public may be found a fine assortment of pure drugs and chemicals, medicines, toilet articles, perfumes, soaps, fancy goods and everything usually to be obtained at first-class establishments of this character. The utmost care and discernment is displayed in the selection of this stock to ensure purity and high quality, and the prices are dictated by a spirit of moderation for which the house enjoys a well deserved repute. A specialty is made of the prescription department, the greatest care being devoted by the proprietor to its details, so as to assure beyond peradventure correctness and accuracy and that no adulterated or inferior quality ingredient shall be used. Mr. Nielsen is a gentleman of great experience in all that pertains to the profession of the pharmacist. He is both a graduate and experienced druggist and took his degree at the State University of Copenhagen, in Denmark; also, at the Venezuela University, in Venezuela, South America. He is a registered druggist of the Board of Pharmacy, State of Texas. Concluding, let us add that under his management this house has more than ever become noticeable for enterprise, offering to the public the best of goods at lowest prices in all lines.

MISS L. I. MOODY.
Toys, Fancy Goods, Bric-a-brac, Etc.   Masonic Temple.

We question whether if among the retail establishments of this city any is better known than the one now under comment, which has been before the public of Houston for the past twenty years. It was originally established by Mrs. S. E. Laburzan, and Miss Moody became the proprietress January 15, of this current year. This lady, however, had been with the former incumbent for over twelve years, and to her is familiar every detail connected with the business. The store occupied is in the Masonic Temple—an illustration of which appears in this volume—and it is of the dimensions of 28x100 feet. It is stocked with a large assortment of toys, fine fancy goods, birthday and wedding gifts, holiday gifts, stationery, hair goods, etc. All of these are of admirable selection, equal to the best to be obtained anywhere in the city. Miss Moody, through such a long and intimate familiarity with the business, is a skillful and accomplished buyer, and she thoroughly understands the drift of popular taste, and succeeds in satisfying it entirely. The place has long been a favorite resort with the residents of the city, who are perfectly well aware that here they will obtain the best of goods, the most reasonable prices and courteous attention. We must not fail to mention that Miss Moody is sole agent here for the world renowned Butterick patterns, which are standard throughout the country. We are pleased to accord a brief space to this house in this review of the business interests of the city.

SAM ALLTMONT,
Dealer in Dry Goods, Shoes, Clothing, Etc., 311 Travis Street.

The origin of this old established business goes back to the year 1872, when it was founded by the late Nathan Alltmont, the father of the present proprietor. For over twenty years the senior Mr. Alltmont carried on the business alone, until August 1, 1893, his son, Mr. Sam Alltmont, became a member of the new firm, which was designated N. Alltmont & Son. From 1884 until 1889, Mr. Jonas Alltmont was a member of the firm. Mr. N. Alltmont died December 8, 1893, and the junior member has since continued the business under his own name. His father was a gentleman much respected both in business and social circles in this city, and although of the ripe age of seventy-one at the time of his decease, his death was much regretted by all who enjoyed the pleasure of his friendship and acquaintance. In connection with the business a two-story brick building 25x100 feet in area is occupied. The store is divided into a number of general departments, viz: dry goods, millinery, shoes and clothing. At the head of the millinery department is Miss May Taylor, a lady of fine taste and good judgment; Mr. M. B. Leach is manager of the shoe department, Mr. Theo. Huck of the dress goods department, while as an assistant to Mr. Sam Alltmont in the general conduct of the business, Mr. Noah Alltmont acts as general manager. Each department contains a full stock of goods of the best selection, procured direct from some of the most eminent manufacturers and wholesale dealers in the country. A specialty is made in trimmed hats, and the house has in its employ a skilled trimmer, who goes each season to the various large centers to study the newest fashions of the day, both in imported and domestic novelties, so that oftentimes they may be found at this establishment long before they are on view at many contemporary houses. In other departments this concern is equally abreast of the times, and attractive dry goods, shoes, hats, clothing, notions, etc., are here displayed at the disposal of the public at lowest prices. Mr. Sam Alltmont is thoroughly experienced in all relating to his business, of which he has a life long knowledge. For nine years he was its manager before he succeeded to the proprietorship. He is an accomplished buyer, fully understanding the wants of the public in this direction. The business policy of this house is conducted upon that fair dealing and honorable basis which would be expected of a house that has been in successful operation for nearly a quarter of a century.

NATHAN ALLTMONT
ESTABLISHED 1872

J. R. JETER & CO.,
Land Brokers, 207½ Main Street.

The handling of real estate and the placing it before the public so that it may be purchased to advantage engages the attention of a number of reliable and enterprising firms here, and of these that of Messrs. J. R. Jeter & Co. is one of the most prominent. This house transacts a regular real estate business, handling both city property and farm and fruit lands. They now give their particular attention to the handling of "Pear Land," which is fifteen miles south of Houston on the Santa Fe Railroad. It is in the center of a fruit raising and market gardening country, which for fertility and desirability is probably not surpassed elsewhere. The property is of the extent of 6,000 acres, and this has been sub-divided into ten and forty acre tracts, which are sold upon easy terms to suit. Here may be obtained a farm and homestead for but a small outlay of cash, the balance to be paid in periodical installments from the profits which are sure to be the result of a moderate display of industry and judgment. On these lands can be successfully cultivated strawberries, pears, plums, peaches, sweet potatoes, Irish potatoes, onions, English peas, snap beans, spring turnips, radishes, etc. It is estimated that a pear orchard comes into profitable bearing in about five years, and during the time before it arrives to maturity all kinds of vegetables may profitably be cultivated. A pear orchard in full growth gives a profit of from $450 to $650 per acre. The locality is provided with pure artesian water from wells sunk all over the country. The climate is perfect, being equally free from severe cold or burning heat, the proximity of the Gulf preserving it from the latter. The property is well located as regards easy access to a market, the two cities of Houston and Galveston having, between them, a population of about 100,000 persons. There are no blizzards to retard the work of the agriculturalist, who is enabled to carry on the business of his farm every day in the year. The land is now sold at a cheap price, which is sure to rapidly rise and appreciate, as the section is being rapidly settled and cultivated. Messrs. J. R. Jeter & Co. will be glad to correspond with any who may contemplate exchanging the frigid atmosphere of the North for the balmy climate and fertile soil of this favored section. The firm are also interested in a property known as Woodland Heights, which is about to be placed on the market. This is 200 acres in extent, and it will be cut up into suitable lots for residences. It will undoubtedly constitute a valuable addition to Houston's suburbs. It is situated only one and three-quarters of a mile distant from tha court house, and it is adjacent to the line of the electric street railroad. A beautiful park will be laid out, and altogether it will be made one of the most attractive and desirable properties in the city. Mr. J. R. Jeter is a gentleman of large experience in all relating to real estate matters. He is thoroughly to be relied upon and is truthful and honorable in all his dealings. He is an advocate of all measures tending to the advancement of the city and section, which should conduce to making known to the outside world the real advantages and attractions they have to offer.

HOUSTON TRANSFER LINE.
Office and Stable Corner Congress Avenue and Louisiana Street.

One of the most go-ahead, wide-awake enterprises in the city of Houston is that known by the above mentioned designation. The origin of this business dates back to the year 1876. Since that period the proprietors from time to time bought out several stables and increased the facilities of their own. The premises now occupied consist of a large two story building of the dimensions of 125x250. It is in every way well appointed and fitted up for the purpose to which it is applied. The firm devote

their energies to a regular baggage and transfer business, transporting passengers and baggage to and from all depots, to hotels, or elsewhere in the city. They control practically, all the hotel trade and contracts for shows appearing in the city. Experienced men and special trucks are provided for moving furniture, household goods, pianos, safes, boilers, merchandise, heavy machinery etc., and entire satisfaction guaranteed in every instance, along with reasonable charges. The firm hold the U. S. government contract for the transfer of all mails here. They have a full equipment of horses, carriages, trucks, wagons, etc., from thirty to forty vehicles all told, and about sixty-five to seventy horses. The firm employ about thirty-five hands in the various departments. They pride themselves on their promptness, and baggage or passengers have never been too late for a train through any remissness on their part. A special department is the buying and selling of horses and mules, and the best of inducements in this line are offered the public. They board horses for firms and private individuals, giving them the best of care and skilled attention. Connected with the establishment is a blacksmith, paint and wood shop, where vehicles of all descriptions are made and repaired. Among the conveniences also available is a feed grinding machine, operated by steam. In fact nothing is left wanting to make the undertaking the most complete and perfect of its kind in the Gulf States. The proprietors individually are J. C. Baldwin and H. B. Rice, both of whom are experienced in all relating to the business. Mr. Baldwin is a native of Baldwinsville, N. Y., a thriving town twelve miles north of Syracuse, N. Y. This place was named after Dr. Jonas C. Baldwin, Mr. Baldwin's grandfather. Its founder commenced the settlement of the place in 1807. Baldwinsville is well known as being the center of distribution of an important leaf tobacco growing district. Concluding, we particularly commend the house of J. C. Baldwin & Co. as one where our readers will find all their wants in the above lines promptly and satisfactorily fulfilled.

PHILIP W. HUDSON & CO.,
Real Estate, 914 Texas Avenue.

Prominent among reliable firms of real estate agents in Houston, who are offering on the market full values in real estate, is the firm of Philip W. Hudson & Co., whose business was inaugurated here in 1889. The firm transact a general real estate and brokerage business, buying, selling and exchanging all descriptions of town, suburban and farm property. They have generally on their list large lines of business and house property, homes, lots and blocks in the city and large and small tracts of land to suit all classes of buyers, and particularly adapted for ranches, farms, fruit and truck gardens, lands for rice culture, etc. The firm are the exclusive handlers of what is known as Riverside Park, located on the Washington road, near the Houston

Farm residence of Col. Philip W. Hudson, Pleasant Hill Farm,
on St. Mary's Bay, Harris County.

Heights boulevard. The property is platted into several hundred lots, and it is partly built up with attractive residences and neat homes. It is sold on easy terms to suit purchasers. Another desirable property on their list is Magnolia addition, near Riverside park. This is sold on the same plan as the above. The firm are also offering on the market twenty acre fruit farms, located at the mouth of Buffalo bayou. The property is on the celebrated San Jacinto field of battle. Another desirable property they have for sale is the Oakland addition, on Harrisburg avenue, near the south confines of the city, adjoining beautiful Magnolia park. Messrs. Philip W. Hudson & Co. have many other properties of value and desirability, and their list of fruit and farm lands in the surrounding country is one of the largest in the city. The prices desired for these are remarkably low, and the terms offered place them within the reach of all. investors and home-seekers are invited to call on or correspond with this firm, and they will be met with every courtesy, and inducements placed before them which will clearly demonstrate the advantages derived from an investment at the present time. In another part of this volume has been clearly shown what are the possibilities and accomplishments of this section of Texas, which, with the growing city of Houston, is bound to be the El Dorado of the South, not in the yield of yellow metal, but in its yield of golden fruit, wholesome vegetables, and produce, to feed its inhabitants and to ship abroad for the consumption of the people of the North and West. The individual members of the firm are respectively, Col. Philip W. Hudson and Mr. Richard M. Hudson, father and son. Both are well known residents of this city, thoroughly posted in all pertaining to real estate matters. Col. Hudson is a member of the G. A. R., Knights of Pythias, and various Masonic bodies, Woodmen of the World and other societies. The standing of this house is of the highest, references being permitted to any of the city or county officials, or to any responsible business firm. All enquiries will be met with prompt attention, and all information concerning the garden spot of the Lone Star State cheerfully furnished.

W. H. OPET,
Dealer in Dry Goods, Clothing and Shoes, 1115 and 1117 Congress Avenue.

The retail trade conveniences of this city may be said to be remarkably complete, and the proprietors display more enterprise and push than is usual of places of similar population elsewhere. This is particularly apparent in the more recently established houses, and an example of this fact is seen in the business of Mr. W. H. Opet, who first commenced operations March, 1892. Since that period his store has become popular for first-class goods, offered to the public at low prices. The premises comprise a double store in the three-story brick building of the dimensions of 50x80 feet, where may be examined full lines of dry goods, clothing, shoes and gents' furnishing goods, also other articles suitable to the wants both of the male and female sex. Owing to the expansion of the business the house has recently added to the above the store adjoining it, thus giving it increased facilities to display the large and fine stock carried. The business policy of the house is to sell close, giving the fullest value for money procurable. What we here claim for this concern can be easily verified at a personal visit, and much more pretentious establishments have not the same really valuable inducements to offer. Mr. W. H. Opet, the proprietor, is an experienced buyer, with a thorough appreciation of the requirements of the public, and he obtains his supplies direct from first hands in all cases. He is a well known and popular resident, prominent in society organizations. He is a member of the Knights of Honor and several other of these societies. We are justified in saying that this house is one of the most useful and progressive we have among us with all facilities and advantages at command.

I. H. WEINER,
Expert Law Reporter, 317½ Main Street.

Among enterprises of Houston which may be classed under the heading of professional is that of Mr. I. H. Weiner, who started his business March, 1893. Already this gentleman has become well known and his services appreciated with the class who desire to utilize his expert knowledge and experience. Mr. Weiner devotes his energies to general law reporting, stenography for all purposes, typewriting, etc. His specialty is expert work, the reporting of law cases and general mercantile work. He solicits job work of every description, and all favors extended are promptly fulfilled at the shortest notice. Mr. Weiner has every facility, and he has in his employ two competent assistants to aid him in the work. Those desiring performed anything in this line can with confidence entrust their orders to this gentleman, assured that it will be completed to their satisfaction, and upon a reasonable scale of charges. Mr. I. H. Weiner is a well known citizen of this community. He has been a resident of Houston for ten years, coming from New York city. For five years of this time he was the manager of the Houston branch of the Washburn & Moen Manufacturing Co. of Worcester, Mass. He has the completest experience of every detail relating to his present undertaking and commands the fullest confidence and appreciation of all professional and business men of the city.

A. G. HOWELL,
Provision Broker, Cotton Exchange.

The important position that this city is now assuming in the commercial economy of the State renders a reference to the facilities here enjoyed for obtaining all kinds of food products a fitting theme of comment in this volume. Attention is therefore now directed to the enterprise of Mr. A. G. Howell, who established himself here as a provision broker and manufacturers' agent in the year 1887. His efforts have been largely conducive to bringing into immediate contact the *bona fide* producer and manufacturer and the wholesale merchant. Mr. Howell represents in this market some of the most eminent first hands and original sources of supply in the United States, such as F. Carle & Son, cereals, Kansas City; Dwight & Co., soda, New York; New York Condensed Milk Co.; American Glucose Co., Buffalo; Cudahy Packing Co., provisions, South Omaha; F. Cannon & Co., coffee importers, New Orleans; Aughinbaugh & Co., canned goods, Baltimore; A. Lusk & Co., fruits, California, and other leading firms in various lines. Mr. Howell is enabled to quote to the trade the lowest current prices and to execute all orders without delay. The reputation and standing of the house in trade circles is such that we shall not presume to offer any comment on the subject other than to say that references are invited to the banking house of T. W. House and to the wholesale grocery firms of Messrs. Wm. D. Cleveland & Co. and Carson, Sewall & Co. Mr. Howell has been identified with this department of business for many years, and he is thoroughly familiar with every detail connected with it. He is a well known resident of this community. He is a director of the Texas Savings, Real Estate and Investment Company, and is also of the firm of Smith & Howell, storage and warehousing. This firm have a commodious warehouse along the track of the Southern Pacific Railroad.

S. M. RUSHMORE,
Fancy and Staple Groceries, Wines, Liquors, Confectionery, Etc., Corner Congress Avenue and San Jacinto Street.

We doubt greatly if the celebrated old Roman epicures ever saw displayed before them such an array of good things to eat and drink as are today visible at the well stocked store conducted by Mr. S. M. Rushmore. The business was originally founded by Mr. Chas. Pescay, the present proprietor succeeding in 1886. The store is a handsome and commodious one, comprising the corner store of the new Shaw building, which is located on the corner of Congress avenue and San Jacinto street. It is 25x90 feet in dimensions, and here displayed on every hand are the choicest delicacies from all parts of the world, and indeed, not to weary the reader in enumeration, we will state that at this establishment will be found all sorts, kinds and descriptions of delicious articles, including the finest of imported and domestic canned and bottled goods, sauces, pickles, preserves, fine confectionery, etc., that would tempt a sated appetite or astound an uncultivated one with gastronomic wonder. Mr. Rushmore makes a particular specialty of fine canned goods, which are put up expressly for his trade, and under the brand of "Dew Drop" may be procured the finest quality of canned fruits, vegetables, fish, etc. that comes to this market. The house also deals heavily in all the ordinary lines comprised in the term groceries, and a particular specialty is made in fine teas and coffees. Confectionery of the choicest quality is another particular line, and this succulent luxury may here be obtained in perfection. Recognizing the importance to families and others of procuring choice and unadulterated wines and liquors for home consumption and for medicinal use, the house is prepared to furnish the best imported and domestic goods of all kinds both in small and large quantities. Much of the foreign wines and liquors are imported for this establishment, and domestic goods are obtained from the distillers and producers direct. In all departments the facilities of this establishment are of the best, and the prices will be found eminently just and reasonable. Mr. S. M. Rushmore, the proprietor, thoroughly understands his business, and he is a gentleman of wide awake enterprise, striving by all legitimate means to consolidate and increase his already wide spread patronage.

HOUSTON CROCKERY HOUSE,
Jno. McClellan & Co., Proprietors; Dealers in Crockery, Glassware, Etc., 610 Main Street.

The Houston Crockery House conducted under the proprietorship of Messrs. Jno. McClellan & Co., began operations here May, 1893. The house at once sprang into prominence in view of the superior quality and character of the wares which it offered to the public. The premises occupied consist of a two-story brick building 25x100 feet in dimensions. Here may be seen a remarkably fine display of china, glassware, queensware, lamps, table cutlery, silver plated ware, etc. These goods are obtained direct from the makers in this country or specially imported from Europe. In some lines the products of American factories, at least equal, if they do not surpass the goods made abroad. Of these Messrs. Jno. McClellan & Co. carry in stock some of the choicest and finest. There are, however, certain lines in which European manufacturers still bear the palm of superiority from all competitors. Of such the houses of Haviland & Co. of France, and Alfred Meaken of England, are prominent exponents. Messrs. Jno. McClellan & Co. make particular specialties of their wares, and they are the sole importers of the celebrated English Iron Stone China, made by the latter house. While, as before mentioned, the finest quality of goods is handled, a complete variety of standard articles are also carried. The trade of the house is both wholesale and retail, and every inducement is offered to dealers as well as to the general public. The facilities of the firm enable them to quote the lowest prices, and nothing is left undone to make business transactions between themselves and their customers mutually pleasant and profitable. A visit to this establishment is well repaid even if immediate purchases are not made, and the most courteous attention will be extended visitors by the proprietors and their employees. The members of the firm individually are John McClellan and L. Kaminski, both gentlemen of business acumen and experience. Mr. McClellan was superintendent of Bradstreets at Galveston for three years, but he is originally a Houston man, and identified with its interests. He is also president of the Local Board of the Michigan Savings and Loan Association. Mr. Kaminski comes from St. Louis, where for twenty-five years he has been engaged in the crockery business, and therefore every detail connected with it is thoroughly familiar to him.

McWILLIAMS & CO.

Real Estate. 913½ Franklin Avenue.

The scale upon which this city is growing, along with large outlying territory being rapidly settled and cultivated, augmented by a constantly increasing population, all combine to give real estate investments a stability, with assurance of rapidly enhancing values, which would be difficult if possible to duplicate elsewhere. Messrs. McWilliams & Co. occupy a prominent position among leading and reliable real estate agents of this city, and they possess the best of facilities for doing business. They have a large list of property on their books, and they make a particular specialty of county property, farm and fruit lands, much of which is their own property. The firm control what is known as GLENDALE, which is located about four and a half miles from the court house in this city, and one mile from the new fair grounds. This property is divided up into ten and twenty acre tracts, and it is especially desirable for fruit and truck raising. Farms are sold on this property at a low price, and upon terms to suit the purchasers. The location of this tract is admirable, it being so close to the city of Houston, which affords an unfailing market for the products raised on its soil. Messrs. McWilliams & Co. also have for sale a large tract near Hitchcock, which is also highly desirable, and which is offered upon the most reasonable terms. The firm are prepared at all times to buy or sell any description of desirable farm property, and they have real estate of this class at all times to offer to investors and homeseekres. It is manitestly to the advantage of the above class of the public, either here or afar, to investigate the attractions herein offered, and a substantial profit is certain to be the result of judicious investments in South Texas real estate. The firm are in the enjoyment of the best of facilities for assisting the purchaser to make a profitable investment, and they may be depended upon for fairly and honestly representing what they have to offer. As evidence of their standing in financial circles, they invite references to the Omaha National Bank, of Omaha, Neb., and the Planters and Mechanics National Bank of this city. The individual members of the firm are Messrs. H. L. McWilliams, and F. G. McWilliams, both thoroughly experienced in all relating to the real estate business. Correspondence is solicited from any part of the United States, and cheerfully and promptly responded to. It is now that the opportunity offers to plant the seeds of a future competence, and a full crop is sure to follow in due season. Finally let us add that this firm is in every way a well balanced one, and a reliable authority on real estate values.

BAYOU CITY LUMBER COMPANY.

Dealers in Lumber, Shingles, Sash, Doors, Blinds, Etc.; Office and Yard, Tenth Street, on H. & T. C. R. R.

The lumber trade may be regarded as one of the most important branches of business carried on at Houston, and it has been greatly stimulated owing to the marked progress and advancement of the city during recent years, and the growth in building operations. An enterprise comparatively recently instituted to supply this demand is that conducted under the title of the Bayou City Lumber Company. The enterprise was founded during the past year, and it at once became prominent in the trade owing to its complete facilities and ample resources. At the above indicated location the office and yards are situated, and the premises occupy a space of about two and a half acres, on which are contained the office building, lumber sheds, storage conveniences, etc. The company deals in all kinds of lumber, carrying in stock at all times upwards of 1,000,000 feet to fill current orders. They also handle extensively shingles, sash, doors, blinds, mouldings, cypress cisterns, builders' hardware, etc. They are in the enjoyment of every facility for advantageously supplying the trade, all products being obtained from original sources, placing them practically on the same footing as *bona fide* makers of the goods. The company have their manufacturing done at Beaumont, Texas, where are located some of the largest mills in the country. At the present time dealers will find, that the company are amply adequate to satisfy all demands made upon them, and the largest orders are promptly filled. The quality of the products leaves nothing to be desired, and they offer the best of inducements in the way of terms and prices. The president of the company is Mr. Massena Wiess, and Mr. Joe. W. Davis, is secretary and treasurer. Mr. Wiess came from Round Rock, Texas, previous to identifying himself with this industry. Mr. Davis is a Houston man, always identified with this locality. In conclusion we may say that already the standing and general reputation of the company for promptness and enterprise is fully established and appreciated, and it today enjoys the esteem of the trade and community generally.

M. F. McILVAINE & CO.,
Manufacturers of Mattresses, Spring Beds Etc., 206 and 208 Milam Street.

The old stuffy feather beds of our ancestors are now generally discarded and are no longer considered essential to comfort. A well made spring bed or mattress, constructed according to approved modern methods, is far superior, and at the same time is much more cleanly and convenient. The business carried on by Messrs. M. F. McIlvaine & Co. was inaugurated December, 1892, and already has demonstrated indications of a pronounced and permanent success. The premises occupied are contained in a two-story building of 50x100 feet. Here all required tools and appliances are available and from eight to a dozen skilled work-people are given employment. The firm are manufacturers of mattresses, spring beds and bedding supplies generally. In the manufacture of these goods the greatest care is exercised as to detail to ensure the very best quality of raw material, the best workmanship and superiority in the general character of the product. Altogether it may be said of the goods made and sold here, that they are, in all their essentials, equal to the best on the market; at the same time the prices are based upon a scale of fairness and moderation which induces a permanent and satisfactory patronage. The range of products here turned out includes woven wire mattresses, spiral spring beds, all grades of mattresses, mosquito bars, pillows, comforters, cots, etc. The trade of the house, while largely local, also extends to neighboring sections and is steadily increasing. Mr. M. F. McIlvaine is a gentlemen of thorough experience in all that pertains to the business, and he exercises the closest care and supervision over all the operations. As illustrating the growing diversity and expansion of the industries of this city, we are glad to accord a measure of our space in this volume to this young and enterprising concern.

WM. J. LEMP BREWING CO., ST. LOUIS,
Houston Branch Corner Commerce Avenue and San Jacinto Street.
A. Moser, Manager.

Many of the great brewing enterprises have largely extended their sphere of usefulness during late years, away from the ground where they have taken root, and they thus afford to the inhabitants of distant localities the advantages of being able to

procure in perfection a grade of lager beer often otherwise unobtainable. Such has been the course of the Wm. J. Lemp Brewing Co. of St. Louis, who, in addition to supplying a large home demand in that city, have established branches and agencies at very many of the principal centers throughout the country. To attempt any description of the plant or facilities of this immense concern in these pages would be impracticable. We may, however, state that at St. Louis the brewery covers three city squares, the main buildings are seven and eight stories high, and the equipment is as complete as the ingenuity of man could devise. The annual output of the brewery is over 300,000 barrels, and the total sales exceed $3,000,000. An elaborate bottling department has a capacity cf 100,000 bottles daily. Five hundred refrigerator cars are in constant use in transporting the beer to distant localities. Seven hundred men are employed, and over one hundred horses. The business at Houston has been established for the past twelve years and the beer is standard on the market here. The company have an ice factory and warehouse on the Central Railroad where they have storage facilities for six carloads. Southern Texas is supplied from this point, and orders are filled with promptness and dispatch. The reputation of the products of the company for well nigh a half a century is soundly established; however, we might as well reflect here the general verdict, which is, that for flavor, purity, wholesomeness and general excellence this lager beer has never been surpassed. Mr. A. Moser, the manager at Houston, is a well known resident, who thoroughly understands the business confided to his charge. To his efforts are largely due the success of the enterprise at this point, and the continued satisfaction of patrons. The location at Houston of this branch of the Wm. J. Lemp Brewing Co., materially adds to Houston's trade conveniences and facilities.

SID WESTHEIMER.
Livery, Sale and Transfer Stable, and Undertaker, Commerce Avenue and San Jacinto Street.

Among enterprising establishments in Houston, which have significantly contributed to the general advancement and growth of the trade facilities of the city, must be classed that conducted by Mr. Sid Westheimer, who founded his business here September 1883. Since that time it has gained greatly in the favor of our residents, due to the facilities it possesses and the inducements it offers to the public. In connection with the business, premises are occupied and owned by Mr Westheimer,

which comprise a large two story brick stable 100 feet square in area. This is thoroughly well equipped, and appointed in a way that is altogether suitable for the well-being and comfort of horses. The operations of the house include the conduct of a first class livery establishment, where may be obtained on hire every description of vehicle or rig suitable either for business or pleasure. Mr. Westheimer also boards horses at reasonable prices, giving them the best of care and attention. This gentleman also buys, sells and exchanges horses and mules, and generally has on hand a large stock of Kansas, Missouri and Texas horses. He makes a specialty of gentle horses for family trade, and one thing that the public can here rely upon, and that is, that in no case are any misrepresentations made, but fair dealing and fair trading are the inviolable rules from which there is no deviation. To the observance of this policy, and to enterprising and energetic modern methods in transacting business, must be ascribed the large success which has been achieved by the house. About April 1st Mr. Westheimer will add to his enterprise a first class undertaking establishment, with all facilities provided, including hearses, carriages, and a full stock of caskets and supplies. Mr. Westheimer is a large real estate owner here, and has always real estate to sell or trade in this thriving and growing locality. Business transactions of any character with him may be depended upon as leading to ultimate advantage, and to the mutual satisfaction of all concerned. Since the cut representing Mr. Westheimer's building was made, a number of alterations have been introduced, which afford him handsome offices and warerooms for his undertaking business, making it altogether one of the most complete and desirable establishments of the kind in the city.

C. SCHWARZ,
Manufacturer and Dealer in Carriages, Buggies, Etc., 601, 603 and 605 Preston Avenue.

Among carriage manufacturers in South Texas, who have gained a reputation for their products, none stand higher in the estimation of the public than does Mr. C. Schwarz, who with lengthened experience and at the head of his present establishment for the past sixteen years, is today fully prepared to execute in the best manner all work entrusted to him. Using nothing but the best materials, carefully selected and well seasoned, employing only the most experienced and skilled workmen, and enjoying the best of facilities, this house turns out a line of carriages, buggies, spring wagons, etc., made in any of the approved styles, and equal to the finest which the skill of the present day can produce. The manufacturing facilities of the house embrace a two-story factory 100x125 feet in dimensions, which is sub-divided into painting, trimming, blacksmithing and wood-working departments, and where the services of about a dozen or more skilled mechanics are employed. All details of the work are performed on the premises, every part of the vehicle being made here under the supervision of the proprietor, who is eminently a practical man in the business. Mr. Schwarz generally keeps a stock of carriages on hand to fill immediate orders, and he also handles harness in large and useful variety. Mr. Schwarz is agent in Houston for the celebrated Studebaker, Old Hickory and Tennesee wagons, equal to the best made of their class. This gentleman is a well-known resident, interested in the city's advancement and progress, and he is identified as stockholder in some of Houston's most important industries. Our readers may enter into business relations with this house with the full assurance of receiving fair and liberal treatment and manifest advantages in the way of terms and prices.

H. H. DOOLEY.
Real Estate. 415½ Main Street.

In this city a real estate concern which enjoys the benefits of a long establishment, and a complete familiarity with the locality, is that conducted under the proprietorship of Mr. H. H. Dooley, who commenced operations as long ago as the the year 1867, and who therefore for over a quarter of a century has been before the public. This gentleman devotes his services to all the details connected with a general real estate business, handling city property, farm and fruit lands, etc. He also collects rents, and takes charge of property for non-residents, and generally attends to the interests of investors and property owners. The entire charge of estates is undertaken by him, including collection of revenues, paying taxes, instituting improvements, etc. He has on his list many desirable properties, which he offers at low prices, and upon easy terms to suit. Intending settlers will do well to consult with him when contemplating a purchase, and the tried results of his lengthened experience are placed at their disposal. We have elsewhere devoted much space to the exploitation of the great advantages of this section, and Mr. Dooley is well in a position to bestow large benefit on all who may enter into dealings with him.. He is a well known resident of this city, with a high reputation for fair dealing and integrity, and we are certainly justified in according him due share of notice as perhaps the oldest established real estate man now engaged in the business in the city of Houston.

J. A. TEMPEST,
Architect, 914 Franklin Avenue.

The city of Houston is rapidly advancing, and from an architectural point of view this fact is particularly prominent. Among gentlemen engaged in the profession of the architect here is Mr. J. A. Tempest, who adopted Houston as the theatre of his operations in 1891. He is technically and practically conversant with everything connected with his vocation, having had many years experience. He began the practice of his profession in Toronto, Canada, one of the finest cities, architecturally speaking, on this continent. For twelve years he carried on his business successfully half of which time was spent at Buffalo, N. Y., but recognizing the field open to him here he removed to this city at the date mentioned. Already have his services been properly appreciated by capitalists and residents, and some noticeable work has been done by him in this city and locality. Mr. Tempest made the plans for the new Baptist church at Marshall, Texas, Christ Church, Houston, an illustration of which appears in this volume, and eight mission churches in the neighborhood. Another exponent of his skill is the San Felipe public school, which cost $18,000, and this is perhaps the only public building in Texas which has been fully completed without one cent of extra cost above the contract amount. This is a tribute to Mr. Tempest's carefulness and attention to the smallest details of the work undertaken by him, also worthy of mention is Mr. W. B. Chew's residence, and that of Mr. H. S. Fox, two of the finest in the city. Many other residences and buildings have been constructed from his plans, we only giving here the more noticable. Mr. Tempest is prepared to furnish plans and estimates for the erection of all kinds of building, and to superintend the same if desired. The endorsement he has already received speaks eloquently as to his skill and capabilities. Enquiries will be met with the promptest attention and nothing will be left untried which will make a business connection with him satisfactory and pleasant to all concerned.

JOHN C. TURLEY & CO.,
Furniture, Auction and Commission Merchants, 209 Travis Street.

Affording the public of Houston and vicinity great conveniences in the way of making advantageous purchases, the above business has been carried on with steadily increasing success since February, 1893, when it was founded as John F. Morriss & Co. On October 1, 1893, the present firm of John C. Turley & Co. became the proprietors. The firm now enjoy the best of facilities, and the enterprise is ranked among the leading and favorite trading headquarters here. One of the finest buildings on Travis street is occupied, which is of three floors and covers an area of 60x90 feet. All conveniences for the rapid and economical transaction of business are here available, including an elevator. Here may be inspected a full assortment of furniture of all kinds, obtained direct from the manufacturers, or otherwise under exceptionally favorable conditions, so that the goods are offered the public at rock bottom prices. The varied assortment gives every opportunity for the most advantageous selections to be made, and the requirements of all classes are here to be obtained in perfection. Goods are sold for cash or on the installment plan, payable periodically in sums to suit the wants of patrons. The firm also handle a large stock of buggies, saddlery, harness, carpets and matting. The firm in addition transact a general auction and brokerage business, and goods of any description are advantageously sold, either by public auction or private sale. Auctions are held as occasion arise, and these sales are very popular here and are numerously attended by the general public. The house invites consignments of merchandise and goods of any description, and the facilities of the house are such that quick sales and prompt returns may be depended on. The members of the firm individually are John C. Turley and Wm. J. Francis. Mr. Turley comes from Kentucky, where he was in the general merchandise business. Mr. Francis is from Cincinnati. Both gentlemen are progressive, active and energetic business men, striving to do everything in their power to conserve the interests of their patrons. In every instance all representations made can entirely be depended upon, and fair dealing and honorable principles of doing business are the rules from which there is no deviation.

A. WHITAKER,
Nurseryman, Florist and Seedsman; Office, 503 Travis Street.

Adjacent to the Fair Grounds Addition of Houston is to be found the nursery, floral and seed establishment of Mr. A. Whitaker, who commenced operations here in 1859, and who converted that which originally was but little better than a barren waste into a fitting shrine of the goddesses Flora and Pomona. The grounds cover altogether a space of about ten acres. There are here four rose houses, respectively 20x60 feet in area, with an L attachment to each. There are also four ordinary greenhouses of the same dimensions. Altogether there are at least three hundred sash of glass and over nine hundred running feet of frames. In rose plants Mr. Whitaker has a specialty, and he has many varieties in his collection of this the Queen of Flowers. Of fruit trees there is an abundance, and here may be seen 2,000 bearing pear trees, all of which are of the best selected variety. Figs, plums and other fruits also grow here and with the pears are sent to market in the season. The very best of appliances are here in vogue in every department. The reputation of this establishment is spread over a period of over a third of a century and it bases its claims to patronage solely on the merits of its products. The house has a store in the city at 503 Travis street, and here at all times may be ordered by telegram beautiful and rare cut flowers for a young man to send to his girl; also, floral designs, wreaths, etc., for weddings, parties, funerals, etc. The trade may be said to be both wholesale and retail, cut flowers, etc., being sent to all parts of the State and beyond, Mr. A. Whitaker, the proprietor, is a native of England, belonging to an influential family in that country. He is an educated botanist, and he has made the study of flowers and fruits his dominant pursuit for the past forty years, during which he has been a resident of Texas. He is the agricultural editor of the Houston Post, and his "Arcadia" articles in that journal have been copied all over this country and in Europe. He gives his closest personal attention to the details of his establishment, which in every way is a decided acquisition to the city.

J. N. TAUB,
Wholesale and Retail Dealer in Cigars, Tobacco, Etc., 1007 and 1014 Congress Avenue.

An important enterprise of this city devoted to the sale of cigars and tobaccos at wholesale and retail is that of Mr. J. N. Taub, who in the year 1888 became the sole proprietor of the business originally established by Mr. R. Lawrence in 1880. The house has largely progressed with the lapse of years and it now transacts a very important business in this city and neighboring localities. The premises occupied comprise two distinct establishments. At 1007 Congress avenue a three-story brick building 30x60 feet in area is used for the wholesale departments and at 1014 Congress avenue another three-story structure is utilized for the retail trade. Mr. Taub carries a full line of cigars and tobaccos, smokers' articles, etc., all of which are of the best selection, specially suited to the trade of this locality. The cigars of his own brands are made especially for him, and they can be depended upon for uniform quality, desirability and popularity. He makes a specialty of all the popular brands of smoking and chewing tobaccos, of which he carries a very large stock, and his facilities enable him to supply these both to the trade and public at lowest prices. He enjoys the most intimate connections with manufacturers, affording him manifest advantages in competition. All orders from out of town are promptly filled to entire satisfaction. Mr. Taub is a native of Hungary, and came direct from there to this city, which he has adopted as his home. He is a well known resident and an enterprising and honorable business man. He gives his full attention to his industry, assisted in his work by his two sons, who have grown up with the business. The house is in every way a representative one, demonstrating the advantages and advancement of Houston as an favorable wholesale and retail source of supply and purchasing center.

L. E. MILLER.
Electrical Supplies. Office, Foot of Main Street. Shop Corner Runnels and Gabel Streets.

An enterprise of a most useful character, and one which contributes materially to the attractions of the city, as a source of supply, is that conducted by Mr. L. E. Miller, and established by him about four years ago. The shop is contained in a three story building, which is fitted up with all necessary appliances which are operated by electrical power. Mr. Miller manufactures, deals in, and keeps in stock, all kinds of electrical supplies, making a specialty of the execution of every description of electrical work, including re-modeling, repairing wiring, putting in complete light and power plants, electro-plating, the installation of electric fans, electric motors of any capacity, etc. The experience of the proprietor, who is a practical and skilled electrical engineer, assures the fullest confidence that work of this character will be efficiently carried out by the house. Mr. Miller was formerly with the Houston Electric Light & Power Co., having been its manager for eight years. We will here instance some of the more important contracts he has carried out in this locality. He wired the electric plant of the Southern Cotton Oil Co., installed the entire city works at Brenham, Texas, wired the National Cotton Oil Co. of Corsicana, supplied the complete lighting plant of the McFadden Compress Co. at Brenham, and a large number of public buildings and private residences in Houston. He is now filling a contract for the installation of a complete city lighting plant at Corsicana, also in the Hutchins House in Houston, supplying to this hotel about five hundred incandescent lights. Mr. Miller solicits correspondence and enquiries, and prompt replies may be depended upon. The scale of charges is moderate, and the house is in every way to be commended to the public with the assurance that in its particular line no more reliable concern can anywhere be found.

C. W. HURD. (Successor to H. F. Hurd.)
Manufacturer of All Kinds of Buggies and Spring Wagons. No. 50 Commerce Street.

The old established enterprise to which we now accord a measure of our space was founded as long ago as 1853, by Mr. H. F. Hurd, he transfering it to his son, the present proprietor in 1892. The plant covers two lots, and comprises a two story brick building, 50x55 feet in dimensions, and a frame structure adjoining, of 25x50 feet. All required tools and appliances are here in operation, and a force of about eight or ten skilled workmen is given employment. The house lends its energies to the manufacturing of every description of buggy, carriage and spring wagon, indeed it is safe to say that here can be made everything in the way of a wheeled vehicle, from a wheel-barrow to a landau. The goods turned out here are essentially first class, embodying all the elements of beauty of design, strength, durability, lightness in draught, the best of materials and excellence of workmanship. The prices will be found to be altogether fair and reasonable. Particular attention is also given to repairing in all its branches, horseshoeing, blacksmith work of every description, and indeed, we might say, everything in iron that can be produced in a blacksmith shop. Mr. C. W. Hurd is a thoroughly practical man, brought up to the business, and no detail of the work is unfamiliar to him. His father, Mr. H. F. Hnrd, is the oldest living blacksmith in Houston, and although now retired, he still takes an interest in the undertaking. The enterprise was started 'in a very small way, but today may be considered as one of the best known concerns in this section. Concluding we may add that those who want a *cheap* carriage or *cheap* work will not find it here, but those who require a *good* vehicle and *good* work at lowest prices, can do no better than in dealings with this house.

A. F. LUMM,
Manufacturers' Agent and General Broker, 118 Main Street.

The wholesale houses here are doing their full share towards the expansion and development of this city, and an important adjunct and aid to the wholesale trade is the business transacted by what are generally known as manufacturers' agents and merchandise brokers. This important division of commerce is represented in Houston by the enterprise of Mr. A. F. Lumm, who in 1889 succeeded Mr. Geo. Waggaman, who first instituted the business in 1885. Mr. Lumm represents in this market a number of the best known and most responsible firms and organizations in the country. Among these may be mentioned the Elgin Condensed Milk Company, of Elgin, Ill.; Reed Bros., packers, of Kansas City; Wolff & Reissing, importers, of New York; J. C. Grant Baking Powder Company, of Chicago, and as many as from fifty to seventy-five first-class manufacturing and importing houses, handling almost every article connected with the grocery trade. Mr. Lumm sells strictly to jobbers only and generally in car-load lots, which are dispatched direct from the original sources of supply to destination. His facilities enable him to quote the lowest current rates and to assure the prompt filling of all orders. This gentleman is a well known resident of this city, where he has lived for the past seventeen years. He is originally from Kentucky and is an old time commercial traveler, and he was for many years in the employ of the world-renowned Standard Oil Company. He is qualified by his practical knowledge to entirely understand the requirements of this market, and those having dealings with him repose full confidence in all representations made. His enterprise is a valuable one, bringing into immediate contact producer and seller, and it is fully worthy of brief mention in this volume.

S. L. SAM,
Dealer in Boots and Shoes, 315 Main Street.

A large surrounding country naturally seeks supplies here, and the demand has been amply provided for by the enterprise of our merchants. All lines of trade are well represented, and engaged prominently in the boot and shoe business is the house of Mr. S. L. Sam, which was originally founded as Sam Brothers in 1878. In 1883 the style of the firm became S. L. Sam & Brother, and Mr. S. L. Sam became sole proprietor in 1884. The premises occupied for the business are well arranged and centrally located, and comprise the three story brick building at the above address, which is of the dimensions of 21x90 feet, The salesrooms are replete with all the latest novelties in fine boots and shoes for ladies, gentlemen and children, representing all the choicest qualities of some of the best manufacturers in the country. A great deal of the stock is made expressly for the trade of this house, and among the specialties here handled are the goods of Hanan & Sons mens' fine shoes, Brooklyn, N. Y.; Wm. Dorsch & Son, mens' shoes, Newark, N. J.; Rockland & Co., mens' shoes, Boston, Mass.; J. & T. Cousins, ladies' and childrens fine shoes, New York; Stribley & Co., ladies' and childrens' goods, Cincinnati, O.; those of G. P. Dodge & Co., and the Newburyport Shoe Co, Newburyport, Mass. and others. Thus it will be seen that this house obtains its supplies direct from original sources of importance, and under the most favorable conditions, carrying a stock made up of the most reliable goods known to the trade, it is incumbent on buyers in the advancement of their own interests, that they bear in mind this establishment where inducements are offered, and benefits conferred in the way of price and quality difficult to duplicate. The motto of the house "push things and look cheerful" is pithy and to the point, and this is the corner stone of the business policy here adopted. Mr. Sam is a well known and popular resident, identified with many of Houston's enterprises, and he takes every interest in its advantage and progress.

B. R. LATHAM,
Dealer in Furniture, Carpets, House Furnishing Goods, Etc., 701 and 703 Main Street.

A house that has been in continuous existence for a period considerably over a half century, of necessity, merits special recognition in this volume. Such an enterprise is that now conducted by Mr. B. R. Latham, who in 1892 became the proprietor of the business originally founded by his father, Mr. L. J. Latham, in 1839. This gentleman was one of the earliest of American settlers in what is now the State of Texas. He was a pioneer of modern industrial pursuits in this section of the country, and today the house ranks as the oldest established in its line in the Lone Star State. Mr. L. J. Latham died March 20th, 1886, regretted by all who had the honor of his acquaintance and friendship. The premises comprise a three-story brick building of 50x85 feet, besides a warehouse adjoining, which is 30x70 feet. Thus ample accommodations are afforded for the display of a remarkably choice assortment of fine furniture, comprising everything incident to a complete line, carefully selected and superior in quality. The intimate relations the house enjoys with the original sources of supply and the extent of its operations place it in a position to offer marked inducements to the public. A special department is that of carpets, which are carried in stock of all makes and qualities suitable to the requirements of all classes. Mr. Latham is prepared to plan carpets to fit any apartment, make them and lay them to complete satisfaction, promptly and efficiently, with the least inconvenience to patrons. A full stock is also handled of house furnishing goods, toilet sets, rugs, etc., and in all departments the completest facilities are available. The distinguishing character of this house's stock is its high quality, the best class of trade being catered to. Mr. B. R. Latham, the proprietor, is a well known citizen. He has had a lifelong experience of his business, every detail of which is familiar to him. He is a member of the B. P. O. Elks and other societies, and is otherwise socially popular.

E. R. BROWN,
Ticket Broker, 418 Main Street.

Among the greatest conveniences to travelers in all important business centers are those gentlemen who follow the vocation of ticket brokers, and through whose means material saving is often effected in the prices of railroad and steamboat tickets to all parts of the country. In this city this business is represented by Mr. E. N. Brown, whose office is at the above address. This gentleman generally has tickets for disposal at reduced rates to the various leading centers of the United States, and to many minor points in this section of the country. He is prepared at all times to give good prices for unused portions of regular and excursion tickets, either buying or exchanging the same, as may be desired. Mr. Brown is a member of the Guarantee Ticket Brokers Association, which warrants all tickets purchased of any of its members, thus affording purchasers of tickets here full guarantee from loss by seeming misrepresentation or other cause. Mr. Brown comes to this city from Ft. Worth, where he had been engaged in a similar enterprise. He succeeded September, 1893, to the business originally established in Houston by Messrs. Barnett & Co. in 1892. He has every experience in railroad and ticket transactions, and can be depended upon for fair dealing and honest representations. Those about to take a journey or temporarily in the city will do well to call at his office before taking their departure. He is well posted on routes and ways and means, and will cheerfully furnish all information required.

DRS. WILLIAMS & WILLIAMS,
Dentists, 213½ Main Street.

In but few vocations have such great advances and improvements been made as in dentistry. No so long ago the pulling of teeth was in the hands of barbers and blacksmiths. That was the extent of dentistry up to 1840, when Dr. Chapin A. Harris founded the Baltimore College of Dental Surgery, the first and for a long time the only dental school in the world. At that time dentistry, as a profession, was born; the infant being a healthy one and giving promise of arriving at full stature some day, and being of vast benefit to mankind and offering great opportunities for talent and ingenuity, naturally attracted men who professed the above qualifications, who invented many appliances, enabling them to accomplish wonders—onward and upward until today dentistry takes rank with the learned professions. In advance of medicine, dentistry adopted a three years' course. Drs. Williams & Williams, the gentlemen whose names head this article, and who are established at 213½ Main street, are thoroughly identified with the city and its interests, having bought homes here. These gentlemen are young, progressive and enterprising, and are always on the alert for anything new in their line. They pride themselves on their painstaking and thoroughness in every operation performed by them, and the public can rest assured that they are strictly up with the times in every respect and possess all the knowledge and skill that a complete course of study and a number of years of experience can impart. Dr. Thos. P. Williams, the senior member, is one of the clinical instructors in the Northwestern Dental College, of Chicago, and is a regular graduate from the Baltimore College of Dental Surgery, with fourteen years experience. Dr. George J. Williams is a graduate from the Vanderbilt Dental College, of Nashville, with a practical experience of seven years. Both gentlemen have had the honor of serving on the State Examining Boards, and can proudly refer as their patients to many of the prominent families of Houston, as well as South Texas.

SWEENEY, COOMBS & FREDERICKS.
Jewelers.   301 Main Street.

With the advancement of any community, in wealth, intelligence and culture, the fine arts of decoration and adornment prosper, and the skill and taste of the jeweler and silversmith are brought more constantly and generally into requisition. Of course those long engaged in the business have done no little to educate and direct the public taste ; a work which probably no house in Houston has accomplished more effectually than that of Messrs. Sweeney, Coombs & Fredericks, whose establishment was instituted as Sweeney & Coombs, January 24th, 1874, the present firm being constituted in 1889. The premises occupied consist of a handsome store 100x25 feet in dimensions and the stock, valuing many thousands of of dollars, contains an assortment which for beauty and artistic elegance cannot be surpassed in the state. It includes special lines of ladies' jewelry in sets, diamonds, and other precious stones in large variety, plain and ornate rings, French bronzes, marble and ormolu clocks, ceramic and bronze ware, artistic china and bric-a-brac, watches of all the reliable makes, silverware, pitchers, services, card baskets, and tableware, and in short an endless and *recherche* assortment of those choice and artistic goods which belong only to the highest class in the trade. The house makes direct importations of diamonds and foreign goods, and having the most intimate connections with manufacturers in this country they are enabled to offer the most desirable goods to the public at lowest prices. A special department of the business is fine watch and jewelry repairing and diamond setting. The most expensive and complicated time piece may be entrusted to the care of this house, with the assurance that it will be skillfully treated and restored in perfect order. Articles of jewelry are made according to individual design if required, or manufactured from pattern and design furnished by the firm. The individual members of the firm are Messrs. J. J. Sweeney, E. L. Coombs and Gus Fredericks; all of whom are well known residents, bound up and identified with the advancement and progress of the city. Messrs. Sweeney and Coombs are the owners of the opera house, an illustration of which appears elsewhere in this volume. These gentlemen are among the largest real estate owners in Houston, and they are also identified with other interests of importance. Mr. E. L. Coombs is a director of the Planters and Mechanics Bank, and also of the American Brewing Association. Closing this sketch it is but right to say that the house of Sweeney, Coombs & Fredericks is one of the most popular resorts in South Texas for those in search of genuine values in diamonds, jewelry and silverware—a question which is never in dispute on entering into business relations with this house.

J. P. KINDRED.
Real Estate. 502½ Main Street.

An accession to the real estate business here is noticed the enterprise of Mr. J. P. Kindred, who August, 1892 came to this city from Galveston, where he had carried on a similar business since 1874. He devotes his energies to the transaction of a regular real estate business, giving particular attention to rentals and the care of estates for nonresidents. He also negotiates loans and collects interest and revenue, and attends generally to all details connected with his profession. He is also a notary public. Those who may employ the services of this gentleman may do so with confidence, assured that their interests will be well served and considered. He has every experience in the business and a thorough knowledge of real estate values. He invites correspondence and will be glad to furnish all particulars relative to the advantages offered investors and home seekers by this favored section. His offices when enlisted will be found of large value, and he is eminently reliable and trustworthy.

NORTHRUP & CLARK,
Manufacturers of Saddlery and Harness, 1012 Congress Avenue.

One of the most reliable houses engaged in the above trade in this section is that of Northrup & Clark. The establishment of the business took place in 1891, when it was founded by Mr. J. D. Northrup, the present firm succeeding October 29th, 1892. The reputation achieved for making fine goods is of the best character, and has led to the development of a business which is not confined to the city, but reaches out and extends through contiguous territory. The firm occupy a two-story building of 25x100 feet, which affords all conveniences for the business. They manufacture and carry in stock harness of all descriptions, saddles of all kinds, and make a specialty of fine single and double harness of any design and pattern required, only the highest quality of goods being the work of their hands. They are the sole owners of Don's patent seat stock saddle, which is well known for its efficiency and quality. The members of the firm are A. P. Northrup and M. A. Clark, energetic and reliable business people. Mr. Northrup is a practical saddler of eight years' experience, and both gentlemen are thoroughly qualified for the business. Their closest personal supervision is at all times directed in the interests of their patrons, who can be thoroughly well assured that here they can obtain such goods as rank superior in all respects. A large stock is at all times carried and everything is at the disposal of patrons to attract legitimate trade. Both gentlemen are well known members of the community. Mr. Northrup is a member of the Masonic fraternity and other societies, and Mr. Clark is also identified with a number of these organizations. This establishment is entitled to be ranked as among the most useful of Houston's trade conveniences.

CITY SALE STABLES,
Edwin Larendon, Proprietor, 406 to 416 Fannin Street.

One of the best known and most enterprising of the business establishments of this city is that generally familiar to our residents as the City Sale Stables, conducted under the proprietorship of Mr. Edwin Larendon. This gentleman became the owner of the business in 1885, succeeding then Mr. J. C. Baldwin, who had for some time previously conducted it. The premises comprise a commodious stable of 150x100 feet in dimensions, which are in every way adapted to the business. Mr. Larendon buys and sells horses and mules in large quantities, generally having any description of horse on hand. He carries in stock at all times 125 or more animals, and his facilities enable him to obtain these from the best of sources and to offer them to patrons at lowest prices. Another department of the business is the livery stable, and here may be obtained in perfection every description of rig, well horsed and equipped and suitable either for pleasure or business excursions. Orders for weddings, pleasure parties and funerals receive the promptest attention, and careful and sober drivers only are employed by this house. Mr. Larendon also deals in buggies and carriages, carrying a stock of all the prevailing makes and styles. A full line of fine harness is also handled here. This is one of the largest and best equipped establishments of the kind in the State, with facilities surpassed by none. The proprietor is an expert in his business, everything pertaining to horses being entirely familiar to him. Before embarking in his present venture he was for a number of years with House's bank, of this city. He is well known to the entire community, and he enjoys an enviable reputation as an enterprising and honorable business man. About twenty-seven men are employed in the various departments and the business is steadily growing. Those who may be in need of anything in this line can do no better than in leaving their orders here.

F. ILLIG,
Dealer in Furniture, 116 and 116½ Main Street.

For twenty years the above named house has been regarded by the citizens of Houston as an advantageous source of supply for fine furniture and other goods required in the household. The business was instituted by its present proprietor in 1865, and has been conducted by him continuously since that period. The premises utilized comprise a three story brick building 35x100 feet in dimensions, which is filled throughout with a large and well assorted stock of furniture of the finer and medium grades, including some which may be obtained nowhere else in this city. Carpets of all makes and of the newest patterns and styles are also found here at the disposal of the public, also house furnishing goods, etc. A specialty of the house is office furniture, and also that of carrying a class of goods which shall rank superior in all details. Mr. Illig caters to the best class of trade in this city and does not transact an installment business, but the prices, however, will be found as low as the lowest taking the quality of the stock into consideration. The assortment is very varied and includes all styles, allowing a satisfactory selection to be made with facility. Mr. Illig is a well known resident of Houston, thoroughly familiar with every detail pertaining to the furniture business. The reputation of this old established concern is well appreciated and understood, its methods having been always fair, liberal and honorable.

JOHN H. RUBY,
Abstracts of Title, 1008 Congress Avenue.

There is nothing of more vital importance in real estate operations than the validity of the titles to the property transferred. A piece of property with an imperfect title is depreciated in value, and frequently costs the owner a law suit to remedy the defect. These defects in title, often taken advantage of by unscrupulous persons in making abstracts, frequently result in the entire loss of the property to the owner. Therefore, it becomes apparent at once that those entrusted with the examination of the records and the preparation of abstracts of title should be in possession of complete facilities, and should be men of untarnished reputation, and of the highest character and ability. Thus we are led to speak here of Mr. John H. Ruby, who devotes his energies to the furnishing of abstracts of titles to property owners and others employing his services. This gentleman has had many years' experience, and is possessed of special facilities which eminently qualify him for this work. He has had eleven years actual following of the business here, and is thoroughly familiar with city and county property, and with the history of families who have been the owners of property, and how it has descended from the earliest times; facts not always shown by the records. Mr. Ruby is a lawyer, but devotes his whole time to the abstract business. He is conversant with all land laws, including Spanish and Mexican laws affecting titles to property. As no system of laying out the public lands in Texas was ever adopted, but lands were surveyed and located wherever the holder of a land certificate desired, and in any shape or quantity he required, and he in turn sold parcels of his survey in the same chaotic manner, it is apparent that the abstracter should have a good knowledge of surveying; and it is essential that he should be able to map and plat the field notes of each tract of land; know how to construct maps of surveys, to ascertain all conflicts in surveys, as well as other errors in descriptions. Mr. Ruby is especially fitted in this respect for his business. He possesses a good knowledge of surveying and boundary law, besides being a practical draughtsman. He made a map of the city of Houston which was published in 1890, showing how the old boundary and survey lines cross subsequent subdivisions, the whole map being compiled from the county records. The city of Houston being composed of a great many small subdivisions, the plots of which were made without reference to adjoining property, and many of them mere paper sketches, not having been made from actual survey, made the compiling of these and fitting them together into one, a most intricate and complicated work. About a year ago he constructed a map of Harris county for the county assessor's office from the fieldnotes of each survey, as recorded in the county surveyor's office, showing all the distances, abstract numbers, as well as certificate numbers on railroad surveys, so that the several surveys having the same name could be easily distinguished. This is the first map of the kind ever made, and is regarded as the best and most accurate map ever made of Harris county. This proves Mr. Ruby's ability for the work he has undertaken. He has collected quite a number of old maps of early subdivisions and surveys not of record, besides a great quantity of information outside of the records pertaining to titles; all of which is invaluable to an abstracter. There is probably no man as familiar with the records of the county, and as well qualified to prepare abstracts of title as this gentleman. His office is equipped with all the fixtures and data to turn out abstracts of title in every detail on short notice. We have seen several abstracts prepared by him and found them full and complete in every particular with maps and plots of the property. They were neatly and carefully prepared, and contained all necessary information to pass upon the titles without further investigation. Altogether it is safe to say that work of this character confided to Mr. Ruby's care is certain to be performed in the most satisfactory manner. His reputation for integrity and reliability is beyond criticism, and his careful and conscientious attention to the interest of his patrons consolidate every confidence reposed in him. The utility of an institution such as this to the public is self apparent, and we are pleased to set before our readers the above details in regard to it.

THE EMPIRE TRUST COMPANY,
McPherson, Kansas; Houston Branch, 211 Main Street.

We are by no means stating more than the bare facts when we say, that at the present time, the attention of the outside world is directed towards this city and the coast district of Texas generally. An organization which is doing much to demonstrate what are the possibilities and accomplishments of this favored region is the Empire Trust Company, whose headquarters are at McPherson, Kansas, but who have a branch office here at 211 Main street. The management of this organization is in the hands of gentlemen of wide experience in all that pertains to real estate matters, and they have ample capital and every facility. The branch at Houston was opened for business July, 1893, since when much has been accomplished, and large promise is indicated of a much wider sphere of usefulness. The company transact a general real estate business, but their main energies are devoted to the sale of tracts and lots on properties which present the most favorable field for investment. They have on the market at the present time what is known as the Empire Addition. This is a tract of land forty acres in extent, about a mile and a half from the Court House, and which will soon become one of our most attractive suburbs. The property is sub-divided into choice residential lots, which are offered at very low prices, either for cash or on the popular installment plan and there is no doubt that their value will materially increase within a short time. Houston is rapidly growing and her population is increasing, and suitable building sites are not easily obtainable. The Empire Addition is delightfully situated, perfectly healthful in location and altogether desirable. The streets are graded and the electric street car system will soon connect the suburb with the city. Many lots are already sold and residences contracted for, and it will not be long before the property is filled up with contented and happy owners of their own firesides. Another property the company have now on the market is Raywood, in Liberty county. This is located on the line of the Southern Pacific Railway, forty-nine miles east of Houston. It comprises about 6,000 acres, and a part of it has been laid out to form the city of Raywood and the remainder has been divided up into fruit and farm lands of from 20 to 100 acres. The price of these lands is remarkably low and the farms are sold upon terms to suit the purchaser. We have elsewhere spoken freely regarding the attractions of farm and fruit lands in South Texas, and to go into this subject at length here would be but repetition. However, we will briefly state that Raywood presents opportunities to the homeseeker and settler of the most favorable nature. The soil is rich, well watered and easy of cultivation. The climate is almost perfect, free from the severe cold of Northern winters, while the heat of the summer is tempered by the bracing winds of the Gulf of Mexico. Pure water is obtained in abundance with facility, there are good railroad conveniences and the cities of Galveston and Houston afford favorable markets close at hand. Nor is this all, for already the fruits of Texas are rivalling those of California in Northern localities. All the comforts of a high civilization abound, good schools for the children, and cities not far off from which all supplies may be cheaply obtained. As to the soil, it is almost an ideal one. South Texas is now celebrated for producing the most abundant crop of fine strawberries grown anywhere, and for pears it bears the palm from any district. All vegetables and small fruits grow here; corn, cotton, sugar, etc., are staples; sheep and stock-raising have proved very successful; in fact, in cattle and sheep Texas ranks first of all States. Dairying and poultry raising is carried on with signal success, and rice culture is prosecuted here upon equally as advantageous conditions as in Louisiana and South Carolina. South Texas today stands ready to yield the rich fruits of her soil to all who choose to labor honestly, and who are willing to fulfill their duty to the great Mother Nature. Now is beyond question the time to invest, values are rising, and the country is rapidly filling up. Towns are being set out all over the district, and we predict before ten years are over that the population will be more than doubled. The company organize periodically, excursions from the north, and they will refund the cost of the ticket to all who make a purchase. They have really great inducements to offer, as will be realized upon investigation. They invite enquiries, and will promptly reply to all correspondence. The Houston office of the Empire Trust Company is managed by

Mr. A. C. Wilcox, its president. This gentleman has established his residence here, and become thoroughly identified with the welfare and advancement of the locality. He is assisted in the management by Mr. A. G. Robb who is also a resident of this city. These gentlemen are men of high standing and character, thoroughly conversant with real estate interests here and elsewhere, and they devote their full and constant energies to the business.

H. HENKE & CO.
Wholesale and Retail Dealers in Groceries and Liquors. Corner Congress Avenue and Milam Street.

The above business was established in 1873, by Mr. H. Henke, the senior member of the present firm, which was organized in 1888. Commencing upon a comparatively modest scale, the enterprise under able management has gradually and steadily expanded until it has become a controling influence in the trade. The premises occupied have been constructed specially with reference to their present requirements.

The building is the property of the firm. It is of three floors, is substantially built of brick, and covers an area of 100x100 feet. All facilities required for the rapid and economic transaction of business are here available, including an elevator operated by electricity, a patent cash railroad, etc. The business may be said to be divided into three general departments, viz.: The wholesale, the retail and the manufacturing. The stock includes an unusually fine, full and complete line of staple and fancy groceries, condiments, canned goods, relishes, sauces, wines and liquors, tobacco, both imported and domestic, butter and cheese, baking powder, etc., all of which are offered to the trade and public at lowest market prices. Without doubt this house affords an apt illustration of the possibilities of business in this locality, and it stands today in the very front rank of the city's commerce. Independent of its wholesale trade this establishment is the largest retail grocery house in Texas, transacting by far the largest business. In the wine and liquor departments this firm carry large stocks of choice goods, which they sell strictly on their merits. As wholesale dealers in butter and cheese they are leaders. They enjoy the closest relations with the factories in various parts of the country, where these products are made, and they are enabled to carry large stocks at all times, the connection of the house with Henke's Artesian Ice & Refrigerator Co. affording them enhanced facilities in the way of cold storage. The firm are also manufacturers of "Rex" Baking Powder, a standard and pure article. Messrs. H. Henke & Co. are also cotton factors, and they have storage yards located at the corner of Second and Railroad streets. Here they have a storage capacity for about 1000 bales. They handle annually about 6000 bales of the staple, which is mainly wagon cotton. Referring for a moment to their wholesale business, let us say that in every way they are in a position to cater for trade, and quote the closest prices. Their business extends throughout South Texas, and they are represented on the road by three commercial travelers. About forty-five salesmen, clerks and warehouse men are altogether employed by the house. The members of the firm individually are Messrs. H. Henke and C. G. Pillot. Mr. Henke is also president of Henke's Artesian Ice & Refrigerator Co., and Mr. Pillot is secretary and treasurer. The business they conduct in Houston is alike creditable to themselves and to the Hub City of the Lone Star state.

F. S. GLOVER,
Architect, Main Street.

The building interests of a growing city, such as are reflected by Houston at the present time, are among the most important we have among us, and allied closely to these interests and greatly stimulating them is the work of the architect. This profession is represented here by gentlemen of skill and experience, and among such the attention of our readers is now directed towards Mr. F. S. Glover, who began operations in this city September 15th, 1892. His efforts have met with much success and today he enjoys the full appreciation and confidence of property owners, builders and the public generally. His experience has been thoroughly practical, gleaned from various sections of the country. Mr. Glover is a native Texan, but he has followed his profession not only in this State, but in California and other places. Altogether he has been in active business on his own account for the past eight years. This gentleman is prepared to submit plans for any description of public building, private residence, etc., and to superintend the erection of these structures if desired. He has been the architect of a number of notable erections in various parts of the State, and among the more prominent of these we will instance the Mason Block, of Main street, this city; the Surf Side Hotel, a hotel at Portland, Corpus Christi; Woodville court house, Tyler county; Madisonville court house, Grimes county court house and a large number of business blocks and private residences here and elsewhere. Those interested in real estate matters and building may with confidence bespeak the services of this gentleman in the full assurance that everything will be satisfactorily carried out to completion. He is a thoroughly skillful and conscientious architect, giving to the interests of his clients his especial solicitude and conserving them in every available and legitimate manner.

HOUSTON CORNICE WORKS,
Necco & Eisemann; General Contractors in Sheet Metal Ware, Etc.,
Commerce Avenue.

In this city the Houston Cornice Works takes a foremost position in business circles, and the magnitude and scope of its operations are excelled by but few similar concerns in the Gulf States. The enterprise was originally founded about thirty-five years ago by Martin Curtin, who was succeeded by Ernest Necco in 1887, the present firm being formed about five years ago. The plant consists of a building 65x47 feet in dimensions, which is provided with a full equipment of the latest and best tools and appliances suited to the industry. All raw material is procured from original sources of supply, and every facility is at hand for a high grade of production. The Houston Cornice Works turn out everything in the line of tin, sheet iron and copper ware, also galvanized iron cornices, sky-lights, architectural sheet metal work, slate roofing, etc. They supplied the galvanized iron work for a number of prominent buildings in this city and elsewhere in the State. Of such we will mention the United States Post Office, Gibb's building, First and Fifth Ward schools, Opera House, Sweeney & Coombs' building, Henke's grocery house, Perry Block, Kennedy Block, American Brewing Association building, Houston Ice and Brewing Company's building, etc., all in Houston. Outside of the city they also supplied the work for nearly all Harris county's public buildings, also Court Houses in Jefferson, Montgomery, Brazos, Wharton and Hood counties, the Court House at Lake Charles, La., Medical College State of Texas at Galveston, etc. They do all kinds of guttering, spouting and roofing, and special attention is given to repairing of all kinds. The best of work is only performed; and all details are executed under the supervision of the individual members of the firm, who are Ernest Necco and J. Edward Eisemann. Mr. Necco, as before said, bought out the original firm about five years ago. Previous to that time he had been in the employ of the house about five years, but he has had an active experience of the business extending over twenty-two years. Mr. Eisemann came into the business about three years ago, and he also is a practical man of long and extended experience. Both gentlemen are well-known residents, highly respected in the community. Mr. Necco is Chancellor Commander Phœnix Lodge Knights of Pythias, President Protection Fire Company No. 1, which was organized fifty years ago, and which is the oldest fire company in the State of Texas. He is also a member of some other secret organizations. Mr. Eisemann is likewise a member of a number of societies of the above character.

F. GIESEKE & SON.
Dealers in Fine Boots and Shoes. 505½ Main Street.

This enterprise is among the oldest established retail houses here, it having been founded by Mr. F. Gieseke about thirty-six years ago. His son, Mr. H. H. Gieseke, was admitted as a partner March 1st, 1892, and the title of the house was then changed to F. Gieseke & Son. The premises occupied consist of a two story brick building, 50x 100 feet, which is the property of the senior member of the firm. The stock here carried consists of a full line of boots and shoes for ladies,' gentlemen's, and child-

ren's wear, which is of admirable selection, filling all requirements of good quality, style, fit and workmanship. The goods are obtained direct from the makers, and are offered to the public at bottom prices. All sizes, widths and qualities are handled, making it an easy task to here obtain suitable selections. Mr. F. Gieseke, the senior member, is a well known resident and a prominent real estate owner, identified with the progress and development of the city. Both himself and his son are well known and esteemed business men. The house is the oldest shoe concern in the city, and the reputation it enjoys today is fully in keeping with its old time record and character for fair dealing, enterprise and honorable methods of doing business.

☞On March 1st, Messrs. Gieseke & Son transferred their enterprise to Messrs. De Meritt, Matthews & Co., who will continue the business. Mr. H. H. Gieseke, junior member of the old firm, remaining with the new concern. Mr. F. Gieseke desires to thank his old patrons, and recommends the new house to their favor and patronage.

STUART & ADAMS.
Southern Dental Depot. Dental Supplies, 405 Main Street.

The Houston branch of the above well known house, whose headquarters are located at New Orleans, has been in successful operation here for the past six years, and is conducted under the efficient management of Mr. Frank S. Pendleton. The establishment serves as the basis of supply for a wide range of territory, supplying to dentists everything they may require in the way of apparatus and materials for the successful conduct of their business. Even the furniture required in fitting up an office can be obtained from this house. The firm, by reason of their facilities, are enabled to place at the disposal of the profession the very best, most modern and latest improved instruments and tools, which they sell at lowest manufacturers' prices. The range of goods is very diffuse and complete, nothing being omitted that could possibly be of use in the practice of dentistry. They also make specialties of tooth powders, soaps, washes, brushes, etc, and specialties for the mouth highly recommended by leading dentists. In a word, this establishment will be found to be fully up to the times, affording the profession every facility and advantage. The firm of Stuart & Adams is individually made up of Messrs. W. H. Stuart and Chas. A. Adams, both gentlemen of great experience, thoroughly alive to the requirements of their trade, Mr. Frank S. Pendleton, the manager here, has been in charge since the opening of the branch house, and he was also in a similar business in Virginia before being connected with this firm. This enterprise again emphasizes our claim that Houston is the most favorable source of supply in Texas, and that in all facilities and conveniences it is the real metropolis of the state.

I. C. STAFFORD.
Real Estate. 1004½ Preston Avenue.

Today the city of Houston, and continguous territory all around, present advantages for investment and occupation second to no section ef the United States. This fact is fully demonstrated in the great increase of population, which has been characteristic of the locality within the past few years, and in the expansion of manufacturing, commercial and farming pursuits. Contributing to this gratifying state of affairs must be taken into consideration the efforts and accomplishments of the real estate men of this city, and among them, entitled to notice at our hands, is the real estate agency of Mr. I. C. Stafford, who began operations here in 1889. The house transacts a general real estate business, devoting its energies to all details connected with the profession. Mr. Stafford takes the entire care of property into his charge for non-resident investors, collecting rents, paying taxes, remitting revenues, etc. He has on his books a large list of desirable city and suburban properties, farm and fruit lands, which he offers to the public at low prices, and upon favorable terms. Mr. Stafford is part owner of the town of Letitia, which station is about twenty miles from this city, on the M. K. & T. R. R. The town is being rapidly settled, and has a railroad depot, stores, school house and other urban conveniences. The property is divided up into suitable farm and fruit lands, and it has proved in every way remunerative to all who have taken up their home upon it. Around Letitia have been settled in the past twenty-five or thirty years, a number of German farmers, who have been very successful in the cultivation of the land. Nearly all kinds of agricultural products can be grown on this property, and over three hundred bales of cotton were raised during the past season. Mr. I. C. Stafford is also part owner of Cane Island Station, on the M. K. & T. R. R., about thirty miles from Houston. This is also very advantageously situated. Mr. Stafford invites correspondence, and will be glad to communicate with all who are homeseekers, or who are on the search for means of profitable investment. Mr. Stafford has been a resident here for forty-six years, and he refers to any bank in the city. The standing of the house is of the highest, and all business transactions are carried out with integrity and honor, and will redound to the advantages of all concerned.

GUS W. TIPS, Jr.,
Harness, Saddles, Etc., 907 Congress Avenue.

The above enterprise has been familiar to our residents for over a quarter of century, its original inception transpiring in 1866 when it was founded by Mr. G. H. Tips, the father of the present proprietor. In 1885 Mr. Walter Tips acquired possession of the business, and finally in 1891, Mr. G. W. Tips assumed the ownership. For carrying on the business a two story building of 25x50 feet is utilized, and here all conveniences are available. Mr. Tips manufactures and sells saddles, harness, collars, brushes, combs, whips, bridles, halters, saddlery hardware, etc., and indeed everything needed by horsemen for horses. All goods not of his own make are obtained from the most reliable houses and the goods manufactured on the premises may be depended on for quality and first-class workmanship. The saddles and harness made here are the peers of any made in the state, while at the same time, the prices will be found to be altogether moderate. Repairing is also made a specialty of, and is promptly and efficiently performed. Mr. G. W. Tips is a practical workman with an experience of twenty years. Everything connected with the trade is entirely familiar to him. The public when requiring anything in his line will do well to bear him in mind, and they will ultimately realize the advantages of a profitable and satisfactory business connection.

G. W, HEYER,
Druggist, Masonic Temple.

This enterprise was instituted in 1888 by its present proprietor, and it is probably the most elegant appointed and furnished drug store in the state. The entire fittings are of unique and original design, specially made to order, while every line of the woodwork is of beauty and symmetry. The show cases, counters and shelving all match so as to form a harmonious whole, peculiarly handsome and striking. Mr. Heyer carries a full and complete stock of drugs, medicines, pharmaceutical preparations, physicians' supplies, etc., and an unusually fine line of toilet articles, perfumery, fancy goods, etc. The prescription department is a specialty, and it is conducted with a due appreciation of its responsibilities, and only pure and high class drugs are used. Mr. Heyer is a skilled pharmacist, entirely conversant with all connected with his profession, which within late years has been elevated to a much more dignified position than heretofore, and the above named establishment is conducted upon a policy in full sympathy with this advancement.

PAUL FLOECK.

Union Steam Bakery, Confectioner and Grocer.   1210 and 1212 Congress Avenue.

Among the most useful vocations followed at the present time in Houston. is that carried on by Mr. Paul Floeck, who in 1889 succeeded the firm of G. W. Floeck & Bro., established in 1886, and in which he was a partner. His enterprise has achieved a high place in the favor of the public in view of the standard high quality of the products, and for its fair dealing methods of doing business. The store at the above address is of two floors, and is 40x70 feet in dimensions. In the rear is the bakery covering an area of 30x40 feet. The latter is furnished with all required modern devices of merit and utility, conducing to cleanliness and superiority in the products, and they are operated by an eight horse power engine and boiler. Mr. Floeck is a confectioner and grocer, handling a full stock of staple and fancy groceries, canned goods, also candies, confectionery and fancy cakes. His specialty is steam bread made by an improved process, which is warranted of the best and purest ingredients, untouched by hand in the details of mixing. This bread has received the unqualified endorsement of hundreds of Houston's citizens. Mr. Floeck is a practical man, and he personally supervises the operations of his establishment. In his dealings he will be found prompt, honorable and enterprising, and his business is a growing and prosperous one, enjoying the confidence and consideration of a wide circle of custom, and it is no doubt bound to largely expand in the future, and become one of the leading enterprises of the city.

HOUSTON MANUFACTURING JEWELRY COMPANY,

Office and Factory, 317½ Main Street.

Among the latest acquisitions to the city of Houston is the enterprise of the Houston Manufacturing Jewelry Company, which began operations February 15, 1894. The office and factory are located at the above address, and the latter is provided with all facilities in the way of improved tools and appliances, and employment is here given to a number of highly skilled and experienced workmen. The energies of the house are devoted to the making of jewelry for the trade. Anything in the line of diamond and precious stone mounting, ring making, medallions and medals for society purposes or presentations, pins, studs, brooches, ear-rings, etc. can be here produced in perfection, and at moderate prices. The company also execute engraving of all kinds and fine watch repairing for the trade. The industry is a new one in this section and it is of great value to the trade, inasmuch that jewelers throughout this locality are enabled to have their goods made up on the ground, and they thus avoid the otherwise inevitable delays and annoyance of having the work done at places far distant from this center. This fact, we hope, will be appreciated by the trade, and that they will accord their patronage to this new Southern industry, which can fill all their requirements in a manner in every way satisfactory. The manager, Mr. Jack Warfel, is a gentleman who has a thorough practical experience of the business, and he exercises his close and constant supervision over all its details so as to insure as near perfection in the products as is permitted to the work of human hands. We appeal to our readers who are interested to aid the enterprise as far as in their power, by sending it a trial order, and we are assured that this will be the forerunner of continued and permanent business relations.

FRED HOLCOMB,
Jeweller and Watchmaker, 711 Preston Avenue.

The business of the above named house was instituted in 1891, and since then it has become one of the most reliable and favorite in the estimation of the public of Houston. Mr. Fred Holcomb, the proprietor, is a gentleman of large experience in all pertaining to the business he conducts. He has been twelve years connected with the trade. He is originally from Kansas, and was a student of the Chicago Horological Institute, where practical watch-making is thoroughly and efficiently taught. At the above address his store is located and here he carries a stock of watches and jewelry of the best selection, which are offered to the public at lowest prices. Mr. Holcomb makes a specialty of fine watch and jewelry repairing, which work is executed promptly and thoroughly. As eminently a practical and skillful workman, this gentleman is entirely qualified for this business, and the most delicate and intricate time-piece or family jewel may be entrusted to his care with full confidence that it will be returned to the owner as perfect and complete as the day when it left the factory. Another specialty is spectacles and eye-glasses, which are skillfully fitted and adapted to all eyesights. A nice stock of diamonds and precious stones is carried, which are sold strictly as represented and may be depended upon for quality. The house bears the best of reputations for fair dealing and integrity, and all transactions with it will result in the complete satisfaction of its customers and patrons.

W. J. HANCOCK, JR.,
Books and Stationery, 1203 Congress Avenue.

An enterprise which enjoys largely the favor and patronage of the public is the book and stationery business conducted under the proprietorship of Mr. W. J. Hancock, Jr., and established by him here in the year 1879. The premises occupied consist of a three-story brick building of 25x90 feet, which serves as headquarters for the business. Here is contained full lines of standard and school books, office supplies, commercial stationery, etc., and the specialty of the house is essentially fine goods, catering to the best class of trade in the city. Particular attention is given to fine society stationery, visiting cards, etc. A fine line of wedding and birth-day gifts is also to be found here, comprising many beautiful and *recherche* articles not to be obtained at other establishments. Altogether, here the public may procure wares of the character above enumerated equal in quality to any to be found in the best stores in large metropolitan centers. Mr. W. J. Hancock, Jr., is thoroughly experienced in all pertaining to his business, in which he evidences a proficient taste and discernment which has gained for him the appreciaton of his patrons. He is a well known and popular resident of this city, and is the president of the organization known as the Houston Lyceum. The enterprise he conducts may be cited as among the more refined of the commercial pursuits of this city, and in its character furnishes evidence of Houston's progress and advancement in cultured civilization and good taste.

D. G. ROSENFIELD,
Commission Mecchant and Wholesale Dealer in Candies, Foreign and Domestic Fruits, Etc., 912 Franklin Avenue.

The commission and fruit trade is assuredly one of the greatest factors of the wholesale business of this city and locality, and it has greatly advanced within recent years, keeping pace with Houston's great development and increased population. One of the oldest established houses in the trade here is that conducted by Mr. D. G. Rosenfield, who commenced business in the year 1868. This gentleman occupies at the above address a large four-story brick building 40x125 feet in area, besides a warehouse in the rear. These afford the very best of facilities for carrying at all times a very large stock of goods. The energies of the house comprise the handling of fruits and produce, both foreign and domestic, candies, nuts, etc., both on commission and otherwise. In the season the delicate and delicious products of this and neighboring localities find an easy market through the efforts of this concern, and foreign fruits of all kinds are consigned to the house and are received direct from the nearest ports of entry. Consignments of saleable goods are invited in any quantity, and quick sales and prompt returns are sure to be realized. Dealers both in this section and out of town will always find the choicest products of the market at this establishment, and prompt attention and the immediate filling of orders may be depended upon. Goods are invariably obtained direct from producers and manufacturers, and in every thing relating to the commission, candy and fruit trade the house is prepared to transact business after the most approved modern methods. Mr. D. G. Rosenfield, the proprietor, is thoroughly experienced by a long pursuit of the business to understand critically every detail connected with it. He is one of our best known residents, both in business and social circles. He is a member of the Masonic Fraternity, also of the Odd Fellows, Knights of Pythias, Knights of Honor, I. O. B. B., Chosen Friends, Turn Verein, etc., and he has held official positions in many of them. The prominence obtained by this house is such as is accorded only those whose operations have always been characterized by a straightforward system of fair dealing and energetic management.

DUNLAY & GEISLER,
Wholesale and Retail Dealers in Hardware, Sportmen's Goods, Etc., 410 and 412 Travis Street.

As an exemplification of the varied character of the city's commercial undertakings, the above house is entitled to prominent recognition at our hands. The business was founded in 1879 as Comminge & Geisler, the present firm assuming control in 1889. The premises utilized for the business comprise a building of 50x125 feet, where a very large and comprehensive stock of goods is carried, needing the services of fifteen assistants for its care and sale. The firm are wholesale and retail dealers in hardware of all descriptions, also guns, pistols, rifles, fishing tackle and sportmen's goods generally. In the hardware department, which occupies one-half of the establishment, they handle a full and complete line, and in sporting goods the assortment is really a remarkable one, being undoubtedly one of the most complete of its kind in the State of Texas. It includes all the popular and approved makes of fire arms, the best character of sporting guns, such as hammerless guns, shot-guns, etc. The same may be said of the stock of fishing tackle, artificial bait and other needs for those who seek healthful recreation in our woods and forests and along the banks of our bayous and rivers, and on our bays and affluents of the ocean. In a word, it is safe to say that the advantages here placed at the disposal of the trade and public in the above lines are such as are only to be obtained in the largest metropolitan centers. Another department of the house is that of stoves, the firm handling the celebrated Garland and Bellville cook stoves, and they are also agents for the New Home sewing machines and the unrivalled Parker Bros.' shot guns. All goods handled here are indeed of selected quality and are sold at lowest prices. A special department is the repair shop, where all repairs on guns, pistols, sewing machines, locks, etc., are promptly executed at reasonable rates. The members of the firm individually are J. S. Dunlay and A. H. Geisler, both of whom possess a thorough knowledge of the business and its details. The above enterprise may be said to have done its full share toward extending the reputation of the city as a favorable purchasing point, and today Houston can justly claim to be substantially the "Hub" and metropolis of the State of Texas.

B. A. RIESNER.
Manufacturer of and Dealer in Carriages, Wagons, Etc. 813, 815, 817 and 819 Commerce Avenue.

The above named gentleman inaugurated his business here about nineteen years ago. Until 1884 the enterprise was carried on at Preston avenue, but at that time was removed to the present commodious quarters. The plant comprises a three story ironclad brick building, 50x100 feet in dimensions, a single story brick building, 55x100 feet, and other minor conveniences. The entire plant covers five city lots, and is the property of Mr. Riesner. All required facilities are available equally for manufacturing and for the storage of a large stock of goods. The house manufactures and sells carriages, phætons, spring wagons, drays, log wagons, carry-logs, etc., some of which are of its own manufacture, and others are procured from the most reliable makers in the country. Among specialties handled here are the celebrated Milburn wagons, also the Hickman wagons. Repairing in all its branches is a particular and popular department, and this work is well done at the shortest notice on satisfactory terms. Mr. Riesner also deals in oak, hickory and ash lumber, which is sawed to shape as desired. Another specialty is corrugated iron awnings, iron and steel work for bridges and buildings, iron fencing, etc. He enjoys the very best of facilities for supplying this class of work, and as an instance of the appreciation bestowed on him in this line, we will mention that he supplied the architectural iron work for the First Ward school, Mason building, W. N. Shaw building and many others. The business of the house entails the services of from eighteen to twenty-six workmen and assistants, who are all supervised directly by the proprietor, who is himself a thoroughly experienced and practical man. Mr. Riesner is a director and vice president of the Mutual Building & Loan Association, is a director of the Texas Real Estate & Investment Association, also of the American Brewing Association. He is a member of the city council and chairman of the finance committee. He is also director and charter member of Simpson, Hartwell and Stopple Machine Works, and is interested in the Houston Ice & Brewing Co. He is a member of the Knights of Pythias and other societies. He has always taken a keen and active interest in all relating to the welfare and advancement of the city in which he lives and works, and has always enjoyed the respect and confidence of all having dealings with him.

R. D. STEELE,
Architect, 305½ Main Street.

The vocation of the architect has always been an essential and honorable profession. The Tower of Babel must have been built from plans of some sort, however crude, and of the work of the ancient Egyptians, Greeks and Romans are found the fragments which have come down to us. Today in America our architecture falls little, if any, behind that of Europe, and in this city the profession is represented by Mr. R. D. Steele, who inaugurated his enterprise October, 1893. This gentleman, with every experience and technical knowledge, is prepared to submit plans and furnish estimates for the erection of public buildings, business houses, churches, private residences, etc., and also to oversee all details of the work to completion. Mr. Steele began his career as an architect at Velasco, Texas, where he was associated with Mr. Glover. He came to this city July, 1892, and for a period was in the employ of J. A. Tempest, G. E. Dickey and F. S. Glover & Co. He has acquired his experience in the best practical schools and is in every way competent. His prospects are very encouraging and all who entrust their interests to his care may do so with the utmost confidence. He is a skilful draughtsman and is painstaking in the smallest detail connected with his business. It is safe, therefore, to predict for him a wide field of usefulness in the near future, and all interested will do well to investigate his capabilities when requiring the services of a gentleman of the vocation to which he has devoted his energies. Mr. Steele is now preparing the plans for the new office building to be erected by the Houston Co-operative Building Association.

T. WALTER BLAKE,
Dealer in Groceries, Feed, Etc., 1001 and 1003 Main Street.

The most casual observer of Houston's progress may see on every hand unmistakable signs of its expansion and advancement. This fact is particularly noticeable in the increase of the retail establishments here, also in the improved character and facilities of leading houses which make up its best class of trade. Among such should be noticed the enterprise of Mr. T. Walter Blake, who established his present business about three years ago. He now occupies, at the above address, a large double store and basement, which is fifty feet square. He has recently enlarged his premises to accommodate his growing business. This is now the only grocery house on Main street, and it is particularly well located, being in a neighborhood which is destined to become the leading retail section of our main thoroughfare. The stock carried comprises a full supply of everything in the way of staple and fancy groceries, a specialty being made of fine goods for first-class family trade. He also handles corn, bran, oats, hay and fodder, and in all departments his facilities are such that he is enabled to supply the public with the choicest goods at lowest prices. Mr. Blake is a native Houstonian and a well known citizen. He was formerly engaged in business as a wholesale and retail butter and egg dealer, and later was connected with the press in this city. Today his energies are devoted to the building up of a permanent business which shall rank as superior in every way equally in the character of the products as in the courtesy and honorable methods of trading which shall induce the steady patronage of the public. That he has succeeded in so doing is apparent in the growth and prosperity of his undertaking, which is destined to take a leading place among the mercantile enterprises of the city of Houston.

HUDSON & FLEISHEL,
Dealers in Furniture and House Furnishing Goods, 1219 Preston Avenue.

The furniture business of this city has received a valuable accession in the institution of the above house, which, originally established at Tyler, Texas, three years ago by Mr. E. A. Hudson, commenced operations here September, 1893, under the title of Hudson & Fleishel. The firm occupy premises at the above address which comprise a two-story brick building of 40x60 feet, where they carry in stock a full line of furniture, from the cheapest grade to the best, carpets of all makes and textures, curtains, stoves, toilet sets, house furnishing goods in large variety, etc. The stock in every department will be found to be ample, full and complete, suitable to the requirements of all, and placed at the disposal of the public at such prices as cannot fail to command universal appreciation. The object of the firm in establishing their business here, is to supply the residents of Houston and vicinity with goods of reliable quality, under such conditions as shall induce a permanent business connection with the house. Not only to gain trade, but to hold it against all competition, is the business policy of the house, contenting themselves with small profits on large sales, rather than large profits on a restricted business. Goods are sold for cash or on the popular installment plan, in accordance with terms and arrangements to suit their customers. The headquarters of the house are at Tyler, where it is known as the Tyler Installment Company, and Mr. E. A. Hudson has had a wide experience of the furniture business. His partner, Mr. J. P. Fleishel, also is familiar with the trade, and both give their undivided attention to their industry. They are young and enterprising business men, determined to succeed by modern, upright and honorable means.

C. BENDER & SONS.

Manufacturers, Wholesale and Retail Dealers in Lumber, Sash, Blinds, Mouldings, Etc. Corner Willow and Baker Streets.

The above named organization stands prominent among the lumber manufacturing enterprises of the South. The business was established here in 1890, but previous to that period the firm operated mills along the line of the I. N. & G. N. and E. & W. T. railroads, The firm's possessions at the present time are extensive and valuable, and are of such an importance as to place the concern in a leading position in the trade. In this city they have a plant covering two blocks, occupying an area of 250x500 feet. On this is constructed a planing mill, 80x100 feet in dimensions, boiler house and other buildings. The machinery and equipment herein contained embody the latest improvements of the day, in the way of wood-working machines, and includes sixteen planing machines, and many other superior appliances. The motive power is obtained from a fifty horse power engine, and a seventy horse power boiler. The firm have also a saw mill about seventeen miles from here, at a place called Humble. Here they have a capacity for the manufacture of 60,000 feet of lumber daily. They also have a mill at Holohausen, which has a capacity of 40,000 daily. At this point they have a complete plant, including a planing mill, dry kiln, etc. The establishment which they operate in this city is

MR. CHAS. BENDER.

well located on the line of the I. & G. N. R. R., placing it into direct connection with the railroad system here, and enabling the product to be received and shipped with the greatest facility. The firm utilize at this mill about a half million feet of lumber monthly. Including all their plants, they give employment to about two hundred workmen and laborers. An advantage enjoyed by this firm, is that not only are their timber lands owned by them, but that most of the lumber handled is manufactured at their own mills. They use mostly Southern pine, and manufacture and sell rough and dressed lumber, sash, blinds, mouldings, shingles, and a general line of mill work. The trade of the house is both wholesale and retail, and in addition to their local patronage, they make extensive shipments throughout Texas, Kansas, Nebraska, Missouri, etc. They are prepared to quote close prices for carload lots of the staple. The individual members of the firm are Chas. Bender, and his sons, Chas. Bender, Jr. Albert Bender, Eugene Bender and Frank Bender. The senior partner has been identified with the lumber business for the past twenty years, and every detail connected with it is familiar to him. His sons have grown up with the enterprise, and have been admitted to a share as soon as they reached a suitable age. Mr. Chas. Bender, Sr., and his son Eugene reside at Holshausen, Mr. Chas. Bender, Jr. is a resident of this city, and Messrs. Albert and Frank Bender live at Humble. The business is conducted upon a policy which entitles it to the fullest confidence of all who may be brought into contact with it.

HOUSTON PANTS COMPANY,
Merchant Tailors.   Office and Factory, Congress Ave. and Travis St.

An enterprise comparatively new to Houston, but which has at once demonstrated its usefulness and enterprising character is that known as the Houston Pants Company. Established November, 1893, already is the concern well known throughout this and neighboring localities, and the business is steadily extending its scope of usefulness.   The Houston Pants Co. makes a specialty of supplying the public with

fashionable and choice custom made clothing at lowest prices, finding rather its emolument in extensive sales, than in large profits. Goods are made and sold for cash only, so that customers who are honest and pay their debts have no increased charges to pay to compensate for losses incurred from others, who are in the habit of "beating the tailor." Every description of gentlemen's attire can be found here. Full suits are made from $25 upwards, and trousers from $5 upwards. The company carry in stock a large assortment of foreign and domestic materials from which suitable selections are easily made. Everything is first class, including the cloth, trimmings, style, fit and workmanship, and it must not be imagined because the prices are low, that the goods are inferior, the reverse is the case; the main difference being merely that of much lower prices. All goods are made on the premises by skilled custom workers under the direct supervision of Messrs. Teall Bros., the proprietors, who individually are H. N. Teall and W. E. Teall. Both of these gentlemen have a life-long experience of the business, their father before them having been in the tailoring business. The house is eminently a progressive and modern one with every inducement at hand to offer its patrons.

THE BERING MANUFACTURING COMPANY,
Manufacturers of Sash, Doors, Blinds, Rough and Dressed Lumber, Etc.. German Street, near Texas Western R. R. Depot,

Among enterprises of the kind in Houston, the business of The Bering Manufacturing Company is perhaps the most extensive, employing the largest number of work people. It was incorporated in 1891, with a capital stock of $40,000. The plant at the above indicated location covers an area of four city blocks, and the buildings comprise the machinery department a two-story structure 70x150 feet in dimensions; and the carpenter department, a building of two floors 70x130 feet: a two-story warehouse shed of 30x110 feet; a single story store room 30x70 feet; an iron covered boiler house 30x50 feet; an office building, a. shaving honse 18x24 feet, besides lumber sheds, etc. The works are equipped with all of the latest improved wood-working machinery, operated by a powerful Corliss engine and a boiler each of 250 horse power. The force of hands here employed exceed one hundred, many of whom are skilled mechanics. Everything in the way of cypress doors, sash and blinds, frames, rough and dressed, tongued and grooved lumber, exterior and interior finish, brackets, mantels, scroll and band sawing, all kinds of turning, and all other planing mill work is executed to order, and a large stock of goods is also always on hand. Every facility is enjoyed for turning out work promptly and in the best manner. From this house the builder may obtain all his requirements in the way of wood work, and the company carry full supplies of builders' hardware, nails, glass, etc. Of the latter they use about a carload monthly. Their trade is largely in this city, and shipments are also made to various sections of the State. The executive officers of the company are Courad Bering, president; F. C. Bering, secretary and treasurer; A. Teichman, manager and A. C. Bering, assistant manager. These gentlemen are all, so to speak, practical men, having been brought up to the business.

HENRY L. HUBELE,

Dealer in Hardware, Agricultural Implements, Etc., 711 Preston Avenue.

The oft quoted expression "from a needle to an anchor," is scarcely an exaggeration when applied to the stock carried at the establishment of Mr. Henry L. Hubele, whose business was originally founded in 1889, as Schmidt & Hubele, the present proprietor assuming the sole control in 1892. The premises occupied are of three floors, the lower part being 25x75 feet in area, and the second and third floors are 50x75 feet in dimensions. This structure is the property of Mr. Hubele, and the whole of it is utilized for the carrying of the stock, which embraces all kinds of shelf and general hardware, builders' hardware, cutlery, mechanics' and machinists' tools, agricultural implements, stoves, tinware, glassware, and a thousand and one other articles that are in daily request by the builder, the house-keeper, the mechanic and the agriculturalist. Among specialties handled by the house we note the following: Bradley's Disc Cultivators, McCormick's Mowing Machinery, Iron King and Cotton King Cook Stoves, etc. The house has the exclusive agency for these goods here. Mr. Henry L. Hubele is a Houston man, born on the very spot where his building now stands. He has seen the growth of the city and its expansion from but little more than a village to the proud position it now occupies as the metropolis of Texas. He has had thirteen years experience of the hardware business, the details of which are thoroughly familar to him.

MISSOURI, KANSAS & TEXAS RAILWAY COMPANY,

City Office, 204 Main Street.

A new era may be said to have commenced for Houston in May, 1893, for in that month and year the Missouri, Kansas & Texas Railway Company commenced running passenger trains into the city, along their own line and into their new railway station, a very handsome structure erected at an expense of $15,000. This great acquisition to the transportation facilities of the city has opened up a wide expanse of new territory in the State of Texas, and at the same time it gives a new and direct trunk line between Houston and Kansas City, Hannibal, St. Louis, Chicago and the great Northwest. The road has about 2,200 miles of track. The main line from Houston to Hannibal is about 1,000 miles long. The branches are as follows: Hillsboro to Denison, by way of Dallas; Henrietta to Whitesboro; San Marcos to Smithville; Trinity to Colmesneil; Parsons to Kansas City; Parsons to Junction City; Denison to Sherman; Greenville to Mineola; Parsons to Coffeeville; Atoka to Lehigh, where is located the great coal mines of Indian Territory; and Echo to Belton. A new branch line will be in operation on April 1st. This extends from New Franklin, Mo. to St. Louis, a distance of 168 miles. The M., K. & T., or "Katy" as it is familiarly and affectionately designated, is the only railway which runs from Houston to St. Louis, Kansas City and Hannibal the whole way upon its own rail. The road is doing much to open up a new and rich country in this State and Indian Territory. It touches every important town in Texas, and connects with all lines in the State, besides all other diverging roads at Kansas City and St. Louis. The "Katy" was the first road to cross the Indian Territory. The equipment of the road is thoroughly first-class in all its details. It is provided with steel rails and rock ballast throughout. Its service includes the operation of Wagner Sleeping Cars and the American Express system. Every day in the year a through sleeper is run to St. Louis, Kansas City and Chicago, and free reclining chairs are provided all passengers on this and other trains. The M., K. & T. handle and transport immense quantities of freight, and they probably handle more live stock than any other road in the country having the same mileage. The executive officers of the company are Henry C. Rouse, New York, president; Thos. C. Purdy, St. Louis, vice-president and general manager; D. Miller, St. Louis, traffic manager; Jas. Barker, St. Louis, general passenger and ticket agent of the system; W. G. Crush, Denison, Texas, general passenger and ticket agent, lines in Texas. The city passenger and ticket agent, Houston, is Mr. R. B. Courtney, E. B. Connell is assistant passenger agent; W. D. Lawson, traveling passenger agent; R. S. Fife, commercial agent, and J. G. Lindsey, contracting agent.

F. J. TRAPP,
Watches, Jewelry, Etc., 1006 Preston Avenue.

Among those departments of business in Houston which may be classed as of an artistic nature, is unquestionably that of the jeweler, and identified with the trade here is the enterprise of Mr. F. J. Trapp, which dates it establishment from the year 1882, since when it has gained the full confidence of the public. Mr. Trapp carries in stock a well selected assortment of watches, clocks, jewelry, etc. which are of fine quality, and which are placed at the disposal of the public at such prices as invite appreciation. A fully assorted variety is handled, enabling a suitable choice to be made with facility. A specialty is made of diamonds, many choice and beautiful gems being here at the diposal of patrons. Another specialty is eye glasses, spectacles, etc., every kind being handled to suit all sights. Particular attention is devoted to fine watch and jewelry repairing, which is promptly executed to satisfaction. Mr. Trapp comes to Houston from California, where he had previously carried on a similar business. He has been connected with the watch and jewelry trade since 1856, all branches of which are quite familiar to him. The public will do well to inspect his stock and prices when contemplating the purchase of anything in this line.

E. K. DILLINGHAM,
Cornice and Sheet Metal Works, corner Fifth and Washington Streets.

A manufacturing enterprise of great utility to the growing needs of Houston. and one which bids fair to become one of the leading industries of the city, is that established by Mr. E. K. Dillingham on June 8th, 1893. Starting with a small though flourishing business, purchased from Messrs. J. R. Morris' Sons, Mr. Dillingham, by strict attention to work and constant watchfulness of the needs of the trade, so increased the business that his old quarters in the basement of the Hutchins House became too small to meet the growing demands made on them and new and larger quarters became a necessity. After some trouble these were secured, and the removal to the handsome and convenient shop now occupied by Mr. Dillingham may be said to have stamped the enterprise as a firmly established industry of the city. The building now occupied is located on the corner of Fifth and Washington streets, just across the street from the freight depot of the H. & T. C. Ry. and directly on the tracks of that road. It is built of pressed steel brick, covers an area of 50x100 feet and is well lighted by numerous windows and a large skylight, while gas and water are provided for. It was erected for Mr. Dillingham after plans drawn by Mr. E. T. Heiner with special reference to the needs of the work in hand, and is in all respects a model of convenience and utility. From fifteen to twenty-five men are employed in the works, the number varying with the season and the exigencies of the business. The articles manufactured consist of galvanized iron and copper cornices, ridge mouldings, finials, metal shingles, eave troughs, ventilated flues and all kinds of sheet metal work. One branch of the business which is rapidly growing and which daily requires and receives more attention is the manufacture of galvanized corrugated iron cisterns and windmill tanks (Harry's Pat.), which, though comparatively new in South Texas, are extensively used in the northern part of the State. Mr. Dillingham has recently purchased and will at once put into operation special machinery for the manufacture of round beaded eave troughs in ten-feet sections and conductor pipe in same lengths without cross-seam. Though these goods are made extensively all through Ohio, Illinois, Pennsylvania and the East, Mr. Dillingham is the first to undertake their manufacture in Texas. The advantages of these gutters and pipes when compared with the old style made in short lengths, with numerous joints are apparent, and they will no doubt have a ready and growing sale all over the state. Besides the manufacturing business to which attention has been called, Mr. Dillingham is a large contractor for all kinds of roofing and cornice work. Among the buildings in Houston for which he has furnished this kind of work are the Kiam, Mason, Sweeney & Jemison, Scanlan, Shaw and Jones buildings. Other work turned out by this firm are metal frame skylights, corrugated iron awnings with self-supporting iron brackets, shaving and sawdust blowpipes, smoke stacks, breeching for steam boilers, oil drums, etc. In all departments the facilities of the house are of the very best, enabling high class work to be turned out at the very lowest prices. Estimates on work in any of the above mentioned lines are promptly furnished, and contracts satisfactorily fulfilled. The firm solicits an initial order in the first place, and is confident that this will result in a permanent business connection. This volume being illustrative of the industries and advancement of Houston, and at the same time pointing out the most favorable sources of supply, to residents here and in the neighborhood, it is right for us to indicate to our readers the above named house as one where terms and inducements are offered, difficult to duplicate and more difficult still to surpass.

THE CITY OF ALVIN.

Alvin, the center of a fruit-raising, market-gardening and agricultural country, which has no superior in the United States, is located at the junction of, the main line with the Houston branch of the Santa Fe Railroad. It is distant twenty-four miles from Houston, twenty-nine miles from Galveston and thirty miles from Velasco. The town proper contains about 400 acres, sub-divided into town lots, and within the corporate limits were 1,280 acres, now reduced to 640 acres. These are allotted into farm and fruit lands of ten and twenty acres in dimensions. Mr. L. M. Disney and Major G. W. Durant were the original owners of the land upon which the town of Alvin now stands. Since that time the property has passed into the hands of numerous persons, made up largely of actual settlers. Mr. Disney still retains a large acreage, which is offered to settlers and the public at fair prices and on terms to suit. It has become generally known that this locality offers the most favorable inducements to those who are seeking a home location, where with faithful labor and honest industry they may speedily acquire a competence. For fruit farming and vegetable growing Alvin and vicinity cannot be excelled, while for general farming and stock-raising equal facilities are available. A conversation which the writer had with Major Geo. W. Durant, one of the original owners of the tract, illustrates the capabilities of the country in a significant and forcible manner. This gentleman has a farm in Alvin of 183 acres, 165 of which are under cultivation. He has been settled in this locality very many years, having come here about forty-four years ago. He has been in possession of his present farm for about two years. He says: "Any man that comes here and is willing to work is certain to do well. I will give you some idea of what are the average yield and value of the different crops which can be raised from this soil. Pears are very profitable, and until they become sufficiently matured vegetables can be raised on the same land, which not only will pay expenses, but will yield a handsome profit. A six or seven years' old pear tree will yield eight bushels to the tree, and about a hundred trees is a fair number to the acre. This would make 800 bushels to the acre, and say that but the extraordinary low price of fifty cents per bushel was realized, this would give $400 to the acre. But it is not unusual that pears bring as high as $2 per bushel in this section. A man can easily make from $300 to $500 net per acre in strawberries, if he knows his business. Peaches, with 180 trees to the acre, will realize about $800 to that area. All kinds of vegetables do well. Two crops of cabbages can be raised regularly, and each crop, well attended and taken care of, will yield $250 to the acre, which is $500 for the season. Irish potatoes are successful. An average crop, well looked after and properly fertilized, yields 250 bushels to the acre. Garden peas yield about $150 to the acre. German wax beans, if they come on in season, produce $120 to the acre. Peas and beans are early and they can be followed by other crops. Sweet potatoes are a good crop for a new settler. Land in good condition here will produce from one to two hun-

dred bushels to the acre. A crop of last season on twenty acres averaged
219 bushels to the acre. Tomatoes yield a good crop. In years when
these fetch a fair price, to raise them is very profitable. Plums and grapes
do very well. All tame grasses do well. Alfalfa is cultivated with remarkable success and is very profitable. Cape jasmins, the most fragrant
of all flowers, have been grown here within recent years. They are in
season the latter part of April and in May and June. Six hundred plants
can be raised on each acre of land and each plant yields at three years
old from three to four hundred buds each. These buds are in demand in
large Northern cities, and the average price received for them is about
eighty cents a hundred. The buds will keep from fifteen to twenty days
in transit. Of course these flowers are a luxury and the market could
easily be overstocked. Building materials are reasonable in price here,
lumber being about $14 per thousand. Cattle and stock are cheap, and
labor is readily obtainable. Everything required by the settler can cheaply
and easily be obtained in the town.''

We desire to direct the attention of our readers to two experimental
farms in this locality, which are the property of Mr. L. M. Disney, who
wishes thus to forcibly illustrate what may be accomplished here. One of
these farms is 728 acres in extent and it is nine miles from Alvin, near the
town of Manville. It is improved and well stocked, and is leased in tracts
to Swedes, who have been very successful. The other farm is of 640 acres
and is north of Alvin, just outside the corporate limits. Mr. Disney is
cultivating this farm himself, to show what can be done in general farming
and improved stock-raising. The successful culture of fruit and vegetables on these lands is now clearly demonstrated and is beyond question,
and Mr. Disney's idea is to show that the country is equally well adapted
for the raising of all kinds of stock under the most favorable conditions;
also for raising tame grasses and grass for feeding stock. He expects each
winter to feed and fatten from a hundred to a hundred and fifty beeves,
the manure from which will be used to fertilize the land, so as to increase
the yield of feed and grain crops. One of the main points to consider to
achieve success in raising stock here is that the animals should be kept
under good shelter. Lumber and building materials are cheap, so that
the expense of this course is not great and will be repaid manifold. Mr.
Disney is now experimenting with various kinds of crops, and the prospects are that satisfactory results will attend his efforts in most, if not all,
of his ventures. He has under cultivation this season about twenty acres
sown with "Beardless" barley, which is of Californian origin. He has
also planted Kentucky blue grass; Crimson clover, a Louisiana product;
Red Top, Melolotus, a kind of clover grown in Alabama, Alfalfa, a California clover, etc. Rice has been successfully cultivated here for the past
three years. An artesian well has been sunk in the center of the farm,
and at its highest elevation, so that any part of the land can with facility
be irrigated. This well produces about 100,000 gallons of water daily.
A levee is constructed so as to make a lake of about twelve acres, and
outlets to this have been provided, which give control of the water to
allow of the irrigation of the land for rice culture when needed. One of
the essential features of the cultivation of the land on this and neighboring
soils is deep plowing. After plowing with the stirring plow Mr. Disney
has followed with a sub-soiler, which loosens the ground from eighteen to
twenty inches in depth. All of the best appliances required have been
obtained for the proper and improved cultivation of the farm. A great
convenience to the property is the fact that joined to it is a side track from
the village of Superior on the Santa Fe railroad. Mr. Disney is doing

good work on this farm, assured that his efforts will be well repaid by showing that this is not only a fruit and vegetable locality, but that it is just as well adapted for stock raising, cotton raising, corn growing and general farm cultivation.

Alvin possesses all the refinements and necessities of a complete and modern civilization. The population is now about 2,000 persons, and it is rapidly growing. Two churches are already erected, another is being constructed, and money is now being raised for a fourth religious edifice. There are three good schools under State supervision. There are many hundred houses within the corporate limits, and others are going up rapidly. The Santa Fe railroad has just built a new freight house and remodeled its passenger railway station in first-class style, making it a credit to the place. Stores of all kinds abound to fill the needs of the inhabitants, making Alvin thoroughly self-contained and independent. Fraternal societies flourish and prosper, the Masonic Order being very strong, and there are also lodges of the Knights of Pythias, Woodmen of the World, etc. The Masons have a handsome and commodious hall for their meetings. There are no saloons in the place, the sentiment of the people being opposed to their existence. A number of factories are in contemplation, and an electric light plant, ice factory, waterworks and other improvements here will be features of the not far distant future. Altogether the city of Alvin presents today a splendid exponent of the enterprise, thrift and push of the American people, which creates in a short time thriving cities and towns from the lone wilderness, and which makes plenty and contentment reign where formerly the cries of wild creatures were the only sounds which disturbed the silence of the waste.

We here give brief notices of some of the leading business enterprises of the city of Alvin.

ALVIN FRUIT AND PRODUCE COMPANY,
Shippers of Fruit and Produce—Alvin,

The above organization is a recent acquisition to the facilities of Alvin, and it bids fair to develop into one of the most useful in the locality. Many farmers while entirely understanding their business, find more or less difficulty and loss of time in finding means to ship their product where it will find a favorable market. Often in shipping to commission dealers they are obliged to consign their goods to parties of whom they know nothing, not to speak of the anxiety and derangement of their labors which this course entails. The Alvin Fruit and Produce Company has been instituted to relieve the farmer of all trouble and care in the matter, and they are prepared to purchase from him his crops and pay him the cash for the same on the spot. Besides this being a home industry, located in the district and organized and conducted by men of undoubted standing, every confidence is assured. The company invite consignments of all descriptions of fruit and produce in the season, either buying outright or selling on commission, as desired. The highest market prices prevailing in the locality will be paid, and when handling goods consigned on commission advances will be made if desired, and prompt sales and quick returns may be relied upon. The connections of the enterprise assure a ready market, and the products are eagerly absorbed by dealers throughout the North and West. South Texas fruits and early vegetables are now becoming well known throughout the country, being fully up to Californian products in quality and flavor, at the same time that their season is earlier and the distance and expense of transportation is less than half. This company is doing a good work to South Texas in demonstrating thus to the outside world what we are producing here, while to the farmer their assistance is incalculable in obtaining for him a market for his products at his own door. The Alvin Fruit and Produce Company is made up of the following gentlemen: Oscar S. Cummings, cashier, Alvin Exchange Bank; Robert E. Burt, J. H. Mayfield and C. E. Cummings, assistant cashier Alvin Exchange Bank. Mr. Burt devotes his energies to the active management of the business.

W. H. NASH & CO.,
Dealers in Hardware, Stoves, Agricultural Implements, Etc.—Alvin.

In connection with the resources and facilities of Alvin, it is gratifying to have to speak of a house such as that conducted by Messrs. W. II. Nash & Co., to whom much credit is due, as thereby is forcibly illustrated the fact that the locality is eminently self sustained, and that residents and settlers can here obtain all their needs in the above lines of the best quality, and at lowest prices, rendering them altogether independent of outside sources of supply. The business was established in 1893 in a small way, and it has greatly expanded with the prosperity of the town. The firm recognizing the necessity for enlarged premises they built their present headquarters, which have been specially arranged for the business. It comprises a handsome building of two floors, each 36x84 feet in dimensions. The firm here carry a large and complete stock, equal to any handled in the larger cities of the state. It includes full lines of hardware, stoves, agricultural implements, house furnishing goods, farming tools, all of which are of the best selection, procured direct from the manufacturers, and placed at the disposal of the public at remarkably low prices. The firm make specialties of some goods of particular merit. Among such we will mention Prize Panama stoves made at Quincy, Ill., Rock Island plows, Standard mowers, barb wire, etc. The firm also make a specialty of box materials for making crates and strawberry boxes for shipping fruits and vegetables. The facilities of the house in every department are complete, and the diversity of the stock offers the widest field from which advantageous selections may be made. The members of the firm individually are Messrs. W. H. Nash, who resides at Alvin, and J. M. Harrison, who is a resident of Flatonia, Texas. Mr. Nash is also the owner of two farms in this vicinity; one within the town limits is of ten acres, and is devoted to the cultivation of flowers, vegetables and strawberries. The other, about a mile distant from the limits, is of thirty acres, and is devoted to a similiar description of crops. We are pleased to have to chronicle of the existence at Alvin of a business of this important nature, which aids so materially the conveniences and facilities of this growing and prosperous locality.

DARLINGTON-MILLER LUMBER COMPANY.—Alvin.

An important industry allied to the growing resources of this locality is that of the above named organization which was instituted here in 1892. The company's plant and possessions cover about an acre of ground upon which they have erected an office building, lumber sheds, etc. They handle here large quantities of rough, sized and dressed pine and cypress lumber and shingles, sash, doors, blinds, etc, and in fact every description of builders' woodwork. Their facilities are of the best, as they enjoy the closest connections with the producers of the goods. Thus the enterprise is of the greatest utility to the locality, enabling supplies of this nature to be promptly obtained at shortest notice and at lowest prices. The proprietorship of the business is vested in the hands of Messrs. E. R. Darlington of St. Louis, and A. W. Miller of Galveston. Both of these gentlemen have important lumber interests in Texas, Indian Territory, Missouri and Iowa. Mr. C. E. Engle is the manager, and he is a man of thorough experience and practical in all that pertains to the lumber trade. The enterprise serves to illustrate the completeness of Alvin's facilities and tends to demonstrate that new settlers can here obtain all supplies for building, etc., under conditions of the most favorable character.

RICHARDSON & SHIRLEY,
Real Estate—Alvin.

Among reliable real estate agents in Alvin must be classed the firm of Richardson & Shirley, founded about a year since. The gentlemen making up the copartnership are individually Messrs. S. N. Richardson and J. J. Shirley. The first named has been a resident in this locality for about thirteen years, and Mr. Shirley has been settled here for about nine years. Mr. Richardson built the second house ever constructed at Alvin, and for ten years he was the agent of the Santa Fe Railroad. Thus it will be readily seen that they are eminently qualified for their present enterprise, thoroughly familiar with the locality and the real value of property. The firm devote their energies to the handling of property in this and surrounding localities, and they have at the disposal of investors and home-seekers fruit and farm lands, both improved and unimproved, which they offer at low prices and upon terms as may be mutually agreed upon. There never was a time when better opportunities presented themselves for buying lands in this section, and the firm have some of the choicest upon their books. They invite enquiries and will be pleased to receive calls from all who may be paying a visit to Alvin with a view of purchase or settlement. Mr. S. N. Richardson is the owner of a fine farm in Alvin, and has twelve acres under cultivation, planted with fruits, vegetables and flowers, and he also raises here chickens, dairy products, nursery stock, etc. Mr. Shirley has a 56-acre farm about a mile and a quarter west of the town. This is cultivated mostly in pears, peaches, plums, strawberries, nursery stock, etc. Mr. Richardson makes a specialty of growing jasmins of the grand de flora variety and has been particularly successful with them. He ships all over the United States and solicits orders for buds or flowers. Mr. Shirley will ship from 300 to 500 bushels of pears from his orchards this season, and from his nursery he will have for sale this year a hundred thousand young pear trees. This firm, it will be seen, are able to demonstrate to intending settlers the actual accomplishments and possibilities of the country far more forcibly than by any other method. In every way, as a reliable firm with which to deal, Messrs. Richardson & Shirley are entitled to the fullest consideration and confidence.

CARLTON BROS.
General Merchants, Alvin.

The above house began business at Alvin March 1892, and it is now one of the leading sources of supply of the locality. The store comprises a building of two floors, 24x60 feet in dimensions. The firm carry a well selected and complete stock of dry goods, groceries, harness, tinware, boots and shoes, hats and caps, etc., which they supply to the public at prices as low as the lowest, and competing successfully in every particular with Houston and Galveston houses. Indeed, residents of this locality have no necessity to go away from home when requiring anything in the above lines, which they can find here in full and complete variety. The members of the firm individually are T. W. Carlton and L. B. Carlton. Both these gentlemen are from Bullard, Texas, but have now settled definitely in Alvin, and intend to partake of the prosperity in store for this fertile and growing country. The firm own ten acres of fruit lands in the township, which they are now cultivating in pears and strawberries, meeting with gratifying success. Both members of the firm are practically conversant with the business they conduct, having always been identified with this department of commerce. They have every inducement to offer to those trading with them, including courteous attention and fair dealing.

BOSTON BARGAIN STORE,
E. A. Jeanes, Proprietor.—Alvin.

Alvin is rapidly assuming every aspect of a busy and prosperous center, and this result is largely due to the enterprise and energy of the merchants who are here engaged in business. One of the later additions to the trade facilities of the city is the Boston Bargain Store, founded February, 1st, 1894, operated under the proprietorship of Mr. E. A. Jeanes. A two story building 25x50 feet in dimensions is utilized, and here is contained a large stock of goods, which includes dry goods, notions, groceries, canned goods, confectionery, fruits, tin and glassware, crockery, and in fact we may briefly say, everything required in the household, besides many articles of ladies' and gentlemens' attire. The stock being obtained direct from original sources is placed before the public of Alvin and vicinity at lowest prices, entirely justifying the title of the house to its denomination of a "bargain" store. Alvin's residents will soon realize that here they can obtain all their needs in this line under the most favorable conditions. Mr. Jeanes comes here from Lampasas, and is going to make Alvin his home. He is an enterprising business man, upright and fair dealing, striving by honorable methods to attract and hold his full share of public patronage.

W. S. HART.
General Merchant, Alvin.

This is the oldest established mercantile concern in the town of Alvin, it having been instituted June 1889. The business has grown with the development of the locality, and today it is among the more important enterprises of the place. Mr. Hart occupies a store of 24x60 feet, and here is contained a full stock of dry goods, groceries, boots and shoes, hats and caps, harness, hardware, farming implements, etc. The goods are well chosen, and are thoroughly suited to the requirements of this locality. The prices will be found to be fully as low as those of Houston and Galveston, and residents here can procure all their supplies upon equally as advantageous terms as in those cities. Mr. Hart is one of the best known men here, and he has been a resident of South Texas since the war. Those having dealings with him can depend upon receiving fair and liberal treatment, and every inducement offered at their disposal. The house is every way a liberal exponent of Alvin's large and growing trade.

ZYCHLINSKI & CO.,
Real Estate, Alvin.

The above named firm are the successors to the real estate business originally founded in 1892 under the name of Zychlinski & Murdock. The present designation was adopted February 1894. The business of the house consists of the handling of large and small tracts of land in what is known as the Gulf Coast Country of Texas. They have at the present time at the disposal of investors and home-seekers highly desirable farm and fruit tracts of from five acres upwards in dimensions; also, some very attractive and valuable grazing lands in this locality. They likewise have on their books town lots in Alvin, Pear Land and elsewhere, as well as improved and unimproved fruit farms in these towns. The above are offered today at remarkably low prices and upon terms to suit. It is certain that property in this part of Texas will greatly appreciate in value. The past history of the section clearly demonstrates this fact, and we have elsewhere in this volume treated fully on the subject. We may here add that the firm of Zychlinski & Co. have inducements to offer to investors and settlers of the greatest value, and correspondence with them will establish clearly our statement. Mr. W. Zychlinski comes to Alvin from California, and he is thoroughly familiar with all pertaining to fruit culture and the value of fruit lands. He intends to remain in this country, assured that it is destined to become the greatest fruit section of the United States. His experience is both Californian and European and is entitled to credit. He has himself embarked in the business and owns a fruit farm of sixty acres in Alvin, upon which he raises peaches, plums, figs, strawberries, etc., and he has lately planted a portion of the land with pear trees. To all who may be interested in finding a suitable location in which to establish a home and till the soil profitably, we recommend a correspondence with this house, which will, no doubt, result in ultimate advantage and benefit.

TOLER & McGINTY,
Real Estate, Alvin.

The great development and prosperity which have been characteristic of this section within recent years, have naturally largely stimulated real estate operations here. An enterprise in Alvin which has contributed its full share in opening up this country to settlers is that of Messrs. Toler & McGinty, who, March, 1893, succeeded to the business originally founded by Mr. Alf H. H. Toler December, 1891. The firm are general real estate dealers, buying and selling lands on commission, collecting rents and revenues, looking after property for non-residents, making suitable investments for those who choose to defer their residence here, and they have on the list a large variety of improved and unimproved farm and fruit lands in Brazoria, Harris and Galveston counties, the heart of the splendid farm and fruit district of the State. The firm have also at the disposal of their patrons many choice ranch lands in Western Texas. All of the above are offered to settlers and investors at very low prices taking into consideration the fact that they are sure to advance in value within a very short time. We have fully demonstrated elsewhere in this volume the great opportunities which are now presented by Texas lands, and Messrs. Toler & McGinty have some of the choicest to sell upon terms which may be arranged to suit the conveniences of purchasers. The individual members of the firm are Alf H. H. Toler, originally from North Carolina, and J. M. McGinty, who is a native Texan. Mr. Toler has been twenty-one years settled in Texas, and two years in this section, and Mr. McGinty about four years. Both are experienced and honorable real estate men, who may be depended upon to fairly represent what they have to sell. Mr. Toler is the owner of a farm in Arcadia, which is of forty acres in area, and here he cutivates successfully fruits, vegetables, etc., making a specialty of pears, for which this district has become celebrated. Mr. McGinty has also a farm about four and a half miles from Alvin, which is devoted to the growth of small fruits, strawberries, etc. Thus these gentlemen illustrate in their own efforts what can be here accomplished, and they will be glad to demonstrate to intending settlers the truth of our claim that in South Texas an honest competence can be easily gained by all who choose to labor faithfully and well in the service of the soil.

W. Z. WEEMS.
Livery Stable.—Alvin.

Every convenience is at the disposal of the residents of Alvin, and those who visit the town on business or otherwise. Among the facilities of the place must not be ignored the establishment of Mr. W. Z. Weems, who has had a livery stable here for the past five years. He now utilizes a two story building which is 50x80 feet in dimensions, and here he has at the disposal of the public about twenty head of horses and a full outfit of buggies, wagons and carriages suitable for business or pleasure. His prices will be found altogether reasonable, and courteous attention is the invariable rule. Mr. Weems also boards horses for residents, and buys and sells horses and mules, often having very desirable bargains on hand. This gentleman is one of the oldest residents in this locality. When he first came here he conducted a hotel. He is a native of Brazoria county, and is a fair sample of what the climate can turn out—he being the picture of good health and lusty manhood. Mr. Weems owns land in the township, and is identified with the locality. Those who come to Alvin will do well to give him a call, and they will be well treated, and if anything in his line be required they are sure to obtain it here of the best, without being subjected to exorbitant charges.

JESSE HOBBS,
Real Estate, Alvin.

Aiding to demonstrate to the public abroad the advantages and facilities of this garden spot of Texas, must be mentioned the real estate agency conducted under the proprietorship of Mr. Jesse Hobbs, who founded his present business here in 1891. This gentleman transacts a regular real estate business, and he has for disposal a choice list of town sites, farm and fruit lands in this and neighboring localities. These are offered to investors and settlers upon easy terms and low prices. The advantages and facilities of the Alvin country and Gulf Coast section generally, have been fully exploited in another part of this work and we have only to mention here that Mr. Hobbs is in a position to offer marked inducements to those who contemplate an investment or a settlement in this section. Mr. Hobbs is a native Texan, and well knows the country and its possibilities. He has been settled in Alvin for the past ten years, and is an authority on real estate matters. He may be quoted as a thoroughly reliable business man, and is a magistrate and notary public. Those wishing to consult him will receive his promptest attention, and all assistance that may guide them to an advantageous and profitable investment.

SLATAPER & BURGESS.

Grain, Feed and Hay and General Commission Merchants, Alvin.

The above named enterprise was established October 26th, 1893, and it has proved of large utility to the inhabitants of Alvin and vicinity. The firm occupy premises in a building which is the property of its senior member. They deal in grain, feed and hay, also fertilizers of all leading kinds, seeds, wood, coal, lime, etc. They carry full stocks of the above articles, and their facilities enable them to promptly fill orders at lowest current rates. Messrs. Slataper & Burgess are also general commission agents, handling all kinds of country produce. They invite consignments and assure quick sales. Their facilities are of the best in all departments, and are equally at the disposal of both producer and consumer. The firm is made up of Messrs. D. Lee Slataper and T. E. Burgess. Mr. Slataper comes from Pennsylvania, but he has been settled here for a number of years. He is also a prominent real estate dealer here. Mr. Burgess is from Louisiana, and has been a resident of Alvin for nearly three years. Both gentlemen are identified with the locality, and both hold property in Alvin. The enterprise they conduct is carried on with energy and experience, conducing largely to make the home of their adoption self contained and independent. All having dealings with them will realize the profit and convenience of business connections. The second story of their building is occupied by the Masonic fraternity; they having a flourishing lodge of the craft at Alvin.

J. F. DURANT & CO.

Real Estate.—Alvin.

Real estate operations at Alvin and vicinity are naturally active, as might be easily imagined by reason of the great advancement and development of the locality. As is well known by all who have studied the subject, there is no so called boom here; but a solid growth and prosperity brought about by the real value of the land, which is rapidly being filled up by thrifty and hard working settlers from the North and West. Engaged in the real estate business at Alvin is the firm of J. F. Durant & Co., who instituted their present undertaking August 1892. They are prepared with every facility to offer inducements and advantages to those who are seeking a favorable location to make a home, or who are looking for a means of profitable investment. The firm invite enquiries from any part of the country, and will be glad to promptly respond to all correspondence. Of the great attractions of this section we have spoken elsewere at some length, and this firm in the very heart of the farm and fruit lands district of South Texas, have many opportunities at their disposal. They have on their lists desirable tracts in all sections of the Gulf coast country, which are offered at low prices and on terms to suit. The firm are in every way reliable, and they have bound up their interests with the country. Mr. J. F. Durant is the sole proprietor. He was formerly in the dairy business, and he has been a resident here for the past ten years. He has now two farms in this locality, one within the corporate limits of Alvin, which he devotes to the raising of strawberries and vegetables, and the other, about a mile and a half distant from the town, where he has had much success in the cultivation of vegetables, pears and strawberries. Those contemplating an investment in South Texas, the garden of the United States, can do no better than to entrust their interests to the care of this firm.

D. O. CARRAWAY,
Dealer in Dry Goods, Shoes, Hats, Caps, Etc.—Alvin.

The above named enterprise has been identified with the interests of Alvin since September, 1893, when the business was instituted. Mr. Carraway occupies a store of 25x75 feet, where is handled a full and well selected stock of dry goods, boots, shoes, hats, caps, notions, etc., which are placed at the disposal of the public at lowest prices. In the establishment of the above house is again demonstrated that the city of Alvin is altogether self-contained and that its residents can obtain within its borders all their needs and requirements. Full lines are handled in all departments to meet the wants of all classes. Mr. D. O. Carraway comes from Bonham, Texas, where he had been engaged in a similar business for a period of five years. Altogether his familiarity with the dry goods business embraces over ten years' active pursuit of it, and everything connected with it and kindred lines is familiar to him. This gentleman has identified himself with the interests of the locality. He has become the purchaser of several residential lots within the town limits of Alvin, and also a lot upon which he intends to erect a handsome brick store in the near future. His enterprise may be classed as among the more important which are contributing to the advancement and reputation of this growing and prosperous locality.

BAIR & SPEARS,
Real Estate and Insurance Agents.—Alvin.

We have elsewhere fully set forth the great advantages that Alvin and locality present at the present time to investors and home seekers. We now devote a few lines relative to a firm of real estate agents who are doing much to demonstrate to the public the value of the opportunities now offered by this much favored section. Messrs. Bair & Spears succeeded in 1894 to the business originally founded by W. B. Bair in 1892. The firm buy and sell city property, and farm and fruit lands in this section. They have always on their lists many desirable tracts worthy of the attention of the home seeker and investor. They also have improved and unimproved ranches and large and small farms in various parts of the state. Those who may decide to investigate the attractions of Texas as a place of residence will do well to communicate with this firm, and they will be met with courteous attention, honorable dealing, and fair representations regarding what they have at their disposal. Visitors to Alvin will also do well to call upon them when contemplating a settlement here. The firm are also insurance agents, representing reliable companies. The individual co-partners are W. B. Bair, who is from Iowa, and E. P. Spears, who was formerly a resident of West Virginia, and for four years conducted a real estate business at Galveston, Texas. Both are experienced real estate men, having a correct knowledge of real estate values. The benefits of their experience is at all times placed at the disposal of their clients.

SPEARS & OSGOOD,
Grain Merchants.—Alvin.

Nothing better shows the growth of advancement of Alvin than the enterprise displayed by the merchants of the town through whose means the city is rendered independent of outside sources of supply, the needs of her residents being in every way able to be filled within her borders. Among those who have contributed to this gratifying result is the firm of Spears & Osgood, who, April 15, 1893, succeeded to the business originally founded by Mr. B. L. Osgood about a year earlier. The firm in connection with this enterprise, occupy a two story warehouse which is of the dimensions of 30x60 feet. Here they have all required accommodations for the carrying of a large stock of grain, hay and fuel, the commodities in which they deal. These they obtain direct from the original sources of supply, corn; oats, bran and chop from the north, cotton seed meal from this section, and fuel from Indian Territory. All supplies are received in carload lots and are sold to consumers at the very lowest current rates. The firm, besides their local trade also sell at wholesale in the neighboring small towns and villages. Their facilities being so complete they are enabled to offer the most advantageous terms and prices to careful buyers. The members of the firm individually are Messrs. B. L. Osgood and M. Spears. Mr. Osgood is from Mount Pleasant, Iowa, and Mr. Spears is from Emerson, Iowa, where he was engaged in the handling of cattle, hogs and grain. This house is an important acquisition to the mercantile resources of this growing little city.

THE ALVIN EXCHANGE BANK,
Alvin.

The growing importance of the town of Alvin has rendered the extension of its facilities desirable in some directions. Thus a number of capitalists and business men decided to establish The Alvin Exchange Bank, and it opened its doors to the public August 15th, 1893. That its projectors have met with the success they anticipated is fully shown in the amount of business transacted, and the institution is daily growing in public favor. The capital utilized in the business is fully adequate to all demands that may be made upon its resources. The bank devotes its energies to receiving deposits subject to check, discounting commercial paper, granting loans on real estate and other first-class collateral security, making collections at all available points and issuing drafts and letters of credit on all important centers in the United States and foreign countries. The principal correspondents of the bank are the Merchants' Exchange National Bank, of New York City; First National Bank, of Galveston; Planters and Mechanics National Bank, of Houston, and the National Bank of the Republic, St. Louis. The executive officers of the bank are as follows: J. S. Heddon, president; C. S. Cummings, vice-president; Oscar Cummings cashier, and C. E. Cummings, assistant cashier. Mr. Heddon resides at Galveston, being a well known capitalist of that city. Mr. C. S. Cummings is a capitalist of Kansas. The other gentlemen devote their energies to the conduct of the institution here. The bank, with ample facilities, invites the accounts and business of commercial men and farmers generally, and will extend every courtesy and accommodation which lay in its power. It, furthermore, extends an invitation to capitalists, settlers and home-seekers to locate here, and is prepared to offer needed assistance upon a liberal business basis.

D. LEE SLATAPER,
Successor to Durant & Slataper, Real Estate Agents, Alvin.

The above named real estate agency is doing good business at Alvin, and it is prepared with every facility to offer to investors and home-seekers advantageous lands at low prices and on terms to suit. Mr. Slataper has on his list desirable tracts fruit and farm lands, and he invites correspondence from any part of the country relative to Alvin and vicinity. The sole proprietor of the business is Mr. D. Lee Slataper, who is bound up and identified with the growth and advancement of the locality. He is the owner of a fine farm of 120 acres, on which he raises fruits, vegebles, etc. A good deal of experimental work is being done by him in the raising of fruits, and prominent among the varieties may be mentioned grape fruit, olives, peaches, fifty varieties of foreign and native grapes and fifteen varieties of pears. With the latter he is demonstrating that the Bartlett, Seckel, Howell, Lawson and Idaho will do as well as will the Le Conte or Kieffer in this section. He has a large number of Bartlett pear trees in bearing this season. He has also all varieties of Japan plums, many of which will bear this year. He has four acres in cape jasmins, and also has over three hundred thousand cuttings of small fruits, planted in nursery rows. Besides the home farm Mr. Slataper has five improved places of from 18 to 60 acres each, with pear, plum and peach orchards on all, proving beyond a doubt the successful growth of these fruits in this locality. For investors he has a number of houses for sale, on which can be realized from 20 to 30 per cent. in rentals. No better opportunity can be offered for the investment of money than the putting up of moderate priced houses here. In the very near future Mr. Slataper will start a breeding farm, using a 300-acre tract which he owns for the purpose. He has already arranged for a $1,500 imported English coach stallion and thirty good Northern mares. These animals will be used to cut hay and otherwise improve this farm and its surroundings. Taken altogether, Mr. Slataper is one of Alvin's most enterprising citizens, and visitors will do well to call on him and investigate the opportunities he has to offer.

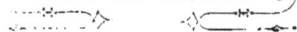

INDEX (CONTINUED)

This volume was printed and bound by CUMMING &
SONS, PRINTERS, 108 MAIN STREET. This house is prepared
with all facilities to execute every description of printing
in the highest style of   the typographical art.
They have one of the   finest cylinder presses
in the South; a full   supply of the latest
style type and all ap   pliances and conveniences. They have   lately removed to their
new central location.   at the above address.
The publishers of this work beg here to thank MESSRS.
CUMMING & SONS for their care as well as courtesy and
promptness which they have displayed in the printing of
this book.

www.ingramcontent.com/pod-product-compliance
Lightning Source LLC
Chambersburg PA
CBHW030606270326
41927CB00007B/1064